Automobile Electrical Manual

A Tranter

Principal, Merton Technical College, London

ISBN 0 85696 818 8 (Hardback)

ISBN 1 85010 005 5 (Softback)

Printed in England

HAYNES PUBLISHING GROUP
SPARKFORD YEOVIL SOMERSET BA22 7JJ ENGLAND
distributed in the USA by
HAYNES PUBLICATIONS INC
861 LAWRENCE DRIVE
NEWBURY PARK
CALIFORNIA 91320
USA

Preface

Progress in vehicle electrical system design is rapid, and the next decade will bring many developments. To cope with this, a background of principles of electricity is the mental equivalent of a well-stocked toolbox – it is the key to tackling any problem. This book is designed to take the reader through basic principles up to an understanding of how modern (and recent) equipment works. Given that base, there should be few problems which cannot be solved. In illustration, service advice is given as appropriate, so that principles and practice are linked.

Professional mechanics, serious enthusiasts and engineering students should find much that is useful; those studying for City and Guilds or TEC examinations were also in the author's mind in preparing this book.

A. Tranter

Merton 1983

Acknowledgements

The author wishes to acknowledge the valuable assistance received in the preparation of this book from the following companies and individuals; in appropriate cases thanks are due for permission to reproduce technical information.

AC Delco Ltd; Austin Rover Group Ltd; Automobiles Peugeot, Paris (Richard Dauman); Robert Bosch Ltd; British Standards Institution (BS Wiring Code for Automobiles from BSAU7: 1968 by permission BSI); Champion Sparking Plug Co Ltd; Chrysler UK Ltd; SA Citroën, Paris; Delco-Remy; Ducellier; EDA Sparkrite Ltd; Ford Motor Co Ltd; General Motors; Gunsons Colorplugs Ltd (Granville Unsworth); Joseph Lucas (Electrical) Ltd (Peter Mountford and staff); Lumenition Ltd; Mobelec Ltd; Pacet Manufacturing Co Ltd (Peter Eva and Tony Clowes); Quinton Hazell plc (Peter Redfern); Salmon Diavia Artico (Derek Eade and Chris Daniel); Sankyo International (Paul Manners); Smiths Industries Ltd; TI Transport Equipment Ltd (John Heath, Crypton Training School); VAG (UK) Ltd (Curt Carthew); Vauxhall Motors Ltd; AB Volvo Ltd.

Introduction

All motor vehicles use an electrical system and the mechanic cannot progress very far without an understanding of its operation.

There is no need to have a feeling that electricity is a difficult subject because 'it can't be seen' – after all, the expansion of gases in a cylinder, heat flow through a metal, the gas content of an exhaust, etc are all things which are accepted without question by the mechanic, yet equally well cannot be seen.

This book sets out to explain how motor vehicle electrical equipment works, and no prior knowledge of electricity is required. True, a range of new terms must be used, but it is surprising how such quantities as voltage, current, magnetic fields and electrons quickly become familiar and are easily imagined – all that is required is an open mind, a little time and patience.

Chapter 1 really starts at the beginning of electrical ideas by explaining what electricity is, and it will no doubt be a surprise to some to learn that all matter – even the reader – is made up of particles carrying electric charge. To produce electric current, all that is necessary is to pump certain of these particles along a wire path which is nothing more than a convenient highway.

The topics of Chapter 1 are only a selection from electrical theory but are all relevant to the automobile and its electrical system.

Some matters, such as the operation of the transistor, rectifier, thyristor (SCR) and other electronic devices are treated in the chapter in which they are applied to equipment.

Being a general book on principles and practice, specific details on any particular type of vehicle will not be found except by way of illustration. While it is hoped that up-to-date practice is adequately described, no apology is offered for the presence of some older equipment and systems, for not only do they lead in logically to the present state of the automobile electrical art, but often are still in service in millions of vehicles.

Contents

The Complete System

It is best to look at the electrical requirements of the motor vehicle as a whole before a detailed study can be made. In this way the reader sees the complete picture of what is happening, just as one uses large and small scale maps.

The accompanying illustration shows the main electrical circuits and how they are supplied with energy. The ultimate source is the fuel, for this drives the engine which propels the vehicle and also runs the generator giving the electrical supply to the circuits.

It should be noted that the battery is for storage purposes only, to keep the electrical equipment operating when the engine is stationary, and for engine cranking at start-up.

Charging and storage

All present-day cars require a battery to store energy. This implies the use of a direct current (dc) system because a battery will store and release dc energy only. There is no known way of storing alternating current energy.

Direct current is required to charge the battery and for many years direct-current generators (dynamos) were employed. The dc dynamo is now obsolescent, although many are still to be found on older vehicles. Present practice is to use an alternating-current generator (alternator) with means of converting the alternating current (ac) into direct current (dc) before reaching the battery.

Direct current generators require more maintenance than alternators and cost more to produce. Furthermore, the electrical output is poor compared with the alternator which, unlike the dc generator, will produce a charging current right down to tickover speeds, and so is useful to maintain a good charge for city commuter vehicles where average speeds are low.

Both dc and ac generators require some form of regulation so that the electrical output is fairly constant over the engine speed range.

Ignition

All petrol engines operate on a four-stroke or a two-stroke cycle during which there is a requirement for a spark to ignite the compressed charge of turbulent air and petrol vapour. This spark must be accurately timed to occur so that the resultant burning of the compressed vapour in the cylinders will give maximum power output consistent with economic fuel consumption.

Today all ignition systems are electrical, but in early engines other forms of ignition were used; for example, slide-valve exposure of a gas flame in a tube. For some specialised applications such as race and aircraft engines the magneto is employed, and the flywheel magneto is widely used in small motorcycles. Road-going motor vehicles generally use the coil-ignition circuit. The ignition coil is a specialised type of transformer and its action is to convert the low voltage of the vehicle system, typically 12 volts, up to some thousands of volts for operating the sparking plugs. Transformers do not work on direct current, however. The essential requirement to transfer energy from one coil to another by magnetic means is that the current in one coil changes. This change is brought about by the use of a contact breaker which is an engine-operated switch connected to the primary coil and the battery. At the precise time when the spark is required the switch is opened, the primary coil current falls rapidly to zero, thus transferring energy to the secondary winding and to the plug in the form of a spark.

In recent years the equivalent task is carried out by electronic means, giving rise to a range of equipment known as electronic ignition. In principle, however, the concept of changing the 12 volt battery supply to become a high voltage at the sparking plug remains.

Lighting and signals

Lighting requirements vary from one country to another, but in

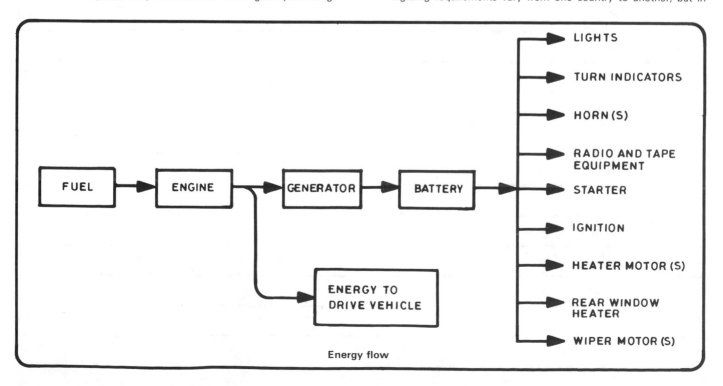

Energy flow

FUEL → ENGINE → GENERATOR → BATTERY →

LIGHTS
TURN INDICATORS
HORN(S)
RADIO AND TAPE EQUIPMENT
STARTER
IGNITION
HEATER MOTOR(S)
REAR WINDOW HEATER
WIPER MOTOR(S)

ENERGY TO DRIVE VEHICLE

general front and rear lighting is essential. Headlamps with main and meeting (dip) beams are standard for all vehicles; variations occur in permissible power ratings and colour of the emitted light according to the country of use.

Again the battery is vital, in that lights must be operable without the engine running, and low wattage lamps at front and rear are installed for night time parking.

Rear lights are vital to safety and are generally coloured red. In recent times it is common to see extra, higher powered rear lamps fitted for driving under adverse conditions.

Brake-operated rear lights are fitted as standard and have a high intensity, using lamps of the order of 21 watts (UK).

Lighting of vehicles features in all vehicle regulations according to the country concerned, and the above is but an indication of typical practice.

Flashing turn indicators are standard original equipment in all countries, the lamp rating being typically 21 watts and coloured amber (in US – red at rear). A warning light of about 2 watts is fitted on the dashboard or elsewhere within the driver's view; on some vehicles an audible warning is provided.

Lighting regulations for trailers require careful interpretation (see Chapters 9 and 10).

Starting: engine cranking

Vehicles are equipped with a direct-current starter motor which is designed to give a high torque (turning ability) at standstill. It is at standstill that the peak effort is required to turn over a cold motor and consequently the current demand can be high – of the order of 300 amperes.

Such heavy loading requires a battery to be in good condition, as must be the cables and connections to the starter motor.

Safety

Hazards are present for those working on automobile electrical equipment. Rotating machinery, high voltages and the presence of a lead-acid battery are a combination which can give rise to accidents; mechanics should be aware of danger points and always adopt appropriate safety measures.

In addition to the normal safety precautions, the following notes apply:

Rotating machines and asbestos filler

(a) Neckties and loose cuffs can easily become caught up in the alternator/dynamo/fan pulley.

(b) Electrically-driven fans may start, whether or not the engine is running.

(c) All starter commutators, some dynamo commutators, and alternator slip-ring assemblies use asbestos filler. Machining these components results in the possibility of dangerous dust being breathed.

Advice on safe machining may be sought from the Asbestos Research Council, PO Box 18, Cleckheaton, Yorks or from Joseph Lucas Ltd, Great King Street, Birmingham, England.

Ignition equipment

(a) Ballast resistors and ignition coils can reach high temperatures. Accidental contact can give rise to burns.

(b) Coil ignition can cause an unpleasant shock but is rarely harmful to healthy persons. Electronic ignition, however, delivers a substantial energy pulse and can give harmful shocks.

(c) Ignition coils should not be incinerated when discarded unless the case is first punctured and the oil drained.

Screen wipers and washers

(a) Link mechanisms, though slow running, operate at high torque. Care should be taken not to trap fingers.

(b) Screen washer fluid often contains antifreeze and it is not unknown for fluid to come into contact with the eyes of an operator who may be adjusting jet directions. Should this happen the eyes should be rinsed well in cold water and medical advice sought.

Lighting equipment

(a) Mercury is used in certain switches (eg to switch boot (trunk) or bonnet (hood) lamps). Should spillage occur, the work surfaces touched should be treated with a thin water-paste containing equal parts of flowers of sulphur and slaked lime.

(b) Halogen lamps should not be touched with the fingers since the glass may fracture or burst at switch-on. Clean the surface when cold with methylated spirit if accidentally touched.

(c) Glass bulbs have only limited strength and undue force when fitting or removing may result in fracture. Removal of corroded bulbs may be difficult; a cloth should be used to hold the glass bulb when removing in this case.

Lead-acid batteries

(a) If acid comes into contact with the eyes or skin, wash with plenty of clean water. Seek medical advice if necessary.

(b) Batteries give off highly flammable gas when being charged. Explosion with resulting acid spray can occur through smoking in the vicinity of the filler vents or by disconnecting cables with the current switched on.

(c) Some form of protective clothing should be worn when handling batteries. After touching batteries, wash the hands.

(d) Do not place metal tools where they may fall across the battery terminals.

(e) Batteries are heavy. Use approved lifting techniques whenever practical, ie when lifting up or lowering a battery keep the back straight and bend the knees.

General

(a) Look out for worn drivebelts. A fracture at speed can be dangerous to a nearby operator.

(b) Remove the battery earth lead when removing or installing electrical equipment.

(c) Cardiac pacemakers are affected by the electromagnetic fields of the ignition system.

Conclusion

Many of the notes given may seem obvious, but it is easy to relax with familiarity of working on automobile electrical equipment. *IT IS TOO LATE AFTER AN ACCIDENT TO REALISE THE DANGER.*

Chapter 1 The Essentials of Electricity and Magnetism

Contents

1 Introduction

1 If the reader is well experienced in electrical matters he may skip this chapter, but if he has never followed a course of instruction, or his knowledge is rusty, then time spent in reading will be an investment.

2 To read manufacturers' manuals, it is essential to have a clear understanding not only of electrical principles but also of the correct use of terminology; this is the reader's mental toolbox and is in every way as important as his practical toolkit.

2 The atom, electrons and protons

1 · Quite a few people begin to read a book on electricity and give up when it comes to visualising what is happening in the circuits. A much simplified picture, sufficient for our purposes, is all that is needed:

2 It is now well known that all matter consists of complex arrangements of particles, some of which have a positive (+) electric charge and are called protons, and others which have a negative (−) charge − these are electrons. A complete unit of these particles is known as an atom.

3 All materials are formed of different combinations of atoms, but it is the atom itself which gives the clues to the behaviour of different classes of materials − for instance those which do not conduct electricity (insulators) and those which do (conductors). Another class is the semi-conductor, which will be dealt with later.

4 Two of the simplest atoms are shown in Fig. 1.1 but most materials are far more complicated. The nucleus consists of protons (which are 1800 times as massive as electrons) and usually some electrons, with other electrons orbiting the nucleus; together the total number of negatively charged electrons equals the number of positively charged protons.

5 Because of the ponderous mass of the nucleus, it may be regarded as fixed in place in solid materials, but it is the mobility of the orbiting electrons which is of greatest interest to us.

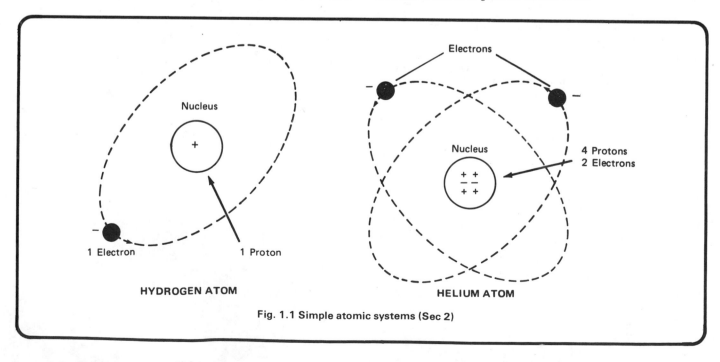

Fig. 1.1 Simple atomic systems (Sec 2)

3 Free electrons (conduction)

1 An atom is, in practice, a very complicated structure; the outermost orbital electrons are sometimes held very loosely to the nucleus like a very distant planet may be to the sun. Collisions may occur, which result in some electrons being driven from their normal path and drifting through the material lattice (Fig. 1.2). These are called **free electrons**. Some materials are rich in them and others have few, or none at all. A material with many free electrons is a **conductor** and without free electrons is an **insulator**.

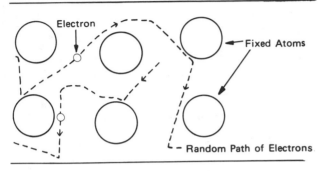

Fig. 1.2 Free electron drift (Sec 3)

2 Imagine a copper wire as a mass of heavy copper atoms with swarms of free electrons in the spaces between them. These electrons are so small that there is plenty of room for them to fly about in all directions, but on the whole they do not progress very far in any one direction; their motion is random.

4 Electron flow = current

1 If a cell or a battery (a battery is merely a collection of cells) is connected to the ends of a copper wire, the free electrons drift along it, all in the same direction, just as when a pump is started, sending a current of liquid along the pipes to which it is connected.

2 It is important to understand that a battery does not make the electricity any more than a pump makes a liquid. The battery and the pump are merely agencies to set in motion something which already exists.

3 Carrying the analogy further, it might be said that it is not the pump which moves the fluid, but the pressure difference which the pump creates that causes the motion. This is a valuable idea because without stating the method used, it is the pressure difference alone which causes fluid flow. This also applies to electricity. Any device (eg battery, dynamo, alternator) which will set up a **potential difference** in an electric circuit can give rise to electric current flow.

4 As a pump produces a certain pressure, so a battery or dynamo produces an electromotive force **(EMF)** measured in **VOLTS.**

5 The complete circuit

1 A circuit, as the name implies, is a complete uninterrupted path round which current may flow.

2 The battery or generator which pumps electrons round the circuit is similar in many ways to an oil pump working in a car. The oil flows continuously round the oil circuit and is primarily used for lubricating bearings.

3 It is helpful to compare the electrical and oil systems of Figs. 1.3 and 1.4.

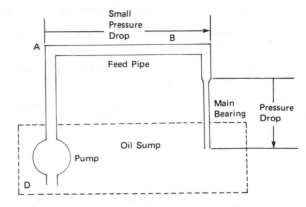

Fig. 1.3 Oil pump and feed (Sec 5)

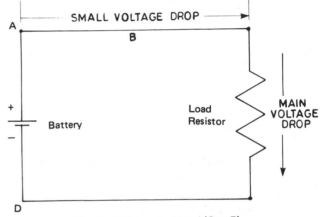

Fig. 1.4 Battery and load (Sec 5)

4 The oil pump produces a pressure difference between points A and D and this causes oil to flow through the feed pipe B to the main bearing where a large pressure drop occurs. This is because of the constriction between journal and bearing and most of the pump energy is expended in forcing oil flow. Ideally, no energy is lost in the feed pipe.

5 Coming to the equivalent electric circuit, the battery produces potential difference (pd) between points A and D and this causes current to flow along the wire B to the load resistor where a large voltage drop occurs. This is because the resistor is made of high resistance wire (or other material) and most of the battery energy is expended in forcing current flow. Ideally no energy is lost in the connecting wires but in practice a small loss will occur.

6 Fundamental quantities

1 The number of electrons set in motion by a battery is astronomically large, so a convenient number (how many does not matter to us!) are lumped together and called a **COULOMB.**

2 Again we are not often interested in the amount of electricity, but the speed of flow round a circuit. The number of coulombs flowing past a point each second is the **rate** of flow and 1 coulomb per second is called an **AMPERE.**

	Liquid system units	Electrical system units
Quantity	gallon	coulomb
Pressure and pressure drop	pounds per sq. inch	volt
Rate of flow	gallons per second	coulomb per second or ampere

7 Ohm's law

1   The load resistor deserves attention, for this is where the electricity will produce the desired effects. For example, an electric fire element consists of a spiral of wire with a resistance much higher than that of the connecting leads.

2   The well known effect is that heat is produced, a phenomenon which will be considered later. Equally, the headlamp bulb of a car is a load resistor and the main effect of current flow will be so much local heat in the filament that white light is produced. Resistance is measured in **OHMS**, the name deriving from the German experimenter Georg Simon Ohm.

3   It is easy to visualise the value of 1 ohm, for it is such that a voltage of 1 volt would cause 1 ampere of current to flow (Fig. 1.5).

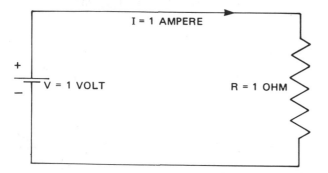

Fig. 1.5 The relationship between volts, amperes and ohms (Sec 7)

4   Georg Ohm is famous for his conclusion that the current increases in direct proportion to the voltage applied.

$$\text{or } V = I \times R$$
$$\text{ie Voltage } = \text{current} \times \text{resistance}$$

Today this seems elementary but its statement in 1826 cost Ohm his job because it did not fit the theory of the day.

Example
5   A headlamp bulb working off a 12 volt battery takes a current of 3 amperes. What is the resistance of the bulb filament?

$$V = I \times R$$
$$\text{or } 12 = 3 \times R$$
$$\text{so } R = 4 \text{ ohms}$$

6   It pays to learn the proper abbreviations for electrical quantities which are written thus:

12 volts	as	12V
3 amperes	as	3A
4 ohms	as	4Ω

8 Series and parallel circuits

1   It is rare that a circuit consists of simply a battery connected to a load resistor. Often two or more resistors are involved and if they are end to end as in Fig. 1.6 they are said to be in **series** and, if as in Fig. 1.7, in **parallel.**

9 Series connection

1   If for Fig. 1.6 Ohm's Law is rewritten it becomes

$$V = I \times (R_1 + R_2 + R_3)$$

Note: The resistances add, and the volt-drops V_1 V_2 V_3 always add up to the total supply voltage V, a point to remember when fault tracing.

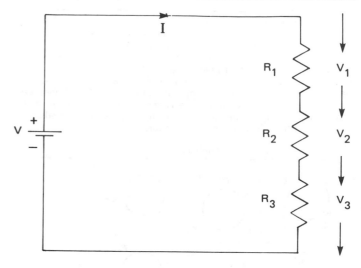

Fig. 1.6 Voltage drop (Secs 8 and 9)

Voltage drops around a circuit add up to the supply voltage

Example
2   To see how this equation might be used in practice, suppose $R_1 = 3\Omega$, $R_2 = 4\Omega$, and $R_3 = 5\Omega$. What current would be drawn from the battery if V = 12 volts?

$$12 = I \times (3 + 4 + 5)$$
$$\text{or } 12 = I \times 12$$
$$\text{so } I = 1 \text{ ampere}$$

3   In practice, the internal resistance of the battery may be significant (especially if it is wearing out) and there may be unwanted resistance in the cables and connections. These undesired resistances would have to be taken into account for some purpose by using Ohm's Law as above. See the example given later.

10 Parallel connection

1   Referring to Fig. 1.7 it is clear that the battery must supply the current to all three branches and that the total current is the sum of the branch currents:

$$\text{that is, } I = I_1 + I_2 + I_3$$

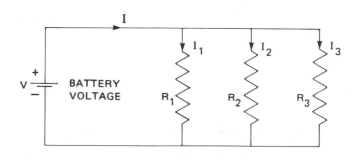

Fig. 1.7 Resistors in parallel (Secs 8 and 10)

2   Each branch has the full voltage V applied to it, so in this case the separate currents may be calculated and added.

3   Note that this is the most frequent arrangement to be met in a car electrical system — for instance R_1 could be the lighting load, R_2 the horn, R_3 the ignition, and the current demand on the battery would be the sum of the separate currents.

Example

4   Suppose again the supply voltage was 12 volts and the load resistors were $R_1 = 6\,\Omega$, $R_2 = 3\,\Omega$, and $R_3 = 4\,\Omega$, as in Fig. 1.8.

$$I_1 = \frac{V}{R_1} = \frac{12}{6} = 2A$$

$$I_2 = \frac{V}{R_2} = \frac{12}{3} = 4A$$

$$I_3 = \frac{V}{R_3} = \frac{12}{4} = 3A$$

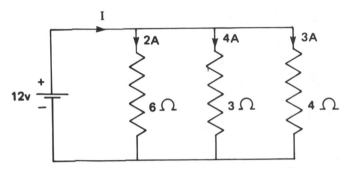

Fig. 1.8 An example of current drain by resistors in parallel (Sec 10)

The total current drain from the battery is therefore $I = 9A$.

5   By using Ohm's Law again, it will be seen that if the equivalent resistance of the 3 branches in parallel, R_T, is worked out it is given by

$$V = I \times R_T$$

$$12 = 9 \times R_T$$

$$R_T = \frac{12}{9} = 1\frac{1}{3}\,\Omega$$

6   The practical case fitting the parallel connection is, in fact, all the components connected to a car battery.

7   For example, if the head and rear lamps take 5A and 0.5A respectively and the ignition coil 1.5A, then if they are all on together the total current drain is:

$$I = 5 + 0.5 + 1.5 = 7A$$

11 Energy and power

1   **Energy** (or work, as it is sometimes called) is measured in **JOULES** where 1 joule is the energy expended when a pressure of 1 volt drives a current of 1 ampere through a load for 1 second.

So   joules   =   volts x amperes x seconds
or, in symbols   J   =   VIt

Example

2   If a 12 volt battery delivers 3 amperes of current to a headlight bulb for 20 minutes, how much energy is used?

Energy   =   V x I x t
         =   12 x 3 x 20 x 60
         =   43,200 joules

3   The joule is not used very much in routine electrical work, but it is of interest to note that it is also the unit of energy in mechanical engineering if SI (metric) units are used.

4   **Power** is closely related to energy, for it is simply the rate of utilising energy. The unit of power is the **WATT**.

$$\text{Watts} = \text{joules per second ie } \frac{\text{joules}}{\text{seconds}}$$

Remembering that joules = volts x amperes x seconds

we have Watts = $\dfrac{\text{joules}}{\text{seconds}}$ = volts x amperes

so   **Watts = volts x amperes** for a direct current circuit

5   In the example described, the battery delivering 3A at 12V is giving a power of

$$W = V \times I = 12 \times 3 = 36 \text{ Watts}$$

Clearly the joule (watts x seconds) is an inconveniently small unit and it is more usual to use the larger time quantity of the hour. Electricity bills are worked out this way, as illustrated:

Example

6   An electric heater works off 240 volt mains and takes a current of 10 amperes. If the heater is switched on for 4 hours how much energy is used?

Energy   =   V x I x t
         =   240 x 10 x 4
         =   9600 watt-hours
or   =   9.6 kilowatt-hours (kWh)
             (9.6 units on your electricity bill)

12 Wiring volt-drop

1   Examination of the wiring loom of a car will show that the wires and cables are of different thicknesses, and that often the wire is not one solid strand, but made up of many strands or filaments twisted together.

2   The designer chooses a cable so that the current flowing from the source to the load does not produce an undue waste of energy in the wires carrying it.

3   It is important to remember that although the wires are made of copper, which is a good conductor, nevertheless there is some finite resistance in which heating loss and volt-drop will occur. This means less power to the load, and inefficiency.

4   The battery shown connected to the bulb in Fig. 1.9 has a terminal pressure of 12 volts and ideally all this voltage should appear across

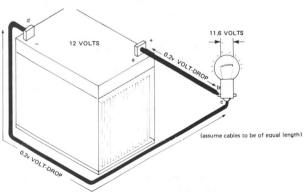

Fig. 1.9 Volt-drop in connecting cables (Secs 12 and 13)

the bulb; however, here the connecting wires have a resistance which gives a loss of 0.2 volt for both go and return, leaving only 11.6 volts to light the bulb filament.

5   The result in this case is poor illumination due to the waste of power in the wires. Better results would be obtained by using thicker cables, but the limits to increasing diameter are determined by the cost of copper and undesirable stiffness of thick wires.

13 Ammeters and voltmeters

1   There is no need to know much about the internal workings of electrical instruments in order to use them, and the basic rules are simple. An ammeter measures the current flowing **through** a circuit; it is connected so that this current flows through the instrument, ie in **series** with the load, as shown in Fig. 1.10.

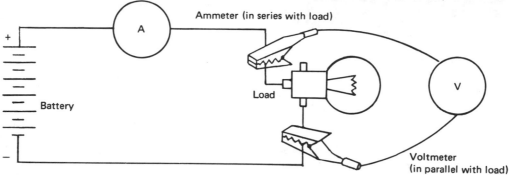

Fig. 1.10 Connections for ammeter and voltmeter (Sec 13)

2   The instrument designer keeps the internal resistance of the ammeter as low as possible; if by accident the ammeter were connected **across** the load, instead of in **series** with it, this would be disastrous. Because of the low ammeter resistance a heavy current would flow, destroying the instrument and possibly melting the connecting wire insulation.

3   Fortunately the voltmeter is not so vulnerable because it is designed to have a high resistance and is less likely to be burnt out.

4   The voltmeter measures electrical **pressure** and should be connected **across** parts of a circuit. For instance, in Fig. 1.9, if connected across a and d the voltmeter would measure the battery voltage; across b and c the bulb voltage, and from d to c or a to b the volt drop in the cables.

5   Sometimes instruments have a switch to give different ranges. Clearly the user will choose the range so that the pointer needle gives a reading well up the scale, for there is a considerable risk of reading error at low readings where the thickness of the pointer may be comparable with the amount of deflection.

6   Instruments should never be regarded as wholly accurate, and very cheap equipment can be a poor investment in terms of reliability of readings.

7   Multi-purpose instruments are useful for workshop testing, but care is even more important – make sure that the right range is selected and alter the range switch with the leads disconnected. The reason for this is that a rotary range switch may pass through current ranges – amperes – before reaching the desired voltage position. If connected to a supply this can spell the rapid end to an expensive instrument.

8   Most test instruments have a moving-coil movement; this type responds to direct current (dc) only.

9   Moving coil instruments may be arranged to measure alternating current or voltage by incorporating a rectifier, usually of the bridge type (see Chapter 4).

14 Electromagnets

1   A limitation to the amount of power generated in permanent magnet dynamos and other electrical equipment is due to the relatively weak magnetic field strength of the permanent magnet. The solution lies in the use of the electromagnet, which consists of an iron core over which a coil is wound.

2   Passing direct current through the coil will induce a magnetic field in the iron, which may then bear a strong resemblance to an ordinary permanent magnet with the differences that:

(a)   the strength of the magnetic field can be controlled (within limits) by varying the current in the coil
(b)   the magnetic field virtually disappears when the current is switched off

3   The arrangement of the electromagnet is shown in Fig. 1.11, together with a graph showing the way in which field strength varies

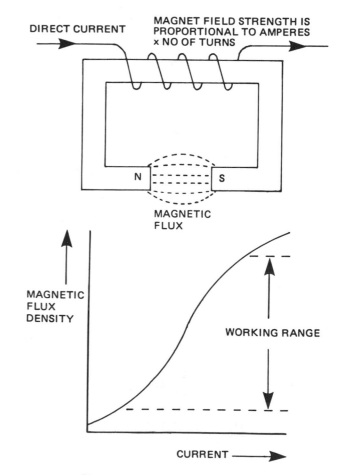

Fig. 1.11 The electromagnet (Sec 14)

with coil current. Note that beyond a certain current the magnetic flux density flattens off — the iron is said to be saturated.

4   The electromagnet finds many uses in electrical equipment for cars; instead of a permanent magnet in a dynamo or alternator it is possible to use electromagnets, with the advantage that the electrical output can be regulated by varying the current in the electromagnet windings. In motor and generator practice, the electromagnets producing magnetic flux are called field poles and the coils are field windings.

15 Electromagnetic relays and solenoids

1   The relay is used to switch heavy current on, or off, by means of a much smaller control current (Fig. 1.12). A typical example is the starter motor, where the current rises to several hundred amperes. In this particular instance, the heavy cable needed to carry this current from the battery must be short to avoid voltage loss, and could not conveniently be brought to a dashboard switch anyway because of the cable stiffness and bulk. The relay overcomes this problem since it is located in the short path between battery and starter and only a thin control cable need go to the dashboard.

2   It is well known that opposite magnetic poles attract each other and will also exert a pull on nearby iron or steel. This effect is used in the relay in which a strip of iron is pulled by the magnetic field created when current is switched on. The movement of the iron strip or **armature** can be made to open or close electrical contacts, which may act as a switch for a variety of uses, some of which will be described later in this book.

3   A simple relay is shown in Fig. 1.13 in which the armature is held in one position by the flat spring until the coil current is switched on. Then the magnetic flux set up by the coil causes the armature to be attracted to the central iron core and so closes the contacts. When the current is switched off the magnetic field disappears and the armature returns to the rest position, the contacts opening. This type of relay is the basis of cutouts and regulators used widely in automotive engineering.

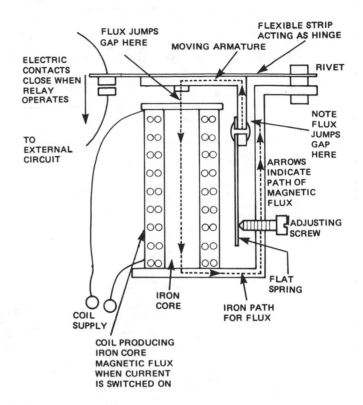

Fig. 1.13 Magnetic relay (Sec 15)

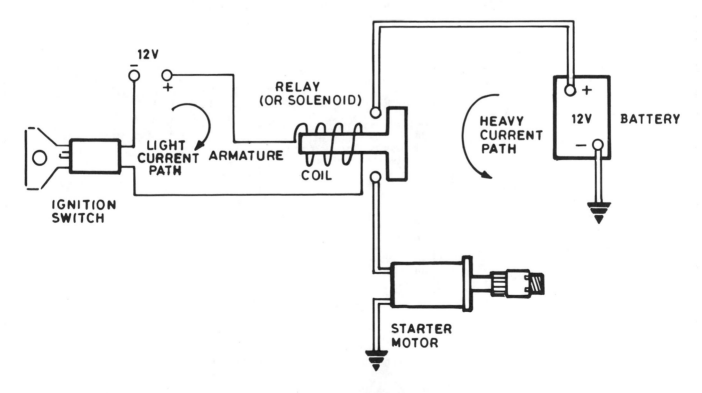

Fig. 1.12 Principle of the relay (Sec 15)

4   A different type of actuating device is the solenoid, often used on starter motors. This relies on the fact that an iron core is attracted towards the mid point of a coil carrying current (Fig. 1.14). The pull exerted on the iron armature can be so great that its movement may be powerful enough to engage the starter pinion gear into a flywheel gear ring and also switch on the heavy current of the starter motor.

16 Magnetic field strength

1   It is found that the magnetic field in an iron circuit depends upon

several factors over which the designer has control:

    (a)   the number of turns of wire on the coil
    (b)   the current flowing (amperes)
    (c)   the iron path details

2   In general, magnetic flux will pass more readily through iron than air and so if a strong field is required, then an iron path of large cross-sectional area is necessary, together with a coil designed to make the product of amperes x turns as large as possible (Fig. 1.15).

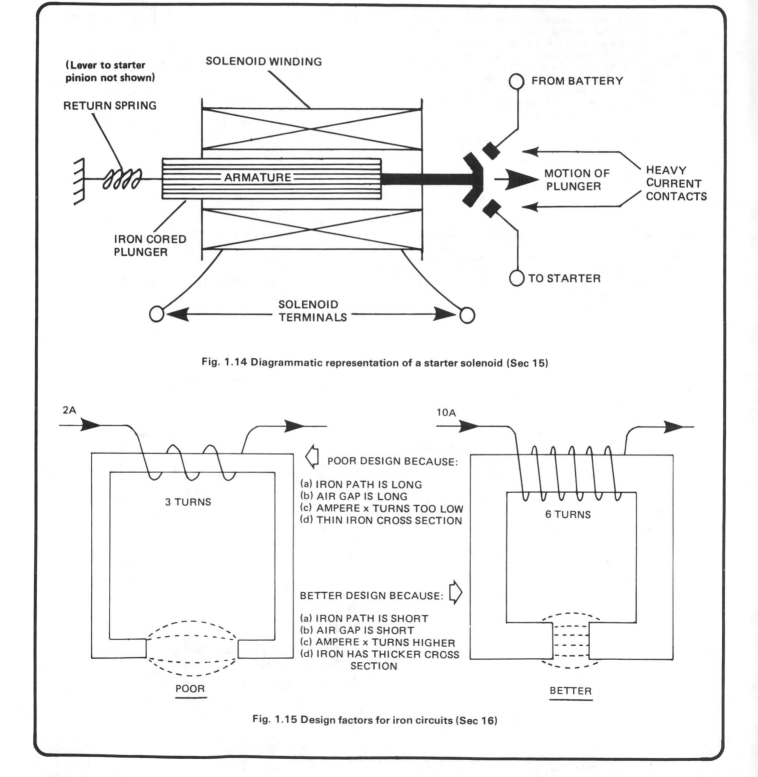

Fig. 1.14 Diagrammatic representation of a starter solenoid (Sec 15)

Fig. 1.15 Design factors for iron circuits (Sec 16)

17 Motors and generators

1   Millions of motors, dynamos and alternators are in use in motor vehicles and probably represent the greatest use of electrical machines in any branch of industry. It is a credit to designers that relatively few failures occur, for these machines are subject to heavy utilisation, need very little maintenance and work in a hostile environment, having to cope with wide temperature ranges, dust, damp and, in the case of generators, speed variations from a few hundred to thousands of revolutions per minute with high acceleration forces.

2   The motor and generator (included here are dynamos and alternators) are not really separate for it is only a question of energy flow. Thus in the case of the direct-current motor, electrical energy is put in and mechanical energy emerges at the shaft. The same machine could be driven by an external prime mover and electrical energy would be available at the terminals. The dc motor and the dc generator are, then, essentially the same device. A similar picture may be stated for the alternator which could be driven as a motor by connecting it correctly to an alternating current supply. The relationship between the dc motor and generator is particularly important here.

3   Most electrical instruments are really a highly specialised form of direct-current electric motor operating over a limited angular range of 90° to 120° only. Designers use the same form of calculations in designing instruments and dc motors.

4   The details of dc generators, alternators and motors will be dealt with in the later chapters of this book. Here the two important principles of motor and generator action are stated, and armed with this information, the way in which machines and instruments work will be readily understood.

18 The generator rule

1   If a wire moves across a magnetic field it is found that a voltage is generated in it for so long as there is motion (see Fig. 1.16). The

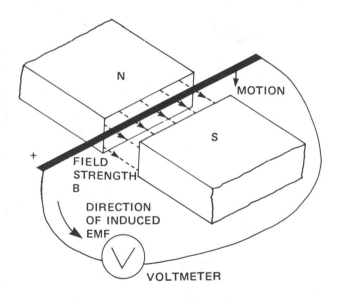

Fig. 1.16 Induced EMF in moving conductor (Sec 18)

voltage obtained is found to depend upon:

(a)   the length of wire in the magnetic field
(b)   the velocity of the wire at right angles to the magnetic field
(c)   the strength of the magnetic field

The actual value in volts is:

$$E = B\,\ell\,V \text{ volts}$$

where: B   =   strength of magnetic field measured in Webers per square metre (or Tesla)
            ℓ =   length of wire (metres)
            V   =   velocity of wire at right angles to the magnetic field (metres per second)

No need to be concerned about any calculations to read further: all that is important is to remember the factors which fix the size of the generated voltage.

2   In order to make a generator, the wire is formed into a rectangular coil and spun round inside the magnetic field. All the rest is detail, but upon this basic rule depends the operation of the dynamo and the alternator. This theme occurs in the book several times — it is well worth remembering.

19 The motor rule

1   This is the converse of the generator situation. Electric current passed down a wire located in a magnetic field will experience a force at right angles to both current and field directions.

2   Fig. 1.17 shows a wire carrying a current. The wire is situated in a magnetic field, the direction of which is conventionally agreed to be from N to S in the air path. The wire will create a magnetic field of its own and this field will interact with that of the motor field giving rise to a force acting downwards. The numerical value of the force will depend upon:

(a)   the strength of the magnetic field, B Webers per sq. metre
(b)   the amount of current flowing in the wire, I amperes
(c)   the length of wire inside the magnetic field, ℓ metres

The force is:

$$F = BI\ell \text{ Newtons}$$

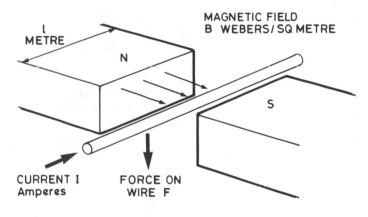

FORCE ON WIRE, F = BIℓ NEWTONS
(For those who think in Imperial Units
1 Newton is approx. ¼ lb force)

Fig. 1.17 Force on a wire carrying a current (Sec 19)

3   If now the wire is bent into a rectangular shape and located within the magnetic field again, the direction of current in the two sides is opposite and so will be the forces acting on them. It now remains only to pivot the rectangular coil on bearings for it to become a simple electric motor, for the two forces will give rise to rotation, Fig. 1.18.

4   This idea of motor operation will be particularly useful when reading the Chapter on Starters, where the subject will be developed further.

5   Torque is an important concept in engineering. In Fig. 1.19 torque is applied to a nut by means of a spanner and is a measure of turning capability. It is simply the force and distance multiplied, but on the condition that the direction of force is at right angles to the direction to the nut centre.

6   Looking again at the simple motor of Fig. 1.18, the coil radius is R, and there are two operating sides each giving a force F, so:

Motor torque = 2 x F x R   Newton-metres
(or pounds-feet in Imperial units)

7   Further developments of these ideas are given later, particularly in the Chapters on Starter Motors and Charging Systems.

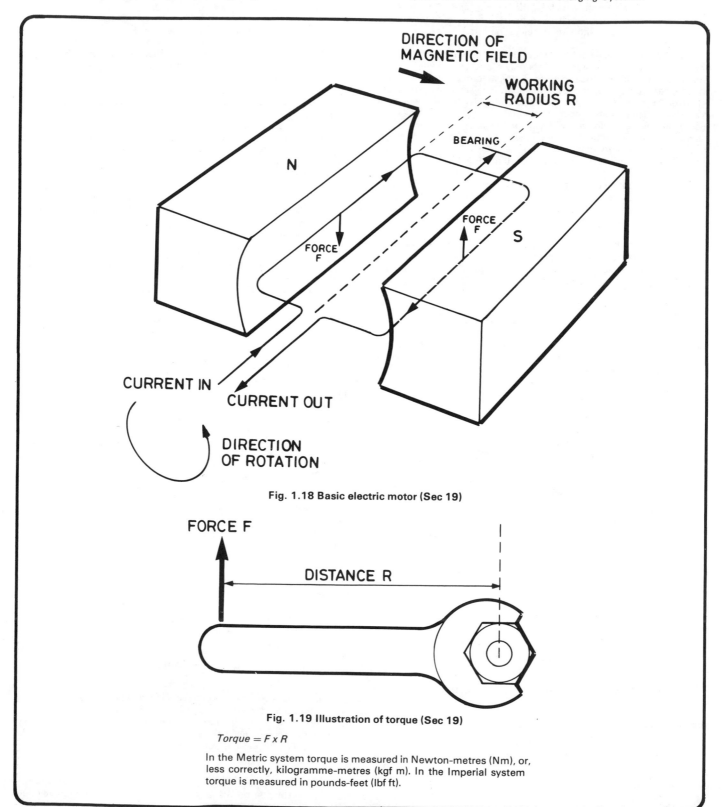

Fig. 1.18 Basic electric motor (Sec 19)

Fig. 1.19 Illustration of torque (Sec 19)

Torque = F x R

In the Metric system torque is measured in Newton-metres (Nm), or, less correctly, kilogramme-metres (kgf m). In the Imperial system torque is measured in pounds-feet (lbf ft).

Chapter 2 Instruments and Auxiliaries

Contents

1 Vehicle instrumentation – general

Instruments are fitted to every automobile, the speedometer being a legal requirement in most countries. In addition there may be a fuel gauge, and possibly others to read coolant temperature, oil pressure, manifold vacuum, charging current and battery voltage.

Some vehicles will also have an engine revolution counter (tachometer), this often being an electronic system.

2 Instrument types

Electrical instrument indicators used in automobiles are found to be in three categories:

(a) Moving iron – used for many years and now less popular
(b) Bi-metal – sluggish instruments requiring a stabilised supply voltage
(c) Air-cored – instantaneous response, self-compensating, requiring no voltage stabiliser

3 Moving iron instruments

1 These depend upon the relative magnetic pulls of two coils upon a small pivoted iron armature to which the dial pointer is attached. Fig. 2.1 shows the instrument in conditions of:

(a) tank empty
(b) tank full

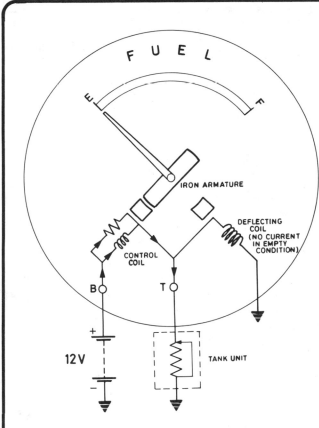

Fig. 2.1a Moving iron fuel gauge – empty (Sec 3)

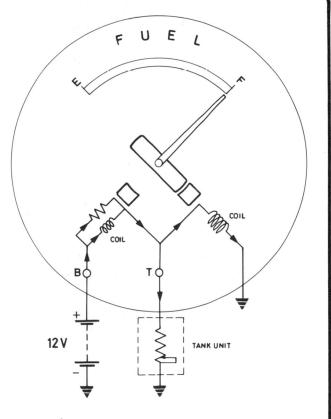

Fig. 2.1b Moving iron fuel gauge – full (Sec 3)

2   The control coil and deflecting coil both attract the magnet when carrying current and the position of the magnet and its pointer are a measure of the fuel tank contents.

3   The variable-resistance fuel level transmitter has low resistance when the tank is empty, and high resistance when full. As the fuel level rises there is increasing resistance to current passing through the fuel level transmitter. Instead, the current passes through the deflecting coil which then attracts the magnet on the indicator needle.

4   There are two disadvantages of this instrument system:

   (a)   the system is undamped and the pointer moves quickly to follow petrol waves and disturbances
   (b)   the difficulty of measuring tank content when nearly empty – just when accuracy is sometimes most needed

5   The instrument has advantages of cheapness and the readings are independent of supply voltage.

4   Bi-metal instruments

1   This instrument is used with several vehicle measuring devices, but as a fuel gauge it employs a variable resistance unit and float in the tank together with a bi-metal current indicator (Fig. 2.2).

2   The instrument consists of a bi-metal strip in the form of a 'U' with a heater coil wound on one leg. As the strip bends due to the unequal expansion of the two different metals used, a pointer moves across the scale to indicate fuel level. The U-shape, as a whole, compensates for any ambient temperature changes – so the instrument always zeros correctly.

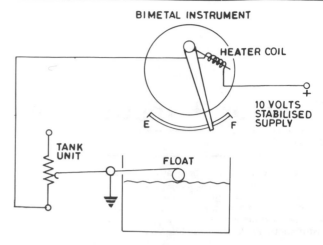

Fig. 2.2 Bi-metal fuel gauge (Sec 4)

3   Sometimes the float is arranged so that its loading weight, and therefore its depth of submersion, varies wth fuel level.

4   At the 'empty' end the float has least submersion and is most sensitive to change. This is further aided by the winding of the tank resistor being graded to give the required scale form on the indicator.

5   Due to the thermal lag, this instrument responds slowly and is not sensitive to fuel surges when braking or cornering.

5   Air-cored instruments

1   This is a relatively recent development to provide an indicator capable of withstanding harsh conditions, self compensating for voltage changes (except when used as a battery voltage indicator), giving instantaneous response and no radio interference.

2   The device may be used to measure fuel level, temperature, battery condition, and pressure.

3   The instrument consists of three coils which are energised simultaneously and, in the centre of the coils, a magnet to which the pointer is attached. To cause the pointer to move, the relative current in the three coils is changed (Fig. 2.3).

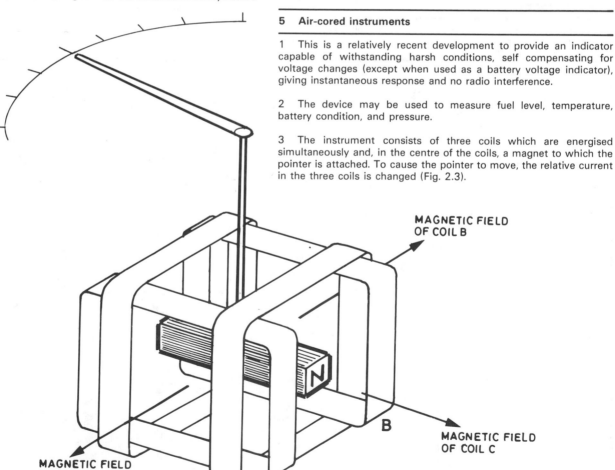

Fig. 2.3 Air-cored indicator (Sec 5)

4 The direction of the magnetic field due to each coil is fixed, but by varying the amount of current in each coil, the resultant vector of magnetism produced by all three can be made to move, and with it the magnet and the pointer.

5 As a battery voltage indicator the three coils A, B, C are connected in series and have current limit and calibration resistors R_1 and R_2 (Fig. 2.4). Across coils A and B is a Zener diode which, once operating, maintains a constant voltage across its terminals and therefore constant current in coils A and B. Current in coil C will, however, rise with increasing battery voltage and the combined magnetic fields of A, B and C will gradually swing round in direction, taking the pointer across the scale, which will be calibrated in volts.

6 For fuel gauges, temperature and pressure indicators, the transmitter unit is connected at the junction of coils B and C. Thus as the measured quantity changes so does the resistance of the transmitter and also the amount of current in C. This causes a slewing of the magnetic field and hence the magnet and pointer will turn.

6 Instrument voltage stabiliser (IVS)

1 This is another example of bi-metal strip application. Instead of moving a pointer, the stabiliser uses the bi-metal heated strip to open contacts which cut off the supply to its own heater and also to other loads connected to it.

2 The strip cools down, the contacts reclose and the cycle continues at a relatively slow rate, depending upon the voltage of battery or generator/alternator. The average voltage is 10 volts for most stabilisers and, since it is designed to supply equally sluggish instruments, the switching on and off has no adverse effect (Fig. 2.5).

3 Stabilisers can become faulty giving rise to erratic readings on instruments. Care must be taken to mount the stabiliser according to manufacturer's instructions, since the attitude is important.

4 The method of testing a stabiliser is to connect a good quality dc voltmeter to the I terminal and earth. The voltage should pulse with a mean value of 10 volts.

7 Temperature transmitters and indicators

1 In earlier vehicles temperature was measured by a liquid capsule connected by a thin pipe to a Bourdon gauge mounted on the dashboard. These were difficult to fit and have now given way to either a thermistor (semiconductor) or the thermal (bi-metal) type.

2 **Thermal temperature units** (Fig. 2.6) use bi-metal elements at both the temperature measuring end and in the indicator. The transmitter is in the form of a voltage stabiliser (Sec 6) in which the contacts open and close at a rate which depends upon the temperature. For higher temperatures the tension between contacts is

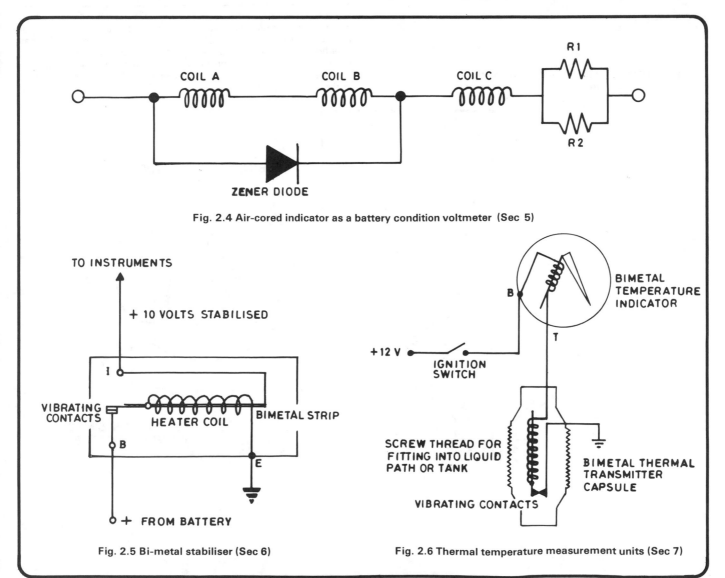

Fig. 2.4 Air-cored indicator as a battery condition voltmeter (Sec 5)

Fig. 2.5 Bi-metal stabiliser (Sec 6)

Fig. 2.6 Thermal temperature measurement units (Sec 7)

lower and they will therefore be closed for a shorter period. It follows that less average current will flow through the indicator.

3   Most current will flow when the temperature is lowest and so the indicator zeros at the hot end of the scale.

4   The effect of the making and breaking of contacts will not be noticed on the indicator due to the long thermal time constant.

5   **Thermistor (semiconductor) units** are based on resistors made from semiconductor material which exhibit a marked negative temperature-coefficient of resistance. That is, unlike most metals, the resistance goes down with a rise in temperature.

6   The transmitter is a brass capsule containing a pellet of semiconductor material in close contact with a brass heat sink to dissipate the

heat generated by the indicator current. The temperature of the liquid surrounding the capsule determines the resistance of the thermistor — at high temperatures the resistance is low, current and scale indication is therefore high.

7   From Fig. 2.7 it will be seen that these transmitters can be used with moving iron or bi-metal indicators; in the latter case a stabiliser unit is required.

8   Pressure indicators

1   Pressure gauges can be of the bi-metal, moving iron or air-cored variety.

2   An example of a bi-metal type pressure transmitter is shown in Fig. 2.8 in which a diaphragm, subjected to pressure, will flex. The movement is transmitted to a bi-metal vibrator similar to that of the voltage stabiliser of Fig. 2.5, but in this case the tension with which contacts are initially held together will depend upon the pressure being measured.

3   The reading will not be independent of supply voltage and so it will be necessary to use an instrument voltage stabiliser in-line with the ignition-switched supply wire.

9   Driver's facility and information systems

1   It is now common practice to fit original equipment devices which will alert and inform the driver of hazards and malfunctions. Most of the technology has been available for years, but routine production has now brought down the price of electronics to an economic level. The following represent some of the equipment available and it is certain that the next few years will see many more applications of electronics in the motor vehicle.

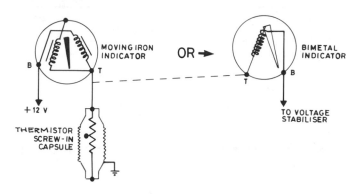

Fig. 2.7 Thermistor (semiconductor) transmitter used with a moving iron or bi-metal indicator (Sec 7)

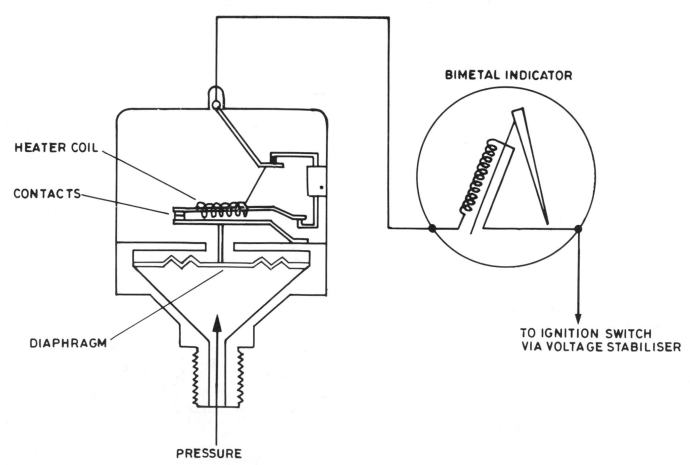

Fig. 2.8 Thermal pressure transmitter and indicator (Sec 8)

Ford Escort Auxiliary Warning System

2   This is fitted to certain models of the Escort range and is a means of warning the driver of low oil level or that the disc brake pads are in need of replacement. Other functions are also indicated.

3   When the ignition is first switched on, all warning lamps light up for five seconds to check that no bulbs are blown. The system is then capable of the following:

4   **Oil level indicator:** The engine oil dipstick contains a thermistor in the lower end which is normally immersed in oil. The thermistor is a pad of semiconductor material which changes its electrical resistance with changes in temperature. If the oil level falls too low the thermistor is no longer directly surrounded by hot oil and the corresponding resistance change lights a warning lamp.

5   **Disc pads wear indicator:** The sensing of worn disc pads is carried out by a metallic electrode built into the pad. When the friction material has worn down to 2mm (0.079 inch) thick, the electrode is exposed and makes electrical contact with the disc, thus switching on the warning lamp.

6   **Coolant level indicator:** A warning lamp is switched on when the level of coolant in the radiator expansion tank falls below a certain level. This is done by a float operated reed switch mounted in the tank.

7   **Fuel level indicator:** A low fuel level is signalled by a sensor mounted in the fuel level transmitter that switches on at 7 litres (1.5 gallons).

8   **Washer fluid indicator:** The windscreen washer fluid level is also measured, so that when down to $\frac{1}{4}$ full a float operated reed switch closes to give a warning.

Seat belt warning

9   Now common practice, seat belt warning devices usually operate by the action of the seat belt clip being pushed home into the socket.

10   The type of warning given varies, examples being a continuously flashing dashboard light or a buzzer timer.

11   It is also possible to find arrangements where the engine will not start unless the seat belts are clipped home. In this, and other systems, the front seats have sensor switches which detect the weight of a driver and passenger.

12   In an arrangement employed by American Motors Corporation, only prior fitting of seat belts will permit engine cranking. If a seat belt is unbuckled while the engine is running a warning light appears when the transmission is taken out of neutral or, for manual gearshift cars, when the handbrake is released. Such a system has the following provisions:

13   **Bounce:** If a seat occupant lifts off the seat momentarily, an electronic logic unit delays the onset of warning for a few seconds.

14   **Restarting:** The engine may be restarted after switch-off, with seat belts unbuckled, provided that the driver has not left the seat.

15   **Override relay:** This is a device mounted in the engine compartment which may be used to restart the engine if the interlock system fails. The ignition is reswitched ON, the bonnet (hood) opened and the relay button pressed and released. Then the ignition switch is turned to START and the override of the relay stays effective until the ignition key is turned to OFF or LOCK.

16   A similar system is used in the Jaguar XJ12 and is known as the sequential start interlock. In this case the engine will not start unless the correct starting procedure is carried out, namely:

   (a)   Sit in car and apply handbrake fully
   (b)   Set the selector lever to N or P
   (c)   Fasten the seat belts

Bulb failure warning

17   Several methods are used to warn drivers of the failure of parking (city) lights and stop-lights.

18   Jaguar use a photocell sensor in a lightproof box behind each lamp. Failure of a particular lamp will cause the sensor to illuminate a dashboard warning light.

19   Another arrangement employs the fibre-optic principle. in which light from the lamp is transmitted down a fibre-optic tube by reflection from its walls, until it is finally displayed at the far end at the dashboard instrument panel. This is non-electrical and promises to find many applications in future vehicles.

Automatic light switching

20   Ford US employs the Autolamp system on the Thunderbird/XR-7, Fairmont/Zephyr, Granada/Cougar and Mustang/Capri.

21   The arrangement provides for a light-sensitive photocell located close to the steering column facing out through the windscreen. The photocell switches on the exterior lights when natural light falls below a predetermined level, and switches off again when the light level is exceeded.

22   The system parallels the manual light switch, which must be in the 'off' position for the automatic function to operate.

23   When the vehicle is parked in the dark, and the ignition key withdrawn, the lights stay on for up to $4\frac{1}{2}$ minutes (controllable), to give the occupants assistance with visibility.

Illuminated entry system

24   Intended to assist vehicle entry during the hours of darkness, by providing illumination of the door lock cylinder so that key insertion may be easier, this system is standard in the Ford (US) Thunderbird and other models.

25   Activation of the system is by raising the outside door handle which switches on the electronic logic module. The vehicle's interior lamps are switched on and a ring of light appears round the two front door lock cylinders. The lock light is from light-emitting diodes (LED) which are gallium arsenide phosphide devices requiring low voltage, and draw a current of as little as 100 milliamperes.

26   The lights are on for about 25 seconds and are overridden by the ignition switch.

27   Opening the doors from inside the vehicle will not operate the system, and should the outside handles be tampered with by being propped up, the module switches off after 25 seconds and cannot be reactivated until the door handle is released.

Anti-skid braking

28   The maximum braking effect occurs just before the onset of skidding. While a squealing stop may sound impressive, better deceleration is obtained just before the squeal (and accompanying skid) occurs.

29   With the availability of electronic control, it is now possible to prevent a wheel skid. This is done by comparing the rotational speeds of the four wheels.

30   Chrysler Corporation (US) have perfected a system using a magnetic wheel (a rotor tone wheel) on each brake disc. A sensor picks up the magnetic field which generates a small alternating current at a frequency directly related to the wheel speed.

31   The alternating signal voltage from each wheel is routed to a logic box which compares the frequencies. If one wheel begins to lock, the rotational speed drops rapidly and with it the signal frequency from that wheel. The logic unit senses the difference, and signals the modulator controlling brake fluid pressure at each wheel to relax the pressure at the decelerating wheel to give a braking force just below the skid point.

Radar headway control

32 Research into the automatic detection of obstacles in front of a motor vehicle has led to a system based on Döppler radar.

33 The protected vehicle has a small frequency modulation radar transceiver with an antenna facing forwards through the front grille.

34 Radar signals in the form of a continuous stream of waves are emitted. These waves will strike a vehicle or obstacle ahead and reflect a fraction of the wave energy back to be picked up by the radar receiver.

35 Now assuming the protected vehicle has a forward speed, it will pass through the reflected waves, their apparent frequency being higher than those transmitted because the receiver is sensing more waves per second.

36 This effect is well known in listening to a train approach and then pass by. In the first case the sound source movement adds to the number of sound waves per second, but as it passes the number of sound waves per second will decrease. Thus the received radio frequency will depend upon the relative speed of the motor vehicle and the obstruction ahead. The signal frequency is analysed and compared with the protected vehicle's speed. When the collision distance and the relative speeds have been calculated, a servo control system can apply appropriate braking. Conversely, it may open the throttle if a constant distance to the vehicle in front is desired.

Trip computer

37 One form of trip computer, used in the Talbot Alpine/Solara, gives information to the driver in the form of an elapsed time since departure, distance travelled, fuel consumed, average fuel consumption and average speed.

38 This is displayed on a digital readout, the calculations being carried out by microprocessor which is fed by the output of a fuel flow meter and a speed/distance sensor.

39 Less sophisticated, but on the same principle, Citroën employ the Econoscope which gives a lamp indication to the driver indicating a poor/good economical driving condition.

Cruise control

40 This has been available in the US for some time, and is now becoming more common in Europe.

41 A cruise control switch is typically mounted on the end of the direction indicator stalk (Fig. 2.9) and is operational only above a certain speed — usually 30 mph (50 kph).

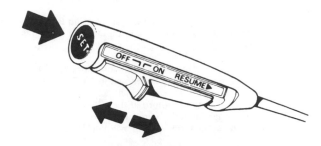

Fig. 2.9 Cruise control switch (Sec 9)

42 With the system ON it is possible to programme a selected speed into a computer by pressing the SET knob at the desired speed. A servo unit linked to the computer then controls the throttle to maintain the cruise speed, allowing for hills, wind change and the different rolling resistance of road surfaces.

43 A touch on the brake pedal instantly disconnects the cruise control until the RESUME switch is operated.

Warning devices

44 Many warning circuits use an audible buzzer in the passenger compartment. The buzzer is available in a convenient form in the Piezo buzzer, with blocking diodes. This buzzer will operate with the range 6 to 24 volts, and may be obtained from electronic component stores; the diode is of the silicon p-n function type and the range IN4000 is suitable.

45 In conjunction with the door courtesy switch (usually located in the door post between the hinges), the diode and buzzer will warn of several possible situations.

46 Fig. 2.10 shows the principle of working in which a warning will be given if the sidelights (parking lights) are left on. As the driver opens the door, the courtesy light switch closes and connects the diode and buzzer to earth (ground). If the sidelight circuit is live ie the lights are on, then the buzzer will sound.

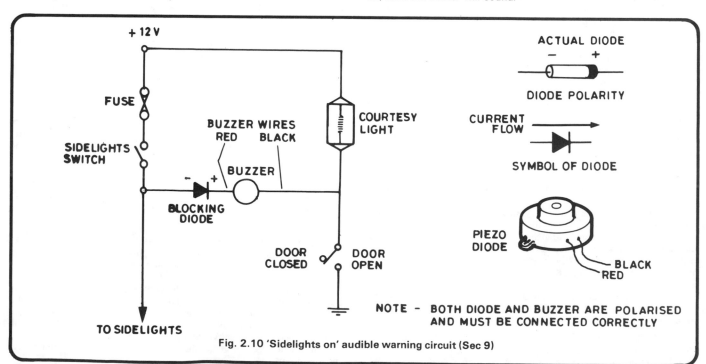

Fig. 2.10 'Sidelights on' audible warning circuit (Sec 9)

47 Note the purpose of the diode which passes current in one direction only; if it were not used then current would leak through the courtesy light, the buzzer and the sidelights.

48 An adaption of this idea to warn when headlights are left switched on is given in Fig. 2.11. A single buzzer may be used, but two blocking diodes are required.

49 Another application, such as an audible warning of the indicators working, uses the same components, but they are connected across the feeds to the left and right flashers and earth. In this case, the door courtesy switch is not used.

10 Fuel pumps – general

1 The majority of fuel pumps are mechanical units operated by an engine-driven cam. However, several vehicles use an electrical fuel pump, which falls into one of two categories:

(a) An electromagnetic vibrator unit mounted external to the fuel tank
(b) A motor driven pump which is submerged in the fuel. This unit is of the high pressure type, running continuously whilst the ignition switch is on, and is used in fuel injection systems.

2 The SU fuel pump is of the electromagnetic type (a) above and works via a pumping diaphragm and activating rod attached to an iron armature. The armature is attracted to the iron core and the diaphragm sucks petrol into the pumping chamber through a non-return inlet valve.

3 The movement of the rod and armature breaks open a pair of contacts (see Fig. 2.12) and the coil is de-energised allowing the

activating rod to return. This pushes the diaphragm and forces petrol out through the delivery valve, simultaneously closing the coil contacts again.

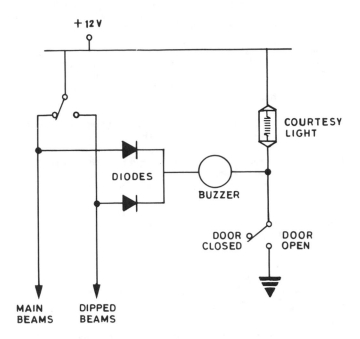

Fig. 2.11 'Headlights on' audible warning circuit (Sec 9)

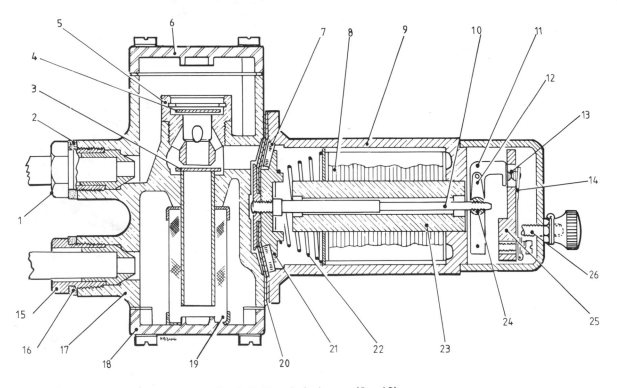

Fig. 2.12 Electric fuel pump (Sec 10)

1 Union outlet	8 Magnet coil	15 Union – inlet	21 Armature
2 Rubber ring	9 Iron coil housing	16 Rubber ring	22 Armature spring
3 Inlet valve	10 Bronze actuating rod	17 Body	23 Magnetic iron core
4 Outlet valve	11 Outer rocker	18 Lower cover-plate	24 Trunnion
5 Outlet valve cage	12 Inner rocker	19 Filter	25 Moulding
6 Top cover-plate	13 Tungsten points	20 Diaphragm	26 Terminal screw
7 Spherical rollers	14 Spring blade		

4   The contacts open and close quickly with an audible click assisted by a spring operated 'throw-over' mechanism which gives a snap action.

5   Electric petrol pumps of this type are often located on or near the petrol tank, but may be mounted on the engine bulkhead. Supply is via an auxiliary circuit fuse and the ignition switch.

6   Such pumps are self-limiting in operation and will slow down and finally stop when the pressure rises in the carburettor supply pipe as the float chamber inlet valve closes. This occurs when the return spring cannot force the activating rod against the petrol trapped in the pumping chamber.

7   Delivery is of the order of 70 pints of fuel per hour to a carburettor located up to 3 ft above the tank, so it will cope with all requirements.

8   Several models are available including a type which will operate a fuel reserve system. In this example the pump has two pumping chambers, but the principle of operation is the same.

9   Servicing is strictly limited, since some models are sealed units and little can be done, save replacement. With some pumps, the SU for instance, it is possible to take the unit apart; when removing it, it is wise to:

(a) work in a ventilated space and do not smoke or have a naked flame nearby
(b) disconnect the earth lead of the battery

Before removal, however, checks should be carried out as follows:

10   Normal operation of the contacts is assumed if the pump gives a series of clicks upon switching on and then the clicks slow down to nil or the occasional click.

11   Take off the feed pipe at the carburettor. Switch on the ignition — the pump should deliver petrol in a series of rapid surges. Be ready to catch the petrol in a container and switch off quickly.

12   If the pump does not click, as in paragraph 10 above, then, with a test meter on the ohms range, or using a test lamp, check that there is continuity between the pump supply terminal and (a) the pump body, and (b) the vehicle body. Pumps sometimes develop a bad earth connection between the pump frame and the vehicle earth due to corrosion. If no continuity exists, this indicates the points are stuck open or an open circuit in the coil.

13   If the contacts are found to be operating as in paragraph 10, but there is no pumping action, the fault lies in the valves or the diaphragm linkages.

14   Sometimes sticky contacts can be temporarily released by tapping the pump body, but this will only be good enough to complete a journey, and remedial action is recommended. Replacement contact sets may be fitted, if available for the particular model, but a temporary improvement to the old contacts is possible by careful cleaning with a points file or glass paper.

15   A diaphragm may also be replaced, and this requires removal of the pump body from the base. The diaphragm may be unscrewed and its replacement carefully fitted.

16   Some pumps have a series of brass or plastic rollers for centralising the internal components, and care must be taken in this operation not to lose them.

11 Immersed fuel pumps

1   A high pressure fuel pump of the roller cell type (Fig. 2.13) may be used with fuel injection systems. This pump is totally immersed in the fuel which flows round the motor armature. Petrol is not combustible under these circumstances, however, so no hazard is present.

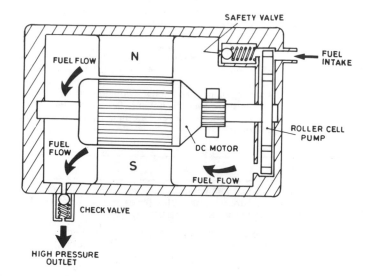

Fig. 2.13 Submerged roller cell fuel pump (Sec 11)

2   Associated with this arrangement is a return pipe from the injection primary pressure regulator which routes surplus fuel back to the tank. Thus there is a circulatory system so that the pump runs continuously so long as the ignition is switched on.

3   The pump body is eccentric with the rotor so that the gap is variable. The rotor is fitted with metal rollers let into slots in which they are free to move and will fly outwards under centrifugal force. Fuel is trapped into a segment between rollers just after the intake port and released at the outlet port into the motor body. It then emerges from an outlet pipe containing a spring controlled check-valve (Fig. 2.14).

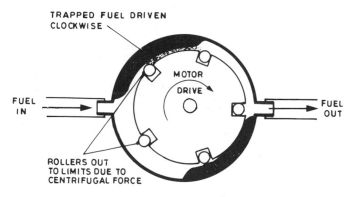

Fig. 2.14 Roller cell pump operation (Sec 11)

12 Thermofans

1   The traditional method of cooling a radiator is by means of a belt-driven fan powered from the engine. It has long been appreciated that considerable power is absorbed by the fan and, moreover, that it cools the radiator irrespective of whether the engine is hot or cold.

2   An improvement resulted from the viscous fan which was still driven by the engine via a belt, but did not drive the blades until a certain temperature was obtained. Today many fans are driven by electric motors and are independent of the engine.

3   Some electric fans operate continuously, as in certain Fiestas, but most have a temperature sensor which switches on the fan motor when the coolant temperature reaches a pre-determined level. The sensor is positioned to have intimate contact with the coolant, possibly plugged into the thermostat housing or into a hose, or simply strapped into the radiator or a hose.

4   Supply is usually via an ignition switch controlled terminal on the fusebox, but some vehicles, among them certain Volkswagens, have a direct battery connection for power.

5   Simple fans are made to fit on the radiator with through-bolts or plastic plugs, or on the water pump. In the case of fitting a thermofan as an accessory (Fig. 2.15), the existing fan is, of course, removed.

6   Although not an electric thermofan, it is worth mentioning the recently developed QH Thermofan. This device fastens to the water pump using the existing pulley mounting bolts and has variable pitch blades (Fig. 2.16). At normal operating temperatures the seven-bladed fan has a feathered pitch; that is, the blades lie almost flat. In the hub a series of rings expand with increase in air temperature to a maximum pitch of 30 degrees. The makers claim a significant saving in fuel, low fan noise, and precise metering of the required airflow.

Fig. 2.15 Typical aftermarket thermofan fitted to a radiator (Sec 12)

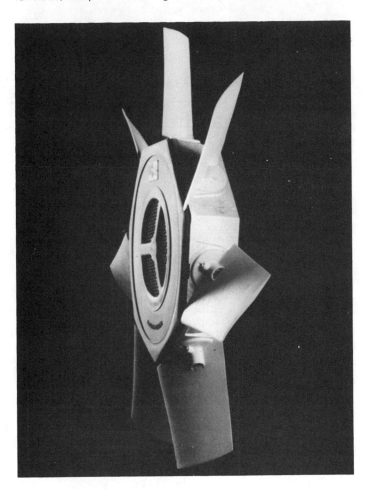

Fig. 2.16 The QH Thermofan with variable pitch blades (Sec 12)

Chapter 3 Batteries

Contents

1 Secondary batteries

1 The primary battery is an expendable device of the type used in torches and portable radio receivers and is of no importance in motor vehicles. The secondary battery, however, is widely used and differs from the primary type in that it is rechargeable after use.

2 Nearly all vehicles use a battery of the lead-acid type, but occasionally a steel-alkaline or nickel-alkaline battery is used. This Chapter deals exclusively with the lead-acid battery.

3 A battery is made up of a number of cells grouped together so that the battery terminal voltage is the sum of the separate cell voltages. A 12 volt battery, for example, has six 2 volt cells connected additively in series (Fig. 3.1).

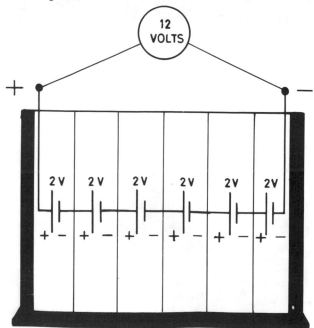

Fig. 3.1 Battery cells in series (Sec 1)

4 In practice, the actual voltage of the battery is not exactly 12 volts, but can reach as high as 14.5 volts soon after being charged, and as low as 10.8 volts in a completely discharged state.

5 The principal features of a lead-acid battery are as follows:

(a) It may be recharged after giving up its electrical energy
(b) The internal resistance is low, enabling heavy starter current to be delivered without too great a terminal voltage drop
(c) The liquid electrolyte is dilute sulphuric acid and, being corrosive, should not be allowed to make contact with eyes, skin, clothing or car paintwork. (Apply copious amounts of cold water in case of accidents with acid)
(d) During charge the electrolyte gives off hydrogen and oxygen. This mixture is explosive and care must be taken to avoid having sparks, cigarettes or naked flames near the battery vents
(e) Water is lost during discharge (except in some maintenance-free batteries — see later) and periodic replacement with distilled or de-mineralised water is essential. NB Tap water is NOT suitable

6 For chemical storage and release of energy, it is necessary to have two dissimilar conducting materials in close proximity and immersed in a conducting liquid, the electrolyte. The car battery uses a lead-antimony grid of several plates per cell and the grid holes are filled with lead oxide paste. After processing these become lead peroxide for the positive plates (chocolate colour) and spongy lead for the negative plates (grey colour).

7 When the battery is said to be in a charged state all or most of the grid contents are lead peroxide and spongy lead, ie differing metallic conductors, but as discharge is approached both plates change chemically and become lead sulphate.

8 Chemically inert separators are used between the plates. Originally they were made of wood or porous rubber, but now use more sophisticated materials such as the inorganic material Kieselguhr (KG) with glass-fibre matting reinforcement.

9 The separators must be strong, for under heavy charge and discharge the plates may swell and distort. Equally they must have a correct pore structure to allow the passage of the electrolyte. Pores which are too small represent an effective internal resistance which would lower the terminal voltage on starter load.

10 Plates are grouped together and are arranged to start and finish with a negative plate so that there are always more negative (-ve) than positive (+ve) plates. Separators are placed between each plate and the ribbed side is towards the +ve plate. Thus the electrolyte is concentrated at the +ve plate (Fig. 3.2).

11 Battery cases were formerly made of pitch and asbestos, but modern batteries use polypropylene (Fig. 3.3) which is translucent, showing battery acid level readily, also having good resilience and low weight.

2 Charge and discharge

1 When a battery is charged, current is forced through it in the opposite direction to normal, in much the same way as filling a tank via its outlet tap (Fig. 3.4). The battery gives a direct current (dc) and so it follows that a direct current is required to recharge it. Clearly if the battery has a terminal voltage of, say, 12 volts, then in order to force current into it, it will require a battery charging voltage somewhat in excess of this, say, 14 to 16 volts depending upon the charge rate required and the internal resistance of the battery.

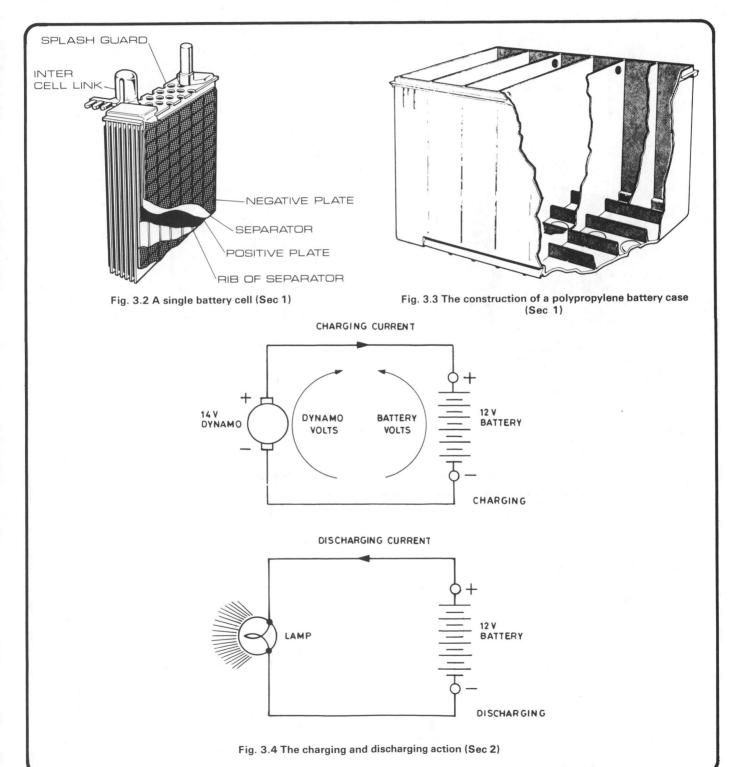

Fig. 3.2 A single battery cell (Sec 1)

Fig. 3.3 The construction of a polypropylene battery case (Sec 1)

Fig. 3.4 The charging and discharging action (Sec 2)

2   Looking now inside the battery (Fig. 3.5), while under charge conditions we see that the flow of current breaks up the electrolyte and that the electrolyte oxygen moves to combine with the lead of the +ve plate to form lead peroxide. Both plates give sulphate to form sulphuric acid in the electrolyte, and the negative plate turns to spongy lead.

3   Thus the two plates are altered chemically and the concentration of sulphuric acid increases, ie, the density, or specific gravity, of the electrolyte goes up as charging continues.

4   When discharging, the flow of current in the cell produces a breakdown of the acid such that sulphate leaves it and combines with both +ve and –ve plates to form, eventually, lead sulphate, so the plates are no longer dissimilar.

5   In addition, oxygen leaves the +ve plate and returns to the electrolyte to form water. Thus the electrolyte becomes diluted and the specified gravity goes down.

6   The hydrometer is a means of measuring the acid specific gravity and so gives information on the state of charge (Fig. 3.6).

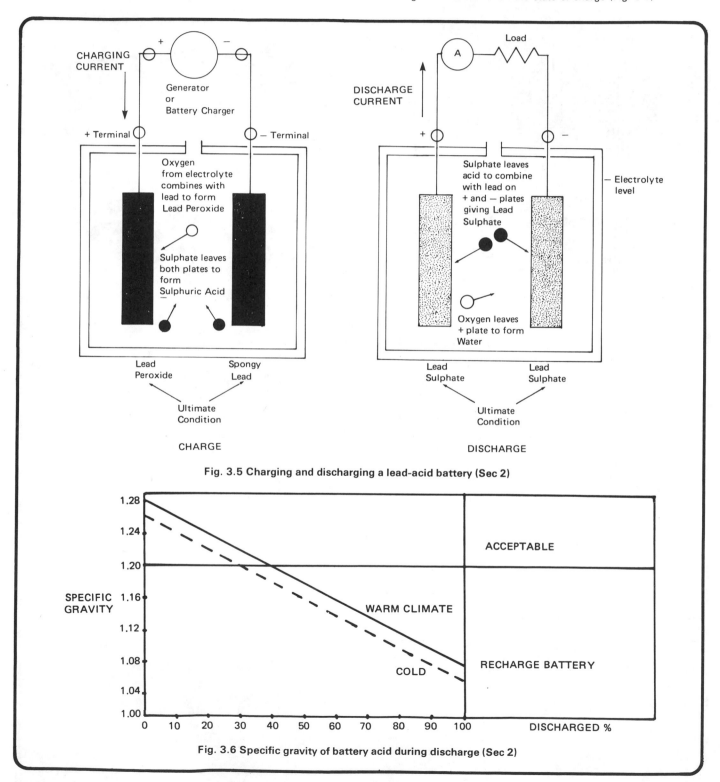

Fig. 3.5 Charging and discharging a lead-acid battery (Sec 2)

Fig. 3.6 Specific gravity of battery acid during discharge (Sec 2)

7   Fig. 3.7 shows an hydrometer which consists of a float inside a suction vessel. The nozzle is inserted into a battery cell and enough acid is withdrawn to read the float. The reading gives a good indication as to the battery charge state, assuming that the correct specific gravity of acid was used for the initial filling.

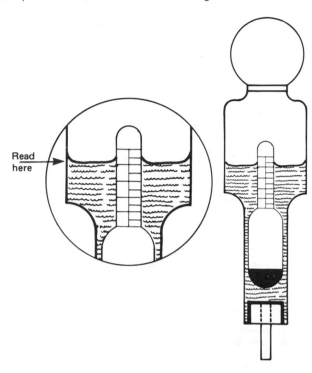

Fig. 3.7 Reading the hydrometer (Sec 2)

8   One formula to correct for very cold or very warm conditions is:

$$S_{20} = S_t + 0.007 (t - 20)$$

where S_t = measured specified gravity

t   = temperature of electrolyte (°C)

S_{20} = specific gravity corrected to 20°C

So that, if the specific gravity reading were to be 1.200 at 30°C, then the reading at the normal temperature of 20°C would be:

S_{20} = 1.200 + 0.007 (30-20)
       = 1.200 + 0.07
S_{20} = 1.27

Note from this the electrolyte will be denser, the lower the temperature.

9   A guide to specific gravity figures in relation to the charge state of a battery is as follows:

Hydrometer reading	Battery state
1.11 to 1.13	Discharged
1.23 to 1.25	70% charged
1.27 to 1.29	Fully charged

3   Ampere – hour (Ah) capacity

1   This is a measure of the total quantity of electricity which can be delivered by a battery from the fully charged condition until its terminal voltage drops to the lowest permitted limit – 1.8 volts per cell, or 10.8 volts for a nominal 12 volt battery.

2   The Ampere-hour capacity is sometimes given at the 10-hour rate and at a theoretical 25°C. The rated current is the steady load current that would discharge the battery in 10 hours, but if the actual discharge rate is higher, then usually the output capacity is reduced.

3   As a specific example, a 36 ampere-hour battery should be capable for delivering 3.6 amperes for 10 hours or 7.2 amperes for 5 hours etc. In practice, discharging at 7.2 amperes would give a somewhat shorter time than 5 hours, but the difference for a battery in good condition would be small.

4   The Ah capacity is also used to work out how long to charge a battery. Assuming the 36 Ah battery to be completely discharged, the theoretical charge might be:

6 amperes for 6 hours   = 36 Ah
or 3 amperes for 12 hours   = 36 Ah
and so on

5   Because the battery is not perfectly efficient, however, the output is never as great as the input, so a rule of thumb would be to put in 1.3 x Ah rating. So, the 36 Ah battery should really receive:

36 x 1.3 = 46.8 Ah input

On 6 hours of charge the current would have to be set at:

$$\frac{46.8}{6} = 7.8 \text{ amperes}$$

It should be noted that some manufacturers quote the Ah capacity at the 20-hour rate.

6   **Reserve capacity** is the time, in minutes, that a battery can hold a discharge rate of 25 amperes. Typically this might be 60 minutes for a battery fitted to a 1300 cc family saloon, and up to 180 minutes for a battery specified for a large luxury car such as a Jaguar.

4   Charging rates

1   On the vehicle the charge rate will be set automatically by the alternator or dynamo regulator. It will depend upon the state of charge of the battery, this in turn being fixed by recent loads and also the age and condition of the battery.

2   If, however, the charge rate on the bench is to be decided then, provided there is no urgency requiring rapid recharging, a suitable figure is somewhere between $\frac{1}{10}$ and $\frac{3}{10}$ of the battery capacity.

3   For example, if the 36 Ah battery were completely flat, then the ampere-hours of input required would be 46.8 Ah (see Section 3), and at the $\frac{1}{10}$ th rate:

Charging current   = $\frac{1}{10}$ x 46.8
                  = 5 amperes approximately

5   Battery filling

1   There may be an occasion to fill a new, dry battery with acid, in which case it is necessary to dilute concentrated sulphuric acid to the correct specific gravity.

2   Great care is required and it is recommended that goggles be worn.

3   To mix the electrolyte, first work out roughly how much distilled water and concentrated acid is required. The table (Fig. 3.8) gives the proportions by volume of distilled water required to 1 part of concentrated sulphuric acid (specific gravity 1.835).

4   **It is important to add the acid to the water and NEVER the other way round.** Considerable heat will be generated, and the acid must be added slowly and stirred until the correct specific gravity is obtained (Fig. 3.9).

SPECIFIC GRAVITY REQUIRED	PARTS OF DISTILLED WATER TO 1 OF CONC. SULPHURIC ACID
1.25	3.4
1.26	3.2
1.27	3.0
1.28	2.8
1.29	2.7
1.30	2.6

Fig. 3.8 Distilled water/concentrated sulphuric acid ratio by volume (Sec 5)

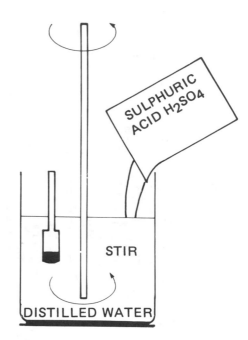

Fig. 3.9 Mixing acid and distilled water (Sec 5)

6 Open circuit voltage

1   The open circuit terminal voltage is that which would be measured at the battery terminals by a voltmeter, but with no external load.

2   It is related to the specific gravity, an approximate expression being:

Open circuit voltage = Specific gravity + 0.84 per cell

Thus if the acid specific gravity measured by an hydrometer were 1.25 then:

Cell voltage = 1.25 + 0.84 = 2.09 volts
Battery voltage = 6 x 2.09 = 12.54 volts

since there are 6 cells in series in a 12 volt battery.

7 Internal resistance

1   All batteries have an internal resistance, but this is very low in the case of a lead-acid battery in good condition. In fact it is because of the inherent low internal resistance that this type of battery is favoured for vehicle work where starting current demand can be very high.

2   Fig. 3.10 shows a battery with its equivalent internal resistance. A little arithmetic will show that if, for example, the internal resistance were to be 0.05 ohms and the open circuit voltage 12.0 volts then, with a lighting load of 10 amperes:

Battery terminal voltage   = 12 - Internal volt drop
                            = 12 - (10 x 0.05)
                            = 11.5 volts

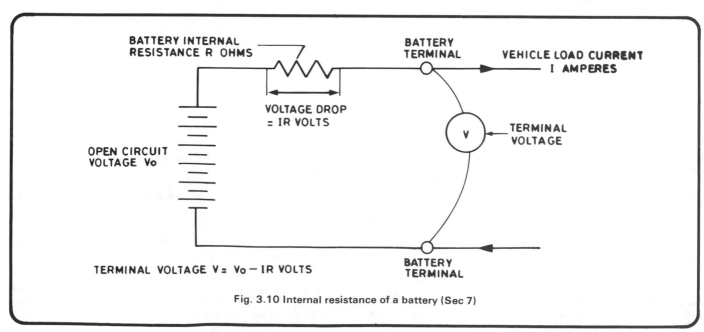

Fig. 3.10 Internal resistance of a battery (Sec 7)

The table shows terminal voltages for this battery under various loads.

Open circuit voltage	Load current (A)	Internal drop	Terminal voltage
12V	10 amperes	0.5 volts	11.5 volts
12V	20 amperes	1.0 volts	11.0 volts
12V	50 amperes	2.5 volts	9.5 volts
12V	100 amperes	5.0 volts	7.0 volts

Note: this example does not represent a good battery in peak condition. A good battery of 12 volt 50 Ah rating should have an internal resistance of about 0.005 ohm at normal temperature.

3   The internal resistance is made up of various individual resistances, namely between electrodes and the electrolyte, the plate resistances, internal connectors and resistance of the electrolyte to ion flow (Ions are particles moving through the electrolyte and carrying a positive or negative charge). Additionally the internal resistance depends upon the state of discharge and cell temperature, the value being higher as the battery is discharged. The designer controls one factor of the internal resistance by the surface area of plates. Batteries with a larger number of plates (and therefore ampere-hour capacity) will have a lower internal resistance.

4   As batteries age, one of the effects is a rise in the internal resistance. Clearly there will come a point where there will be insufficient terminal voltage left to turn the starter motor fast enough for the engine to fire. For a cold morning start, extra torque will be required to free the crankshaft and the minimum engine turnover speed for firing will be about 100 rev/min. It is under these conditions that the end of the battery life is determined.

8   Battery selection

1   The car manufacturer will specify a battery large enough to crank the engine under specific conditions, typically at a temperature of -30°C and assuming a 70% charge.
2   Tests on the vehicle will show the maximum starter current required under the above adverse conditions and from the data a battery of adequate current capacity will be specified.

9   Temperature effects – frozen batteries

1   At low temperatures, the electrolyte will be more concentrated and will have a higher specific gravity, but against this, the chemical reactions within the battery are slower and the overall result is a lowering of the battery capacity with temperature.

2   Fig. 3.11 shows a typical characteristic giving a crossover at -20°C between supply and demand of power for starting a given motor vehicle.

3   The battery should be protected from freezing, particularly when in a low charge state, because then the proportion of water in the electrolyte is higher, giving a greater tendency to freeze. A good state of charge is a good protection against freezing. The dependence of the freezing threshold on specific gravity of the acid is shown in Fig. 3.12, as is the dependence on charge state.

4   A frozen battery will give a very small current only, but does not normally suffer permanent damage, although cracking of cases is not unknown. This is because frozen acid electrolyte does not expand appreciably and remains in a gelatine-like state.

5   It should be noted that recharging in the frozen state is difficult since only a small current can be passed through.

6   Topping up should not be carried out if the outside conditions are below the freezing point of water.

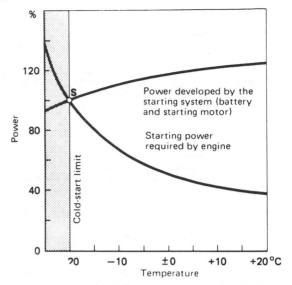

Fig. 3.11 Supply and demand power curves (Sec 9)

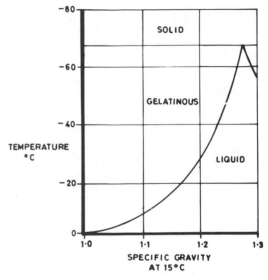

Fig. 3.12a Dependence of the electrolyte freezing point on specific gravity (Sec 9)

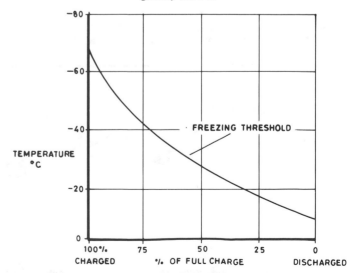

Fig. 3.12b Dependence of the electrolyte freezing point on % battery charge (Sec 9)

10 Batteries with a probe

1   Some batteries have an electrical probe extending to the top surface of the electrolyte, and this is used as an electrolyte level monitor.

2   So long as the probe dips into the acid, then the warning circuit is complete, but as the level drops the probe is no longer in contact and a dashboard warning light is switched on.

11 Dry-charged batteries

1   More correctly the description should be 'unfilled, charged batteries'. The battery plates are first formed by the manufacturer and then given a full charge.

2   At the factory the acid is drained off and the plates dried out, the negative plates being given a chemical preservation treatment. The battery can then be stored without harm for a long period before being brought into service.

3   When needed, the battery is filled with acid of specific gravity 1.28 (corresponding to full-charge acid gravity) and after about 20 minutes soaking time the battery is then ready for use.

4   Should it not be required at this stage, a recharge after four weeks standing is advised. Note that at a first filling some heat may be generated in the battery and sometimes they are filled in two stages with a delay of 6 to 12 hours between stages.

12 Self discharge

1   Over a period, a battery which is not used will gradually lose its charge due to several factors including the following:

2   **Internal chemical processes**: Batteries which have been in service for some time suffer from the effect of antimony deposits on the negative plates. These set up miniature batteries, in effect, which are short circuited upon themselves and use up the charge of the negative plate. In addition, impurities in added water, particularly traces of iron, will result in the self discharge of both positive and negative plates.

3   **Leakage currents**: Dirt and the effects of acid fumes on the top surface of the battery can result in conducting film paths between the +ve and −ve battery lugs. This trouble can be minimised by periodic cleaning of the battery top (and throw the rag away afterwards). Sediment paths at the bottom of the battery case can also lead to leakage paths.

4   Self discharge takes place at the rate of 0.2% to 1% of the battery ampere-hour capacity per day, depending on the age of the battery.

The rate of discharge goes up with temperature and also with the specific gravity value. Batteries of quality use lead of highest purity in the active plate area with the antimony proportion kept small.

5   The remedy for self discharge is, of course, to charge the battery periodically or to maintain a trickle charge approximately equal to the self discharge rate, this being found by trial and error, or by a rule of thumb which gives the trickle charge rate as:

$$\frac{1}{1000} \times \text{ampere-hour rating}$$

For example, a 50 Ah battery might be trickle charged at:

$$\frac{50}{1000} = 0.05 \text{ ampere}$$

6   If a simple battery charger with no rate control is used for this purpose, a good way of reducing the charge rate is to run the battery on charge with a car light bulb in series. Again the bulb is chosen by trial and error with an ammeter in circuit to check the charge rate.

13 Sulphation

1   Under normal discharging, fine crystals of lead sulphate are formed on the plates and, by recharging, these are convertible. If the battery is left discharged for a long period, however, these crystals turn into coarse lead sulphate crystals which are not easily convertible back to the fine state and may ruin the battery.

2   The effects of sulphation are (a) a reduction in the battery Ah capacity and (b) to impede the charging process causing the battery to become very hot.

3   In minor sulphation cases, extended periods of charging at low currents will improve the situation, but in serious cases the battery becomes unusable because of the internal short circuits which result.

4   When a sulphated battery is first put on charge the terminal voltage rises rapidly, whereas that of a healthy battery rises slowly. As the sulphation breaks down the battery voltage falls and slowly rises again as normal chemical changes associated with charging take place.

14 Battery lugs

1   Lugs come into three main categories:

    (a) The die-cast screw-on helmet type (Fig. 3.13)
    (b) The clamp type (Fig. 3.14)
    (c) The Ford type (ie flat lug with nut and bolt) (Fig. 3.15)

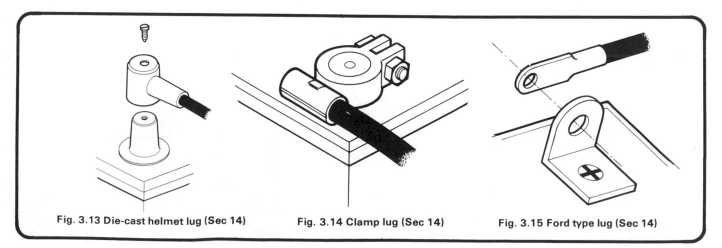

Fig. 3.13 Die-cast helmet lug (Sec 14)   Fig. 3.14 Clamp lug (Sec 14)   Fig. 3.15 Ford type lug (Sec 14)

2 Acid corrosion can cause high resistance contact between the battery posts and the lug. This can reduce the voltage available to the starter and accessories, and can give rise to the phenomenon of an open circuit occurring when the starter is operated. This is signified by a click from the starter solenoid and the dashboard lights going dim. This trouble points to bad contact at the battery or somewhere along the starter cable path – including the earth strap to car body.

3 If the battery lug has bad contact, or if it has developed a white 'fungus', thorough cleaning is necessary and good electrical contact restored by use of emery paper. A light application of petroleum jelly or a proprietary anti-corrosion grease will keep trouble away.

4 Fitting lugs to, or removing lugs from, battery posts should not involve force, especially leverage at the battery, otherwise a small gap will develop and acid will find its way out. If a lug is tight, try soaking a cloth in hot water and applying it to the lug; alternatively a puller could be used if available.

5 Lugs can be renewed by using a kit which consists of a new lug moulded onto a length of starter cable, and also a brass sleeve (Fig. 3.16). Cut off the old lug, strip back the cable by $\frac{1}{2}$" (12 mm) and then solder both cable ends into the brass sleeve using solder flux suitable for electrical work (NOT acid flux). Pull the rubber sleeve provided in the kit over the brass joint.

6 Alternatively a separate clamp lug which can be screwed or soldered onto the existing cable can be purchased from an accessory shop. Some lugs of this type are lightweight and of unknown composition – they invariably give rise to 'fungus growth' corrosion.

15 Filling arrangements

1 Many batteries have screw-in plugs of plastic material, one for each cell. These plugs have small vent holes to allow for the escape of gases during use, and occasionally these holes can become blocked.

For topping up purposes, distilled water is added so that the plates are covered and the level is just over the separators. **Do not fill or inspect while smoking, as the gasses emitted are explosive.**

2 Many patented devices are on the market for the rapid filling of batteries, one of these being the Aqualock incorporated in the Lucas Pacemaker 'A' battery (Fig. 3.17). This battery is of advanced design, the container and lid being moulded on polypropylene, translucent white for the case and red for the lid.

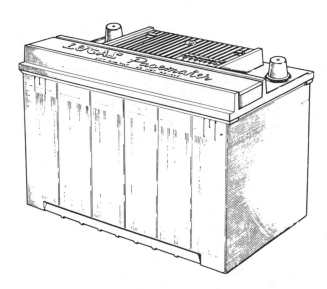

Fig. 3.17 Lucas Pacemaker 'A' battery (Sec 15)

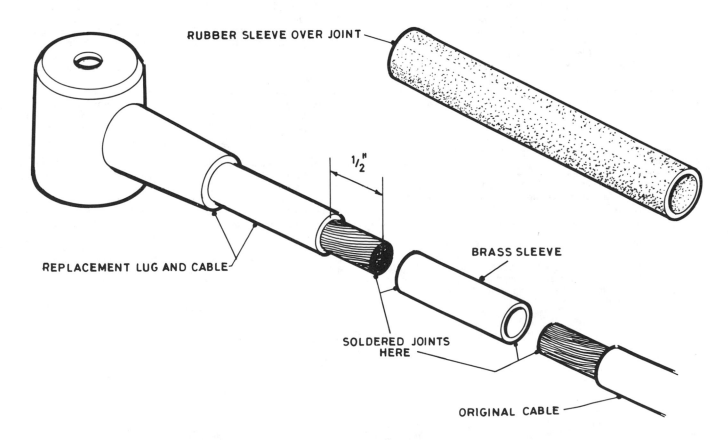

RUBBER SLEEVE OVER JOINT

$\frac{1}{2}$"

BRASS SLEEVE

REPLACEMENT LUG AND CABLE

SOLDERED JOINTS HERE

ORIGINAL CABLE

Fig. 3.16 Battery lug renewal kit (Sec 14)

3   The container and lid are welded together during production with high and low level electrolyte marks moulded into the case. The lid incorporates the ball-valve Aqualock and single vent cover which must be in position except when topping up. Topping up is required when the electrolyte is at the minimum mark on the case.

4   The vent cover is lifted and tilted to one side exposing the filling trough, six vent holes and six rectangular filling tubes. As the cover is lifted and tilted the vent holes are automatically sealed by the balls attached to the vent cover.

5   With the battery horizontal, water is poured into the trough, running into the cells through the filling tubes until the level reaches the base of each tube. At this point an air lock prevents the level rising inside the cell. More water is poured in until all the tubes are full to the top, and the water just covers the bottom of the trough.

6   The lid is now closed down, the airlock is broken and the topping up water runs down into the cells to give the correct level. When charging, the cover must always be in the closed position. It should be noted that recent improvements in design have rendered the quick-fill system obsolescent, although many will still be found in service.

7   Battery developments have resulted in much longer periods between topping up. Typically batteries previously needed topping up with distilled water, say, once a month, depending upon conditions, but now quality batteries need topping up perhaps only once per year. Some manufacturers now produce a battery which is sealed for life, and the only maintenance required is to keep the terminals clean and tight.

8   With the precision of the modern electronic regulator in giving constant-voltage charging it has been possible to develop batteries of high efficiency with lower self discharging rates due, in part, to the use of less antimony in the plate materials. With this comes a reduction in gassing on charge and, consequently, less water evaporation occurs. The new battery is lighter and has lower internal resistance, and a higher maximum current is available for starting conditions. For example, a quality battery of 1969 design would give a maximum starting current of $3\frac{1}{3}$ times the ampere-hour rating, but in 1982 designs this figure can be as high as five times the ampere-hour rating.

9   One further result of less need for topping-up has been that there is little point in providing a sophisticated (but expensive) rapid filling system such as the Lucas Aqualock mentioned earlier, and the present designs use a simple trough filler. Screw-top caps are also again in use. This results in lower production costs and less service time.

16 Fast charging

1   There are battery chargers which can be used for fast or slow charging and also for engine starting. The Crypton AF40 model is shown in Fig. 3.18.

2   Some form of protection against overcharging or overheating is necessary and this can take the form of an automatic cutout based on the time of charging, or when the electrolyte reaches about 45°C (113°F). Another protection is current tapering; the charging current decreases with time to match the rising state of charge and terminal voltage of the battery.

3   Temperature control is achieved by a thermostat mounted in a thin plastic tube, and consists of an expansion bulb containing a liquid which expands with heat, closing a pair of contacts at the prescribed temperature. This in turn is arranged to switch off the charging current until the temperature drops.

4   Towards the end of a charge, battery temperatures rise rapidly and, if uncontrolled, would lead to rapid failure of one or more cells. Because of this, rapid charging should never be used to put in more than 90% of the maximum battery charge.

Fig. 3.18 Crypton battery charger (Sec 16)

5   Charging with a home battery charger is straightforward because of the single-voltage low-current output. Heavy duty chargers can be used with batteries of different voltages and Fig. 3.19 shows the case of 24V, 12V and 6V batteries on charge from one 24V charger.

17 Battery testing

1   Use of the hydrometer has already been described, and readings may be useful when examining a suspect battery. If one cell has a specific gravity reading markedly different from the rest it points to failure.

2   Gassing on charge should be even in all the cells, but look for uneven gassing as a guide to a failed cell. A short circuited cell will not gas like the remainder.

3   The most significant test of a battery is to put it on a heavy-current load while simultaneously measuring the terminal voltage. The heavy-current discharge tester (Fig. 3.20) is marketed by several manufacturers and consists of a resistor mounted between variable spaced prongs to fit the spacing of lugs on different batteries. Built in is a voltmeter which registers the voltage on load. A battery with sulphation troubles or cell internal short-circuit will be immediately shown up as faulty, not only by the low voltage shown on the meter but a faulty cell may also bubble vigorously while under rapid discharge.

4   Individual cell testing may be carried out with a cadmium tester (Fig. 3.21). Two cadmium probes are inserted into the electrolyte of adjacent cells and the instrument is read, indicating cell condition, ie 'recharge' or 'serviceable'.

5   The device reads the voltage between the electrolyte and positive plate of one cell and the electrolyte and negative plate of its neighbouring cell. The cadmium probes are electrically neutral and so make no contribution directly to the reading and act as pick-up probes only.

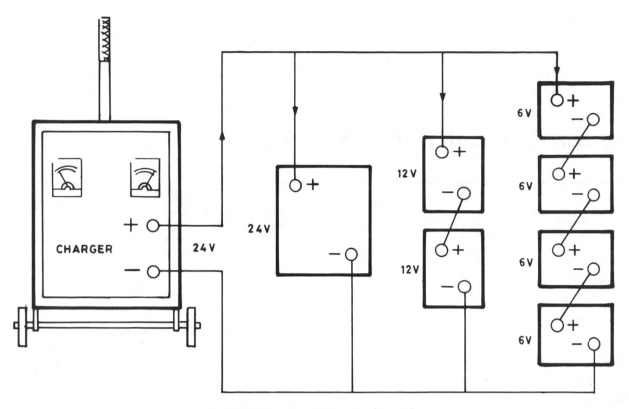

Fig. 3.19 Series-parallel charging (Sec 16)

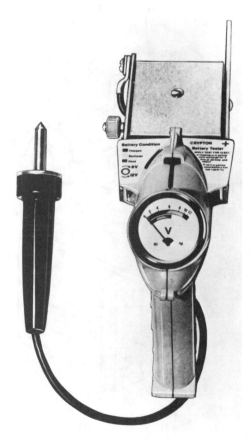

Fig. 3.20 Heavy current discharge tester (Sec 17)

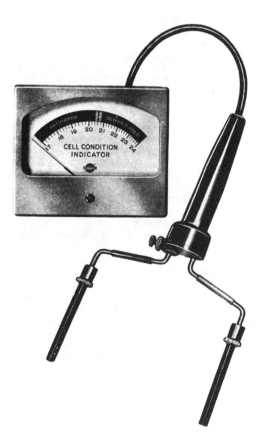

Fig. 3.21 Crypton cadmium battery tester (Sec 17)

Chapter 4 Charging systems

Contents

1 Introduction

The electrical demand for power for ignition, starting, signalling, lighting and other functions requires a generator. Whilst the battery is a power storage device it has only a limited capacity for this purpose and quickly runs down, so some form of re-charging is necessary on the vehicle.

The entire current requirement of the vehicle, including that of battery charging, is provided by a generator driven via a belt by the engine, so the ultimate energy source is the fuel.

Large variations of engine speed mean that the generator requires some form of regulator so that the output voltage is as near as possible constant over the working range of speed.

Battery charging requires direct current, so the generator must either be of the dc dynamo type (now rapidly becoming obsolete) or an ac alternator with a rectifier.

2 Advantages of the alternator

1 It is estimated that city buses spend up to 40% of their peak traffic time standing still, and similar poor operating conditions can apply to the car.

2 The direct current generator does not charge its battery at tickover speed, so traffic congestion, coupled with the ever increasing demand of electrical accessories, meant that this form of generator had reached its limit by the 1960's. Other limitations were concerned with the difficulty in taking off the electrical power through carbon brushes and a commutator. The main current was produced in the rotating armature, the field windings being stationary.

3 Just the opposite occurs in the alternator, in that the main current windings are stationary and the field coils rotate (Fig. 4.1). The field coils are light and can be made to rotate at much higher speeds than can a dc dynamo, so by using a suitable pulley, the alternator is already

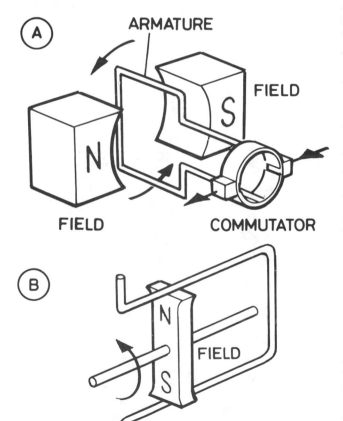

Fig. 4.1 Essentials of the dynamo and alternator (Sec 2)

A   Dynamo – note stationary field
B   Alternator – note rotating field

turning fast enough to charge the battery even at tickover speeds. Fig. 4.2 shows a comparison of outputs from a dc dynamo and an alternator with approximately the same maximum power rating.

4   Finally, the alternator is lighter in weight that the dynamo, requires less maintenance, requires no charging current cut-out, and has a longer service life.

3 Principle of operation of the alternator

1   When an electric conductor and a magnetic field move relative to each other then a voltage (more properly an electromotive force – emf) is generated. Note that the size of the voltage depends upon:

   (a)   the velocity (V) of the wire relative to the magnetic field
   (b)   the length of the wire (ℓ) cutting the magnetic field
   (c)   the strength of the magnetic field (B) thus generated voltage $E = B \times \ell \times V$ volts

This principle, discovered by Michael Faraday in 1834, underlies the operation of both the alternator and the dynamo.

2   In order to increase the length of wire, coils are used; a group of coils is known as a winding. The magnetic flux density is, in practice, always enhanced by using an iron frame on which the field is wound, and this frame is usually constructed of thin laminations stacked to the required thickness. This prevents current being generated within the iron, which would cause wasteful heating and power loss.

3   Imagine now the simple coil of the alternator which is cut by the magnetic field of the North and South poles of the rotating magnet. The voltage or electromotive force (emf) generated in the coil sides will change direction as the poles pass close by in cyclic rotation: N - S - N - S etc. Thus if the coil is connected to a complete circuit externally, the currect flowing will change direction at the same rate, or frequency, at which the poles rotate, hence the name alternating current.

4   The number of revolutions per second of the magnet will also correspond to the number of repetitions, or cycles, per second of the current wave flowing back and forth through the coil.

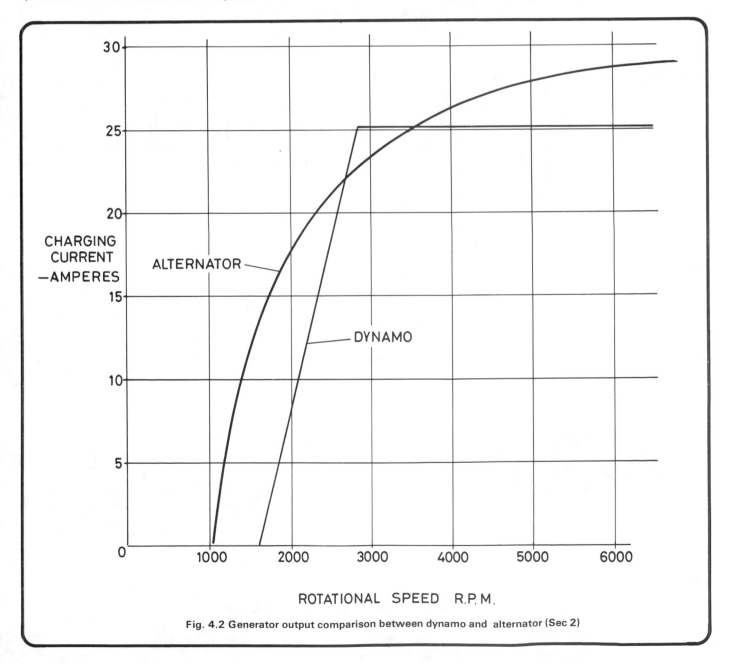

Fig. 4.2 Generator output comparison between dynamo and alternator (Sec 2)

5   Until recently this number was defined in cycles per second, but is now called Hertz (Hz); thus 50 revolutions per second of the magnet will give a voltage or current frequency of 50 Hertz. A graph or waveform of the way in which the electric waves change with time is shown in Fig. 4.3, and is known as a sine wave.

4   Single-phase and three-phase generation

1   An alternator which uses a simple pair of coils will produce a single sine wave of current. For small power requirements this is an adequate arrangement and so, for example, cycle dynamos and older types of motorcycle alternators produced a single-phase output, requiring two wires only. In the automobile, only a few types of small European cars use single-phase alternators.

2   It can be easily imagined that if, instead of two sets of coils 180° apart, the alternator had several sets spread around the iron frame, then the rotating magnet would be able to generate more electricity. This is in fact the case, and it is common to use three pairs of coils to form the stationary winding (hence the name stator), but there has to be a special way of connecting them to bring out the power.

3   If a rotating magnet sweeps past the three sets of coils, then each will produce a sine wave of induced voltage but in sequence. Since a complete revolution of the magnet corresponds to 360 degrees rotation, then each sine wave of voltage wil be 120° apart from the other two (Fig. 4.4). Each coil will have the same voltage generated within it by the rotating magnetic field, but there is a time difference corresponding to the time it takes the magnet to travel from one coil to the next, from 1 to 2, 2 to 3, 3 to 1 etc.

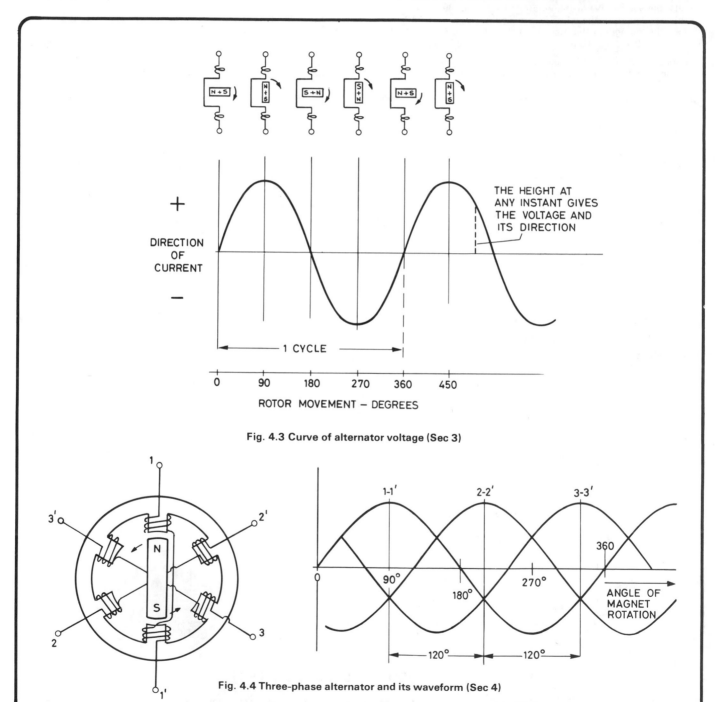

Fig. 4.3 Curve of alternator voltage (Sec 3)

Fig. 4.4 Three-phase alternator and its waveform (Sec 4)

4   It is possible to avoid using six output wires by connecting the coils together in either a 'star' or a 'delta' configuration. Fig. 4.5 shows these connections, both of which are possible for vehicle alternators, although the star is more usual.

5   The star connection will result in a higher voltage between any pair of output terminals than is generated by one coil alone, but will not be twice one coil voltage because of the time phase difference between any pair. In fact the voltage between lines (as the output leads are called) is 1.732 x coil voltage.

6   In the delta connection the output voltage will be that of any coil in value, but the currents generated in each coil will add to give a line current of 1.732 x one coil current.

5   Rectification – converting ac to dc

1   The vehicle battery acts as a storage unit for electrical energy and is a direct current device. Current flowing out from it is direct current as is the current flowing into it when being charged.

2   It is necessary to convert the alternating current from the alternator into a form of direct current before it is useful in a vehicle. Referring to Fig. 4.3, the sine wave shows that alternating current flows first one way round a circuit and then in the opposite direction. If the lower half of the sine wave could be eliminated then current would flow in pulses, but always in the same direction. For battery charging this pulsation of current does not matter, and an ammeter would register the average value of current.

3   A device which will prevent current flowing in one direction, but allow it to flow in the opposite direction is called a rectifier. Modern rectifiers are usually made of semiconductor materials and are highly efficient. Fig. 4.6 shows a simple circuit consisting of an alternator connected to a resistive load, via a rectifier. The lower half of the current wave is stopped by the rectifier, allowing pulses to flow through the resistor, but always in the same direction – that is, direct current. For obvious reasons this is known as half-wave rectification: it is inefficient because the lower half of the current wave is wasted.

4   A better method of conversion is to use full-wave rectification. As the name implies the whole of the alternating sine wave is used, and to accomplish this four rectifiers are used, as in Fig. 4.7. The alternator will produce an output voltage which changes polarity so that it is, in effect, like a battery which rapidly reverses its leads.

5   Current will flow through a rectifier in the direction of the arrow, but not against it, so if the +ve wire at the alternator is traced through, current will flow through the battery and two rectifiers. When the polarity reverses, current flows through the opposite pair of rectifiers, but always in the same direction through the battery. Thus the whole of the ac wave has been caused to pass through the battery. Fig. 4.8 shows the waveforms for both half and full wave rectifiers. The physical layout of one type of full wave rectifier is shown in Fig. 4.9. The individual rectifier elements are often known as diodes, or sometimes as diode rectifiers.

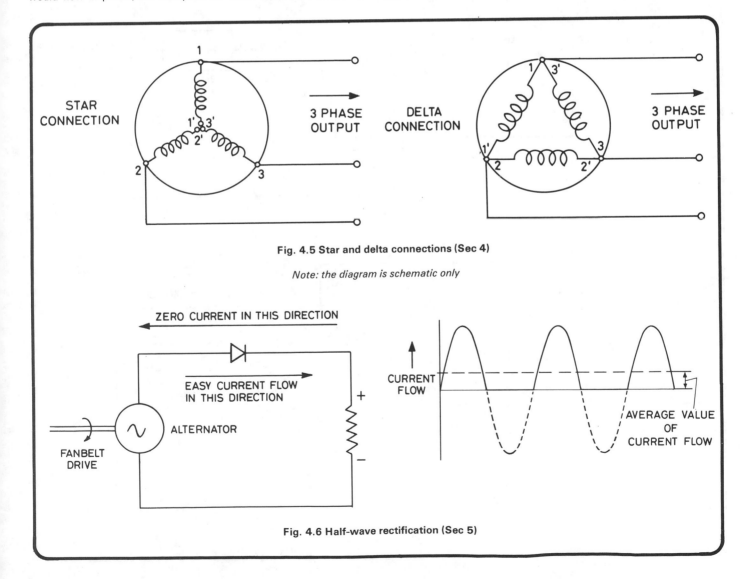

Fig. 4.5 Star and delta connections (Sec 4)

Note: the diagram is schematic only

Fig. 4.6 Half-wave rectification (Sec 5)

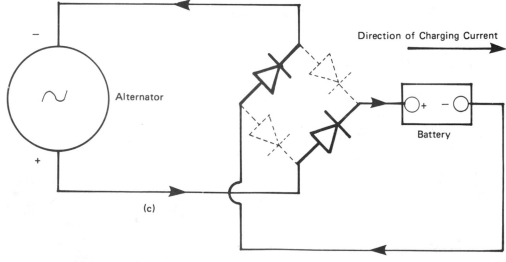

Fig. 4.7 Action of the full-wave rectifier (Sec 5)

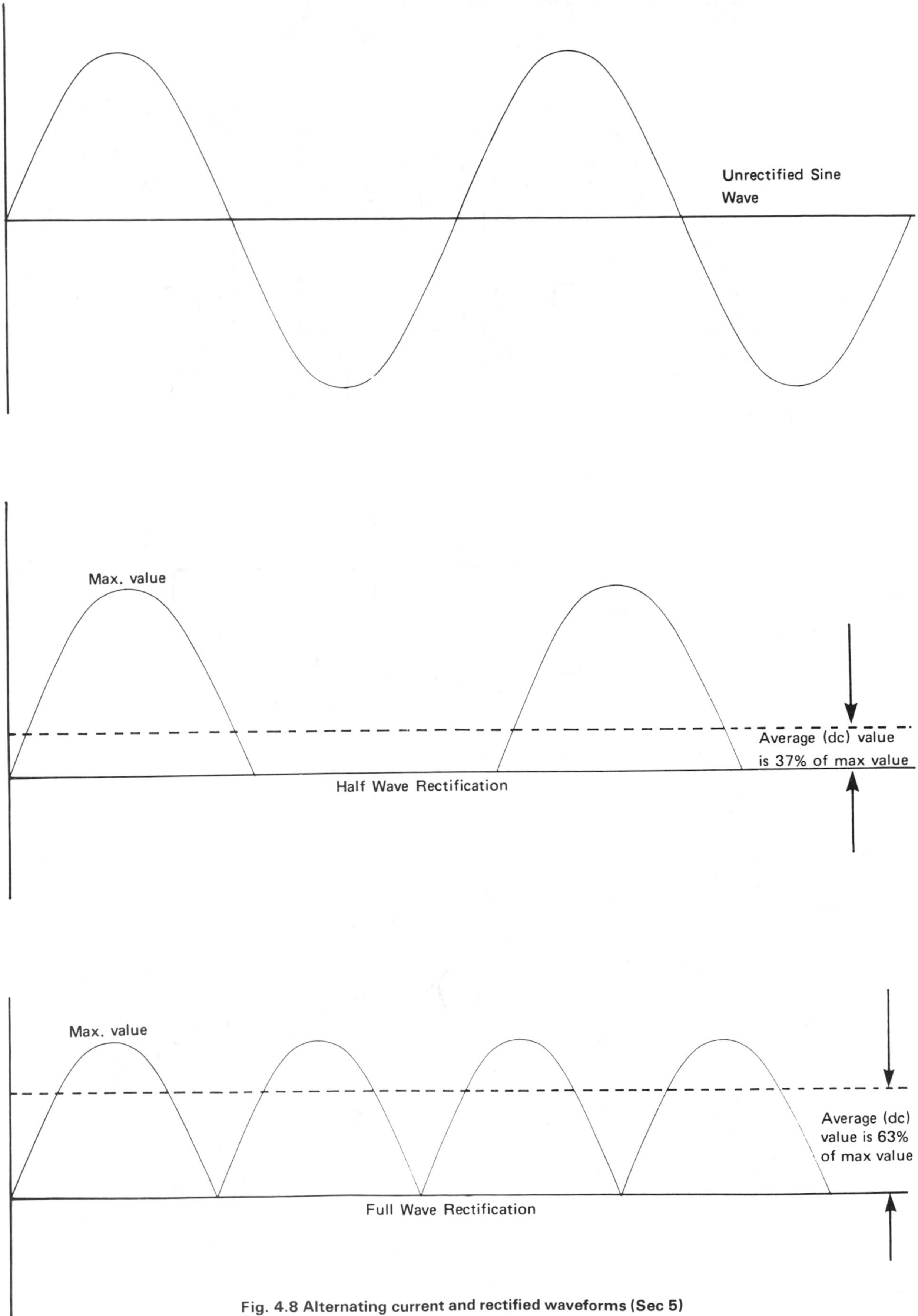

Unrectified Sine
Wave

Max. value

Average (dc) value
is 37% of max value

Half Wave Rectification

Max. value

Average (dc)
value is 63%
of max value

Full Wave Rectification

Fig. 4.8 Alternating current and rectified waveforms (Sec 5)

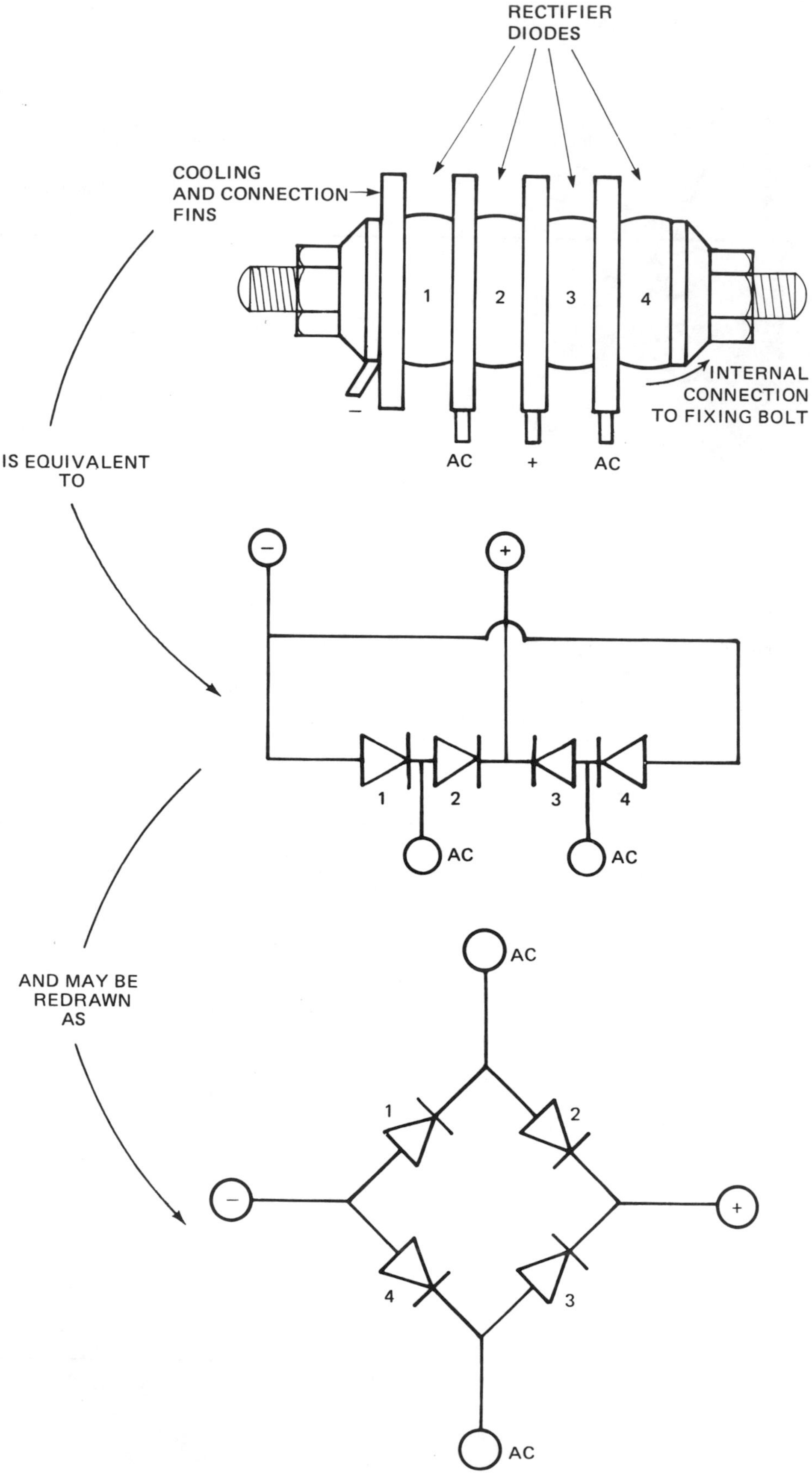

RECTIFIER
DIODES

COOLING
AND CONNECTION →
FINS

1 2 3 4

INTERNAL
CONNECTION
TO FIXING BOLT

−

AC + AC

IS EQUIVALENT
TO

− +

1 2 3 4

AC AC

AND MAY BE
REDRAWN
AS

AC

1 2

− +

4 3

AC

Fig. 4.9 Layout of a full-wave rectifier (Sec 5)

6   Three-phase rectification is along the same lines as the full-wave rectifier shown (often called a bridge rectifier). Fig. 4.10 shows a three-phase alternator connected to a three-phase full-wave rectifier. The effect of reversing each negative half cycle is to give an output voltage or current which has a high average value and a much lower ripple than for the single-phase case. In fact there will be six 'half-waves' per 360° on the diagram shown (Fig. 4.11) and the average value of direction current or voltage is not much short of the peak value.

7   The three-phase alternator is made with this number of phases on the grounds of efficiency, so that most of the stator is used up with windings thus giving high output. Any one of the three windings generates a single sine wave ie a single-phase output.

8   Some French manufacturers use a single-phase alternator in vehicles where the higher wattage output of a three-phase machine is not essential. This single-phase alternator is cheaper to produce and the rectifier stack will be of the simple single-phase full-wave type. The control principles remain the same, in that the alternator output voltage (or battery voltage) determines the direct current feed to the rotating field winding, as explained in the following Section.

6   Field excitation

1   Excitation is a term used by electrical engineers which means the provision of a magnetic field. The simple magnet shown so far in this Chapter will produce alternating current and voltage in the stationary (stator) windings of an alternator but, in general, permanent magnets are anything but permanent when subjected to vibrations and heat.

2   It is usual to make the rotor in the form of an electromagnet, that is, of soft steel or iron in which magnetism is induced by a coil of wire carrying direct current, the coil being wound round the steel/iron. The magnetism will vary in strength according to the coil current and there is the additional advantage of being able to control the magnetic field strength, and hence the value of alternating voltage generated, in the stator winding.

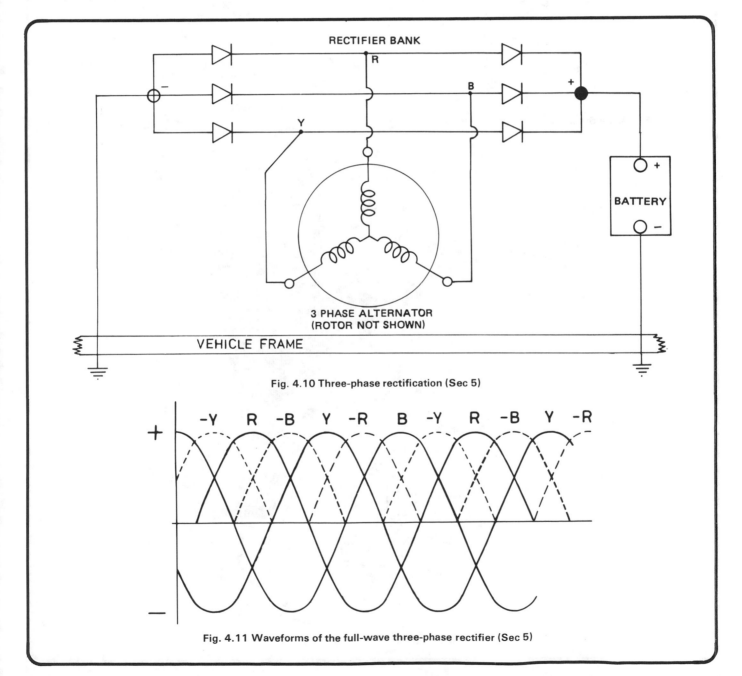

Fig. 4.10 Three-phase rectification (Sec 5)

Fig. 4.11 Waveforms of the full-wave three-phase rectifier (Sec 5)

3   If the rotor coil were wound on an iron frame as shown in Fig. 4.12a, then a pair of magnetic poles, North (N) and South (S), would be produced. Because of the long air path the magnetic field lines would be feeble. Imagine now the ends of the iron stretched out to give two annuli facing each other with a small air gap (Fig. 4.12b). Finally, if the iron ends were shaped to interlock, but without touching like two sets of claws, then the magnetic field lines would pass from N to S, there being considerable 'leakage' externally, and it is this leakage which, when cutting the surrounding stator winding, generates the required electrical output (Fig. 4.13).

4   Note that the rotor must be supplied with dc through brushes and slip rings in order to produce the unvarying North and South poles; two methods of feeding the direct current are in use, battery excitation and self excitation.

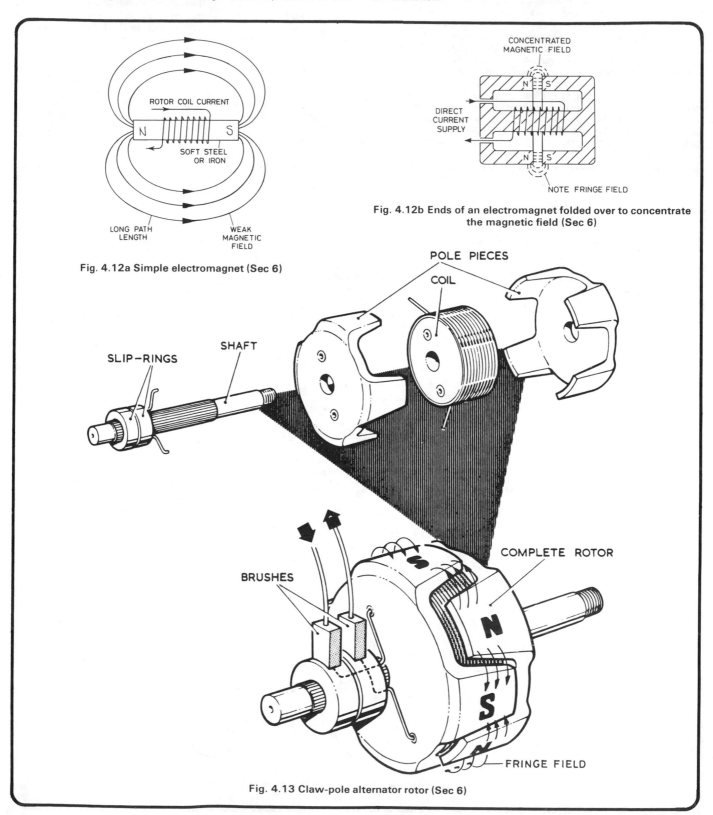

Fig. 4.12a Simple electromagnet (Sec 6)

Fig. 4.12b Ends of an electromagnet folded over to concentrate the magnetic field (Sec 6)

Fig. 4.13 Claw-pole alternator rotor (Sec 6)

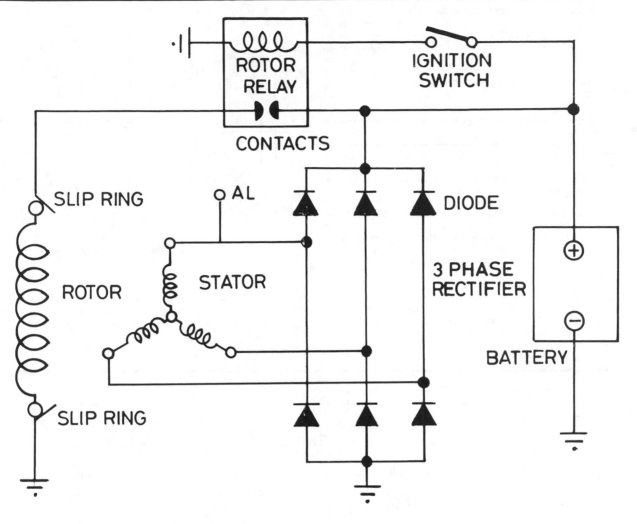

Fig. 4.14 Battery-excited alternator (Sec 7)

Note six diodes. Diagram is schematic only

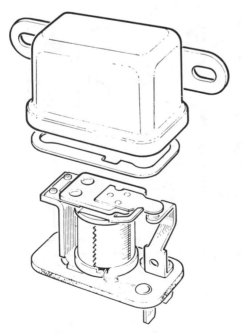

Fig. 4.15 6RA field isolating relay (Sec 7)

7   Battery excitation

1   The vehicle battery supplies the rotor in this method, the means of connection being via a pair of slip rings and brushes. Some means must be provided to disconnect the battery from the rotor (field) when the alternator stops, otherwise the battery would run flat, and this is achieved by a cut-out, or field isolating relay.

2   Fig. 4.14 shows a simplified arrangement of a battery-excited alternator connected to a battery. When the ignition switch is closed, battery current flows through the coil of the relay, pulling the hinged armature down and closing the contacts (Fig. 4.15). Closure of the contacts connects the battery straight on to the field winding of the rotor. The flow of direct current creates the necessary magnetic field to generate ac power in the stator windings.

3   The terminal AL is used to operate a dashboard warning light which will glow at engine standstill with the ignition on, but extinguish when the alternator begins to charge. With battery excitation alternators it is necessary to use a thermal (or similar) control device in conjunction with the warning light, the Lucas system being given as an example in the next Section.

8   Warning light control

1   The Lucas 3AW warning light control has three terminals:

AL   –   to the alternator AL terminal
E   –   connected to a good earth (ground) point on the vehicle
WL   –   connected to the warning light bulb and, through the ignition switch, to the battery.

2   Fig. 4.16 shows a thin, stretched resistance wire, one end of which goes to earth terminal E and the other via a resistor to terminal AL. Note the contacts are closed at engine standstill by the tension of the wire. Thus, with the ignition on, the warning light will glow. When the alternator output builds up, the current from AL heats up the stretched wire which expands; it has less tension, the spring action of the earth connector strip snaps open the contacts and the warning light goes out.

9 Self excitation

1   It is possible for the alternator to produce its own dc to excite the rotor. However, in order to give a good start to the build-up of magnetism, a small current is delivered to the rotor via the ignition switch and an indicator bulb, usually 2.2W.

2   This bulb serves as a no-charge warning lamp and will glow when the ignition is switched on, but when the engine drives the alternator the auxiliary diodes produce a supply to the rotor and the lamp is extinguished, since there will be no voltage difference across it. It follows from this that the rotor is supplied with a voltage approximately equal to that of the battery.

3   In practice, the bulb also has a resistor connected across so the alternator will start even in the event of bulb failure. Fig. 4.17 shows the basic arrangement of the self-excited alternator and is distinguished from the battery-excited alternator by the use of nine diodes.

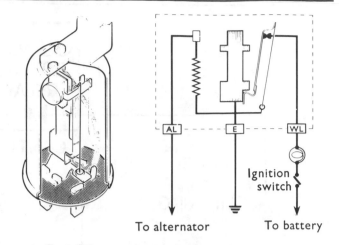

Fig. 4.16 3AW warning light control (Sec 8)

10 Regulator – general

1   Alternators are engine driven and so are subject to a very wide speed range. Without some control the generated voltage would rise to such a point that both battery and alternator would burn out, so a regulator is necessary.

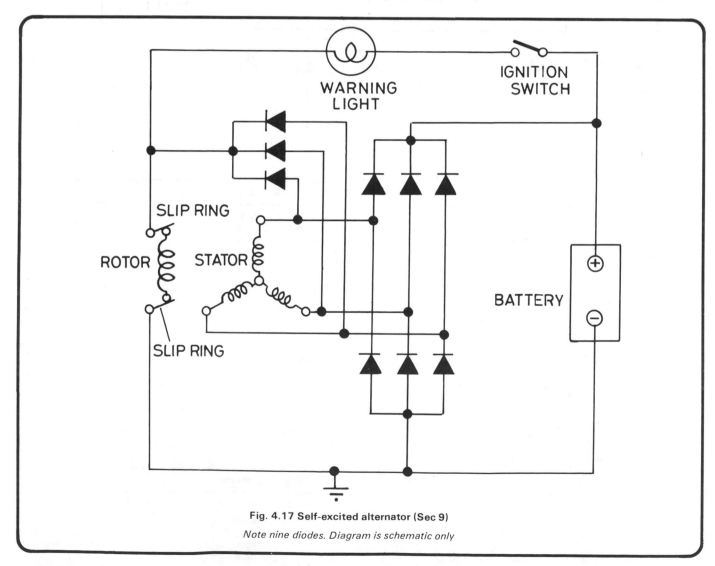

Fig. 4.17 Self-excited alternator (Sec 9)

Note nine diodes. Diagram is schematic only

2 Control of the alternator output voltage is usually carried out by varying the rotor current. Reducing the rotor current results in a weaker magnetic field and therefore the generated voltage in the stator winding falls.

3 Early regulators were of the vibrating contact type, not unlike those used with direct current dynamos, but modern practice is to use a transistor operated version.

4 Whichever method is used, a vital factor is the self-inductance of the rotor winding. Inductance is a property of coils in that current in them cannot change instantaneously, but rises or falls at a rate fixed by circuit parameters. Coils wound on iron frames have a much higher inductance than if air-cored and, indeed, inductance is defined in terms of the magnetic field produced by an ampere of current through the coil concerned. The greater the inductance, the slower will be the rate of current change.

5 Fig. 4.18 shows an iron-cored coil connected to a battery via a pair of contacts which are arranged to open when the current reaches a certain value, i_1, and to close when the current fails to i_2. Note that when the contacts open, current falls because the resistor R is now in series with the coil. The important feature is the time lag for current fall, t_1, and for current rise, t_2. If the contacts can be operated at a fast rate the actual current flow will vary within a small range, and correspond closely to a steady average value.

11 Vibrating contact regulator

1 Though largely superseded by electronic regulators, the vibrating contact type is still worthy of study, for many vehicles in service still have them. They come in two types, namely the single-contact and the double-contact regulator.

2 In the former type, the rotor winding is connected directly to the alternator ouput via a single pair of contacts. When the contacts open, a resistor is connected in circuit, thus reducing the rotor current (and so the alternator voltage) until the lower limit is reached when the contacts close again under spring pressure and short out the resistor (Fig. 4.19).

3 The double-contact regulator has a number of advantages over the single-contact type. For best performance of regulators the resistor should be kept to a low value so that the vibrating contacts handle a small change of current and hence have a longer life. However, at high rotor speeds a high resistance is required to reduce the rotor current quickly when the contacts open. Meeting both requirements is difficult, so a second contact was introduced which earths (grounds) the rotor at the upper end of the alternator voltage range.

4 The advantages are that the voltage falls quickly, and also that a lower value of regulating resistance may be used. A direct consequence is that the contacts can now handle a larger rotor current, a desirable feature in alternator design.

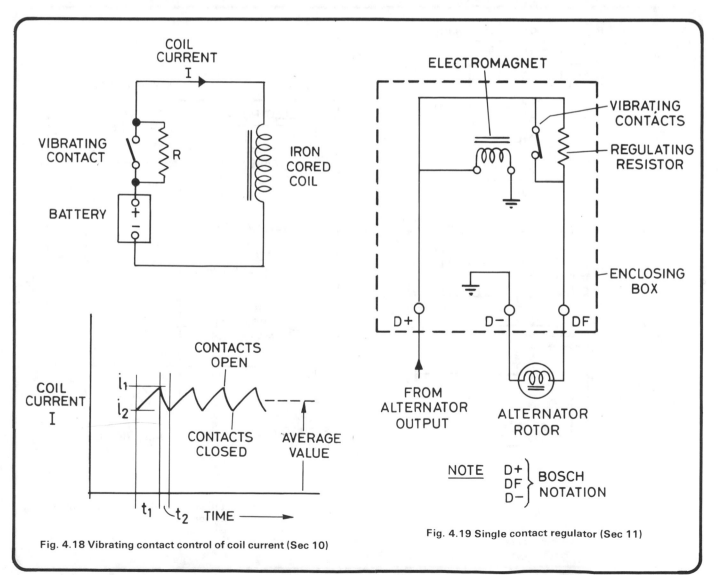

Fig. 4.18 Vibrating contact control of coil current (Sec 10)

Fig. 4.19 Single contact regulator (Sec 11)

5   Fig. 4.20 shows a double-contact regulator. At low speeds the operation is the same as for a single-contact type. When the speed is higher the contacts change over so that the moving centre contact now connects to the earthed contact, thus shorting out the rotor, giving a rapid fall in magnetisation and alternator voltage. As with the single-contact type, spring pressure returns the moving contact to connect with the D terminal, ie alternator output line, and so the voltage rises again.

6   When the contacts open, an inductive voltage will be generated in the rotor winding. In the case of single-contact regulators, a diode may be incorporated across the rotor to absorb transients. Double-contact regulators may use a resistor permanently connected across the rotor, the purpose in both cases being to absorb contact sparks and so prolong contact life.

12 Temperature compensation

1   The voltage regulator bobbin has a shunt coil which has many turns of fine copper wire. Copper wire increases in resistance with temperature at a rate of 0.004 ohms, per ohm of resistance, per degree Celsius (a 0.4% increase for every degree rise in temperature). This means that the voltage applied (ie the alternator charging voltage) will have to be higher to operate the vibrating contacts, a consequence being that the battery will overcharge.

2   Two methods are used to minimise this effect (see Fig. 4.21):

(a) A swamp resistor is connected in series with the shunt coil. This resistor has zero change of resistance with temperature, and is also much higher in resistance than the shunt coil (thus swamping out the effects of its resistance change).

(b) The leaf spring which hold the contacts closed is made of two strips of different metals (a bi-metal strip). As temperature rises one metal expands faster than the other, causing the strip to bend, thus reducing spring tension. This compensates for the fall-off in coil current which is due to the rise in resistance

13 Transistor regulator

1   The vibratory type of regulator can give good long service, but an undoubted improvement occurs when the regulation of rotor field current utilises transistors. It is better, in fact, to refer to 'semiconductor devices' since the transistor is but one form of a whole range based on the ability of semiconductor materials to switch or vary current at a fast rate, with no moving parts.

2   The way in which two important semiconductor devices operate will be given in the following Sections in order to understand the complete regulator.

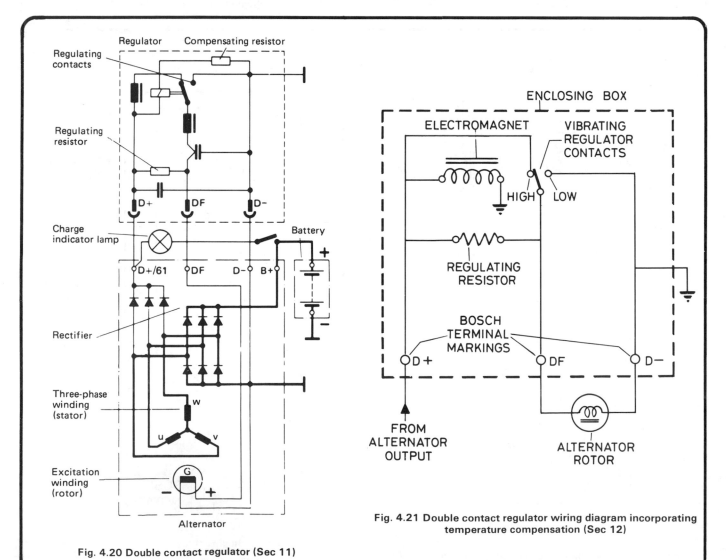

Fig. 4.20 Double contact regulator (Sec 11)

Fig. 4.21 Double contact regulator wiring diagram incorporating temperature compensation (Sec 12)

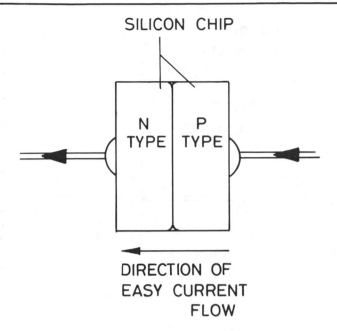

Fig. 4.22 Doped silicon chip as a rectifying diode (Sec 14)

14 The transistor

1   Adding minute quantities of certain chemical impurities to silicon produces remarkable effects. With one type of impurity the silicon is called N type and with another, P type; the silicon is said to be 'doped'.

2   If the impurities are allowed to diffuse into a chip of silicon from opposite faces, then the junction at which they meet acts as a diode or rectifier. Fig. 4.22 shows the direction in which current flows readily; in the reverse direction the current flow would be very small if the battery supply connections were to be reversed.

3   Making a double layer, like two rectifiers back to back (Fig. 4.23) gives the transistor. The three slices are named emitter, base and collector.

4   The main current will flow readily straight through the transistor from collector to emitter on the condition that a small current is allowed to flow between base and emitter. Cut off this base-emitter current and the load circuit current will stop abruptly.

5   Fig. 4.24 shows that, as an example, a base-emitter current of, say, 0.2 amperes will allow 8 amperes to flow from collector to emitter. The life expectancy of this switch is going to be much higher than a switch which breaks the full 8 amperes and, moreover, there are no moving parts within the transistor.

6   It is important to see that the P-N junction between base and emitter is a rectifier diode, in effect. Thus current will flow easily round the loop indicated by the curved arrow marked 'control current' provided (a) the switch S is closed and (b) the battery polarity is as shown.

7   Because only 0.2 ampere is controlling 8 amperes in the load, the transistor is acting as a power amplifier and also as an electronic switch.

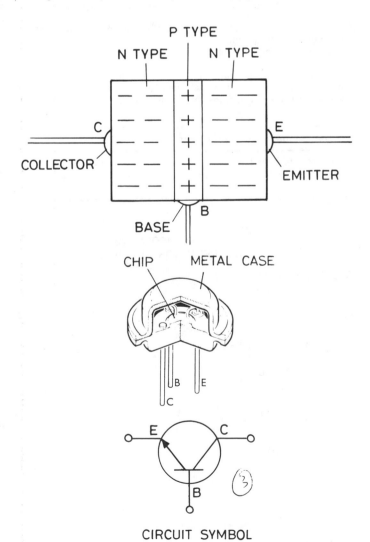

Fig. 4.23 N-P-N silicon transistor (Sec 14)

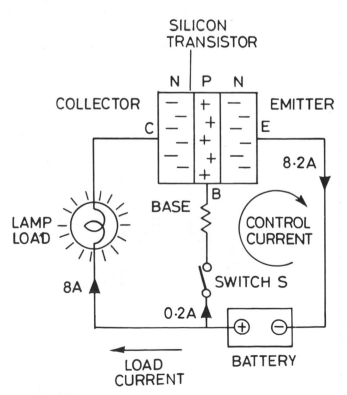

Fig. 4.24 Transistor as a controller (Sec 14)

15 The Zener diode

1   Named after its inventor, this form of diode allows no current through it until the applied voltage reaches a certain value. At the breakdown voltage, current flows easily and so the Zener diode acts as a switch which is conscious of the voltage applied (Fig. 4.25). Note that it is always connected so that the applied voltage is in the reverse direction to that of normal rectifier diodes.

2   Zener diodes are used for a variety of purposes, usually to regulate a supply voltage, and are available for operation in the range of 3 to 100 volts.

16 Regulator operation

1   Reference to Fig. 4.26 shows the Lucas 4TR transistor regulator which controls the rotor field current to obtain the required charging voltage for the battery. The alternator stator is not shown.

2   Operation is as follows. Current flows from the battery, down R_3 on to the base-emitter junction of transistor T_2 and through to the base-emitter junction of transistor T_3. Note that when current is flowing between base and emitter the transistor is switched on, and current can flow from collector to emitter (Section 14). Thus initially:

T_1 is off
T_2 is on
T_3 is on

Because of this, current flows from the battery through the rotor field down through collector-emitter of T_3, ie the rotor is energised, becomes more strongly magnetised, the alternator output voltage is raised and with it the battery voltage.

3   When the battery voltage rises to 14.2 volts, the voltage at the junction of R_1, R_2, and the Zener diode rises to the point where the Zener conducts current which will flow through base-emitter of transistor T_1. This switches on T_1 so that current flows from collector to emitter; the flow down through R_3 causes a voltage drop, so that the base voltage of T_2 falls (cutting off T_2), no collector-emitter current can flow out to T_3 which is also, therefore, cut off and the rotor current stops.

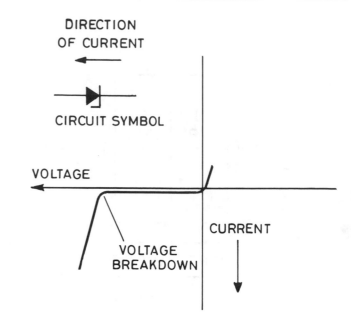

Fig. 4.25 Zener diode characteristics (Sec 15)

4   The stopping of rotor current produces a fall in alternator voltage and therefore battery voltage – the Zener cuts off and the cycle repeats continuously to regulate the system voltage.

5   Diode D_1 is a surge protector, since rapid switching of current in the inductive rotor winding will give rise to dangerous transient voltages which could damage the transistors.

17 The complete charging circuit

1   In order to bring together the separate components a Lucas 11AC negative earth battery-excited alternator set is shown in Fig. 4.27.

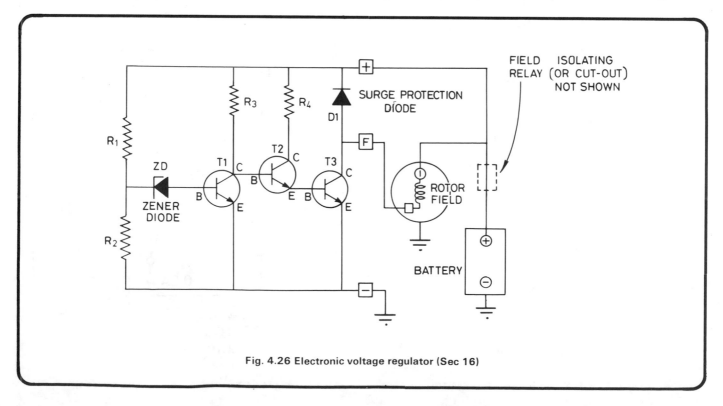

Fig. 4.26 Electronic voltage regulator (Sec 16)

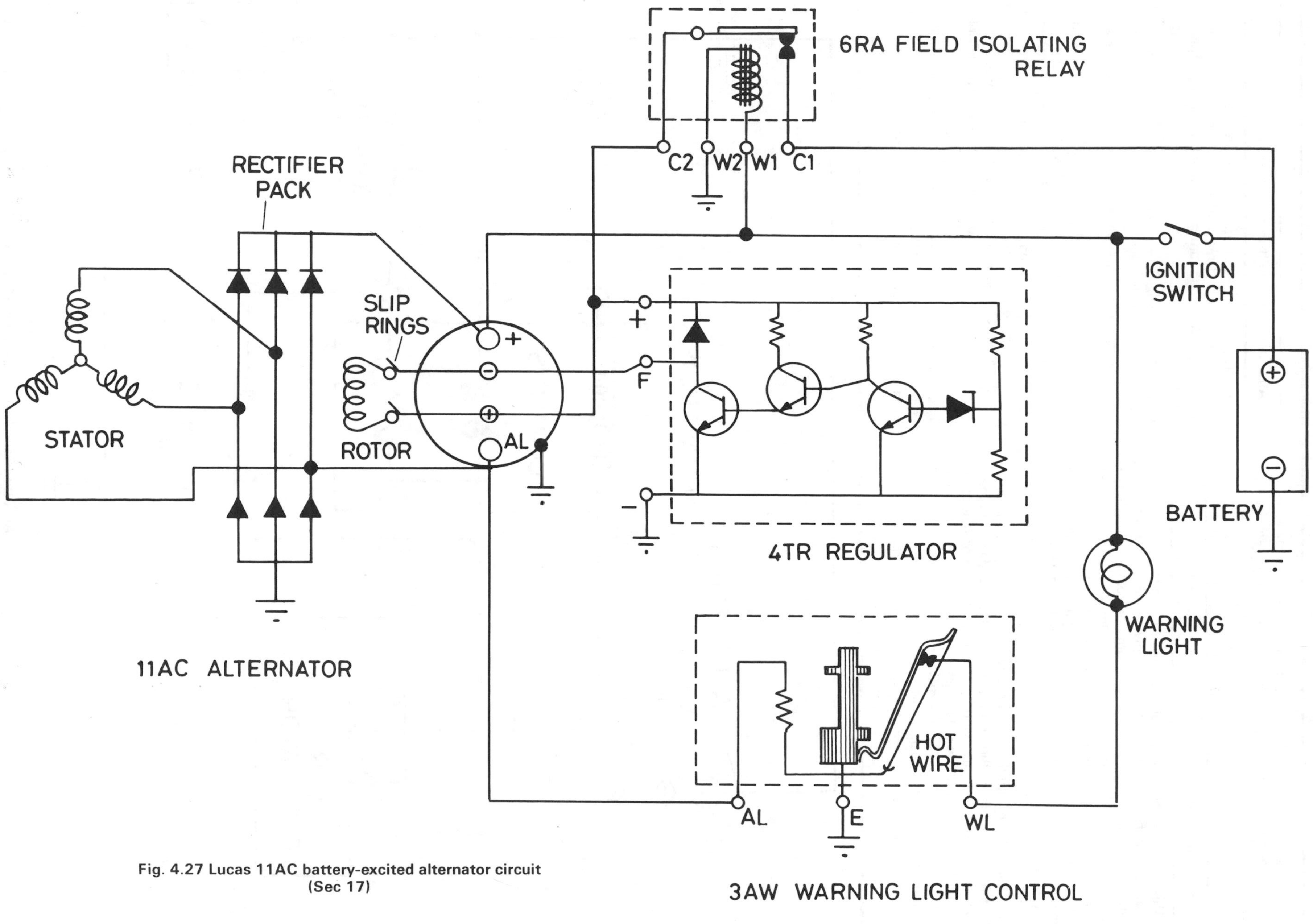

Fig. 4.27 Lucas 11AC battery-excited alternator circuit (Sec 17)

2   The internal circuits of components are given here, but maker's drawings are often encountered where only boxes with terminals are shown.

18 Lucas 16RA relay

1   This relay is offered as alternative equipment and has the advantage that full field current flows only when the alternator is running; in addition the 3 AW warning light control unit is no longer necessary. Fig. 4.28 shows the relay connected into an 11AC alternator system. The sensing point for operating the 16RA relay is the AL alternator terminal and, when the ignition switches on, the warning light and a 60 ohm resistor are connected in parallel with the supply terminals C_1 and C_2.

2   At first, with the ignition on, the contacts C_1 and C_2 remain open, and a small current flows through the warning light, sufficient to make it glow and to feed the rotor winding. When the alternator speeds up, the voltage at alternator terminal AL rises and operates the 16RA relay winding connected to W_1, W_2 at somewhere between 2.5 and 3.5 V. The contacts C_1 and C_2 close, short out the warning lamp and also connect the battery supply to the 4TR voltage regulator.

19 Alternator with built-in regulator

1   As a development of earlier alternator sets, modern alternators have the regulator and rectifier packs built in, so that, in effect, the machine produces a controlled direct current supply for battery charging.

2   Fig. 4.29 shows an exploded diagram of such an alternator, the main features of which are:

   (a) A laminated stator carrying a three-phase star-connected winding
   (b) A 12-pole claw-type rotor carrying the field winding, the shaft having ball-bearings at both ends
   (c) A nine-diode rectifier pack for converting the stator three-phase alternating current into direct current for battery charging purposes
   (d) A micro-chip voltage regulator which works on the same principle as that of the 4TR regulator described earlier (Section 16)

Thus there is no need for either a field relay or a warning light control; the output terminals are blades which fit a socket in one way only to guard against incorrect polarity connection.

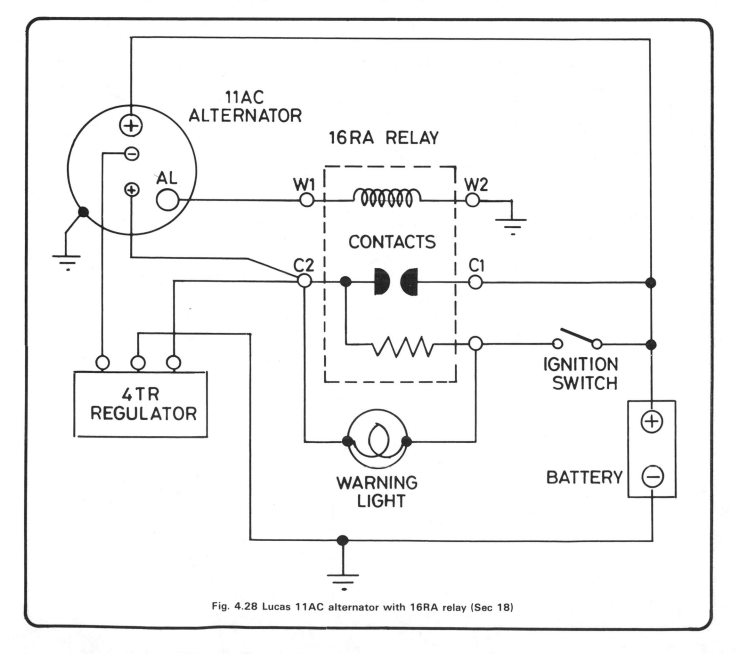

Fig. 4.28 Lucas 11AC alternator with 16RA relay (Sec 18)

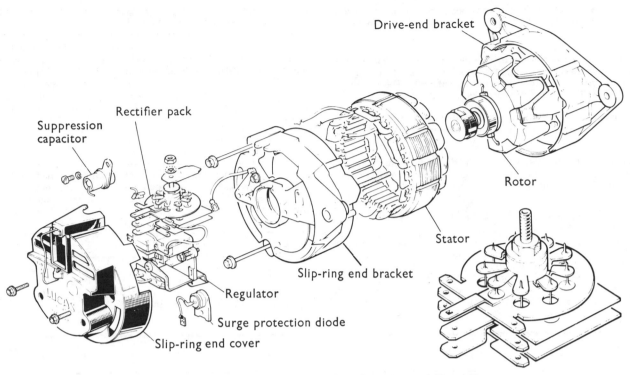

Suppression capacitor

Rectifier pack

Drive-end bracket

Rotor

Stator

Slip-ring end bracket

Regulator

Surge protection diode

Slip-ring end cover

Fig. 4.29 Typical alternator and (inset) rectifier pack (Sec 19)

20 Battery and machine sensing

1   The ACR range of alternators are self-exciting and are in two forms:

    (a)   machine sensing
    (b)   battery sensing

By 'sensing' is meant the point at which the charging voltage is measured.

2   The machine sensing alternator has the regulator voltage sensing circuit connected internally to the alternator output lead, whereas the battery sensing version has the regulator sensing circuit connected to the battery by means of an external direct lead.

21 Machine sensing regulator

1   Fig. 4.30 shows an ACR alternator with the latest type of regulator, the Lucas 14TR microcircuit model. This regulator works on the same principle as the 4TR described earlier, but has feedback components R_5, R_3, C_1 and C_2. The effect of these is to cause rapid switching of the power transistor T_3 between the on and off modes, for it is important from heat considerations that T_3 does not remain in the condition of high internal power dissipation (when the transistor is somewhere between on and off).

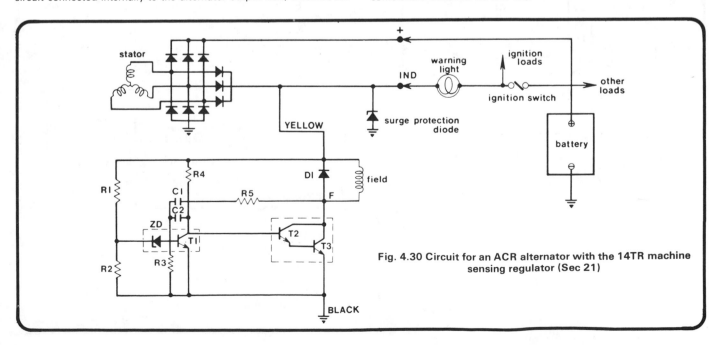

Fig. 4.30 Circuit for an ACR alternator with the 14TR machine sensing regulator (Sec 21)

2   In this type of circuit, should a break occur in the main output lead to the battery, the alternator is controlled to the setting of the regulator.

3   A further refinement giving a fail-safe facility is the dual sensing variation, illustrated in Fig. 4.31. It will be seen that the IND connection supplies only the rotor and transistor T_3. The rest of the regulator circuit is fed from two sources:

  (a)   direct from the battery (white lead)
  (b)   from the alternator +ve terminal via resistor R_6 (red lead)

4   In operation, the transistor T_2 is fed with current from the battery via R_4; current will also flow through diode D_2 to the sensing circuit. Two possible failure conditions can now be considered:

  (a)   **Alternator main lead break:** The load would be thrown off the alternator causing a rise in machine voltage. The alternator voltage would be frozen at a value equal to the normal setting of the regulator, plus the voltage drop across R_6. Thus the alternator and battery would be safeguarded
  (b)   **Battery sensing lead break:** In this case the supply to R_4 would be broken because the diode D_2 would be reversed biassed and would not conduct

It follows that the failure of an external connection would lead to a safe condition in both cases.

5   Fig. 4.31 also shows a further version which may be encountered. Here a temperature dependant resistor is fixed on or close to the battery. With a rise of temperature the resistance falls, thus allowing a higher voltage to reach the regulator via the orange-coloured sensing lead. This would reduce the output voltage of the alternator. Otherwise this version is identical to the 14TR dual sensing arrangement described above.

22 Surge protection

1   ACR regulators incorporate a protection diode which will protect the main transistor of the regulator unit in the event of faulty connections, or removal of the battery leads, when the alternator is running (Fig. 4.32).

23 Battery sensing regulator

1   Schematic diagrams showing this form of connection are shown in Figs. 4.33 and 4.34. The main feature is the connection of the voltage sensing resistors R_1 and R_2 to the battery via terminal B on the alternator and a separate external lead.

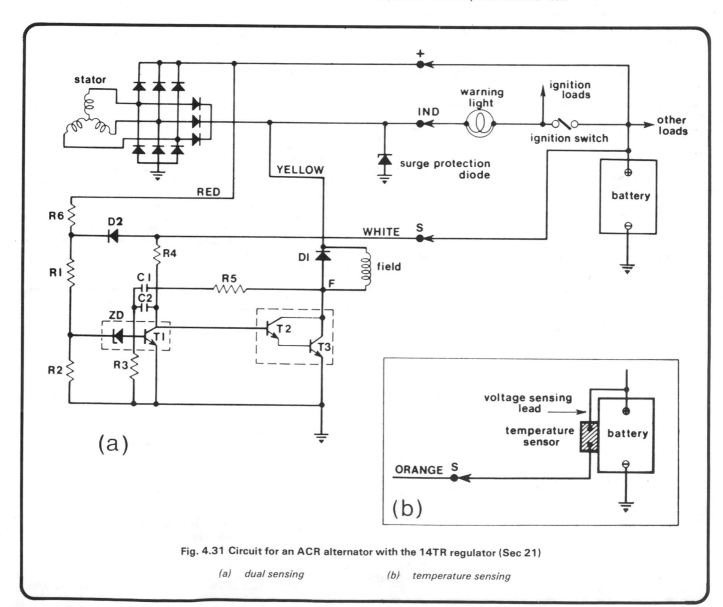

Fig. 4.31 Circuit for an ACR alternator with the 14TR regulator (Sec 21)

(a) dual sensing   *(b) temperature sensing*

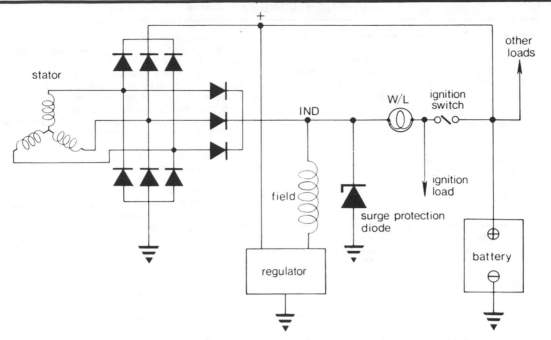

Fig. 4.32 Alternator circuit incorporating a surge protection device (Sec 22)

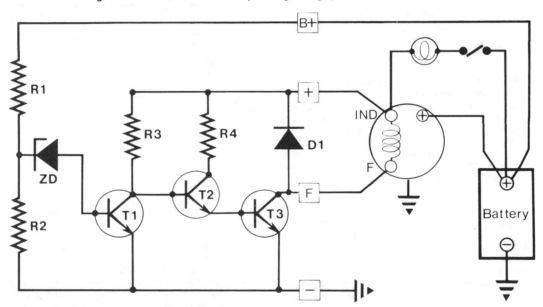

Fig. 4.33 Internal circuit of the 8TR battery sensing regulator (Sec 23)

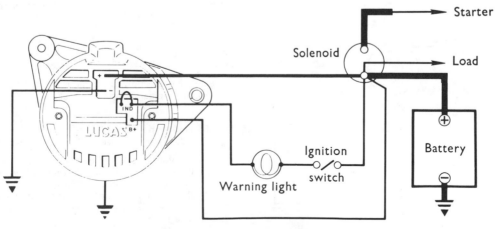

Fig. 4.34 Circuit for ACR alternator – battery sensing system (Sec 23)

24 Alternator testing

1   Little routine maintenance of alternators is required, but periodic checks on the brush length and cleanliness of the slip rings is advisable. Faults in the system can occur in the following:

    (a)   Faulty battery
    (b)   Breaks in cables or poor connections at terminals or plugs and sockets
    (c)   Alternator drivebelt loose
    (d)   Failure of the alternator windings or rectifier pack
    (e)   Regulator failure
    (f)   Fault in any auxiliary units, eg field relay, charge warning bulb, warning light control unit

2   Before examining the system in detail when a fault is present, a visual inspection is worthwhile to check on belt tension, signs of terminal corrosion, whether a battery cell is gassing unusually when on charge, etc. Assuming nothing is obvious then a logical procedure should be followed as illustrated in the following Lucas system; other manufacturers' equipment will be similar.

3   Test equipment need not be extensive, but the following would be required:

    (a)   dc Moving coil voltmeter, range 0 to 20 V (or 40 V if testing 24 V systems)
    (b)   dc Moving coil ammeter, range 10 to 0 to 100A
    (c)   Hydrometer
and desirably:
    (d)   Battery heavy discharge tester

Alternators with built-in regulator (Lucas ACR range)
Test 1: Battery – take hydrometer reading
Measure the specific gravity of each cell. Figures expected for a battery in various states of charge are given in Chapter 3 but look out especially for one cell being markedly different from the rest, (say more than 0.040 specific gravity reading). If the specific gravity is below 1.230 the battery should be recharged before further testing. *Take care that no drops of acid fall on skin or clothes when using the hydrometer. Use cold water liberally if splashes occur.*

Test 2: Discharge test
A heavy current discharge test will straightaway show up a battery fault condition. The test prongs should be applied for up to 15 seconds, during which time the voltmeter should read not less than 9.6 volts.

Test 3: Drivebelt tension
The torque required to drive a loaded alternator is high enough to cause belt slip if it is at all loose; equally it is important not to over-tension the belt to safeguard the alternator bearings. A movement of $\frac{1}{2}$" to $\frac{3}{4}$" should be possible on the longest span as shown in Fig. 4.35.

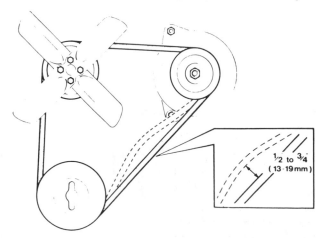

Fig. 4.35 Drivebelt tension (Sec 24)

Test 4: Cable continuity
This is to check that the cables to the alternator are sound. Remove the connection plug from the alternator and with the ignition on, but the engine not running, check the voltage to earth (ground) of each lead in turn. If there is no voltage at the IND lead check the charge warning bulb. Battery voltage should be read on the voltmeter; if not check the leads for continuity. Wiggle the harness about at bends to see if voltage is momentarily restored and check the charge warning lamp connections and ignition switch.

Test 5: Alternator output
This test measures the alternator output current at about 3000 rpm engine speed. Before testing the engine should be run for a few minutes to raise the temperature to that of normal operating conditions. With the engine stopped, remove the battery earth cable and connect the ammeter between the alternator main output terminal and the battery (a convenient point is the starter solenoid – see Fig. 4.36). Remove the connections at the alternator and moulded cover

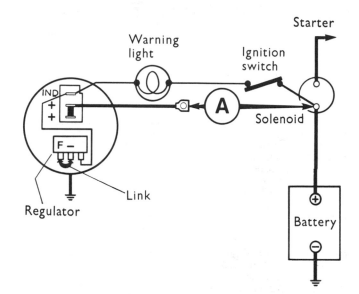

Fig. 4.36 Checking the ACR alternator maximum output (Sec 24)

and re-make them using a jumper lead to short together 'F' and '-' of the voltage regulator unit. (For 8TR units short the green lead and the black (earth) lead. For 8TR 3D units short the green lead to earth. For 11TR/14TR units short the regulator frame to earth). Now reconnect the battery earth cable and slowly run up the engine to the stated speed. The alternator should now be delivering its maximum current as follows:

Alternator model	Ammeter reading
15 ACR	28 A
16 ACR	34 A
17 ACR	36 A
18 ACR	43 A
20 ACR	66 A

The above figures apply to the range of one manufacturer, but are also performance indicators of other makes.

Test 6: Volt-drops on load
Fig. 4.37 shows the test voltmeter being used to measure:

    (a)   the volt-drop V1 from the alternator output terminal to the battery +ve terminal. Maximum allowance 0.5 V with engine at 3000 rpm and all vehicle loads switched on
    (b)   the volt-drop V2 between the battery earth terminal and the alternator body under the same conditions. Maximum allowable 0.25 V

Higher readings indicate a high resistance path, often due to corrosion at terminals and earth points.

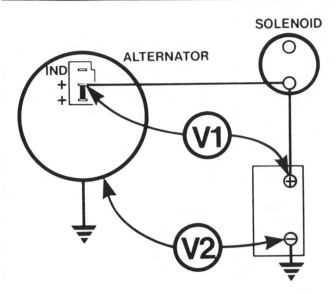

Fig. 4.37 Checking voltage drop in the charging circuit (Sec 24)

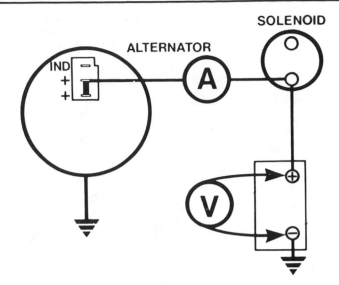

Fig. 4.38 Checking the voltage regulator setting – ACR range (Sec 24)

Test 7: Regulator check

With a healthy, well-charged battery on the vehicle, first remove the battery earth cable. Connect an ammeter between the starter solenoid terminal and the alternator main output terminal as shown in Fig. 4.38; now reconnect the battery earth cable. Connect a voltmeter across the battery terminals and run the engine at 3000 rpm until the charge rate drops below 10 A. The voltmeter limits are 13.6 to 14.4 volts. If the voltmeter reading is unsteady or outside these limits the regulator is faulty.

Battery-excited alternators (Lucas 10/11AC system)

Certain tests will be essentially the same as for the ACR type of alternator, namely battery state, drivebelt tension and cable continuity. Since the 10AC and 11AC systems have the field fed by the battery, additional tests on the field relay and warning light control are necessary.

Test 1: Field relay

Referring back to Fig. 4.27, it will be seen that the relay is intended to connect the field winding to the battery through the contacts, terminals C_1 and C_2 and the ignition switch. Assuming that the fault complaint is that the alternator is not charging, to check the relay connect an ammeter in the alternator main lead as shown in Fig. 4.39, first taking off the battery earth cable. Remove the cable connectors from the contact terminals, C_1 and C_2 and bridge them with a double spade or a short lead with crocodile clips. Reconnect the battery earth cable and run the engine at about 1500 rpm. If charging now takes places the fault lies in the relay, or its wiring. A voltmeter connected across W_1 and W_2 terminals should show battery voltage. If not, then the earth connection at W_2, and the supply voltage at W_1 should be checked.

Test 2: Field circuit check

The simplest way to check the field is to pull the connectors off the

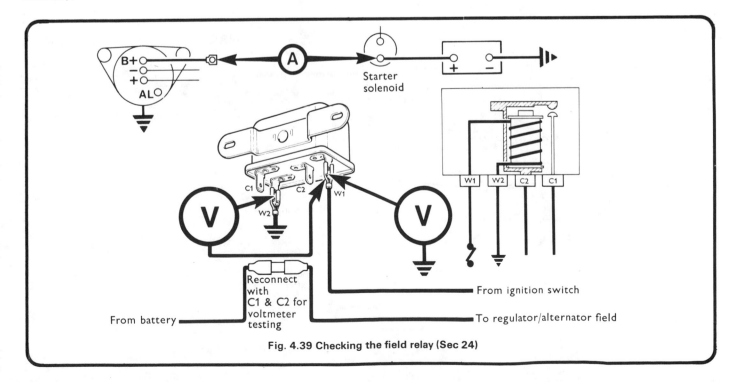

Fig. 4.39 Checking the field relay (Sec 24)

4TR regulator and to bridge the leads going to 'F' and '-' with an ammeter, as in Fig. 4.40. With the ignition switched on, the ammeter should read approximately 3 amperes. If there is no current a break has occurred in the circuit.

Test 3: Maximum output check

With the connectors again removed from the regulator 4TR, 'F' and '-' are bridged, as in Fig. 4.41. The ammeter is connected in the main output lead, and with the engine running at about 3000 rpm the current should be as follows:

Alternator	Ammeter reading
10AC	35 A
11AC	45 A
11AC (uprated model)	60 A
11AC (24 volt)	23 A

A zero, or low figure, points to a faulty stator, or trouble with the rectifier diodes.

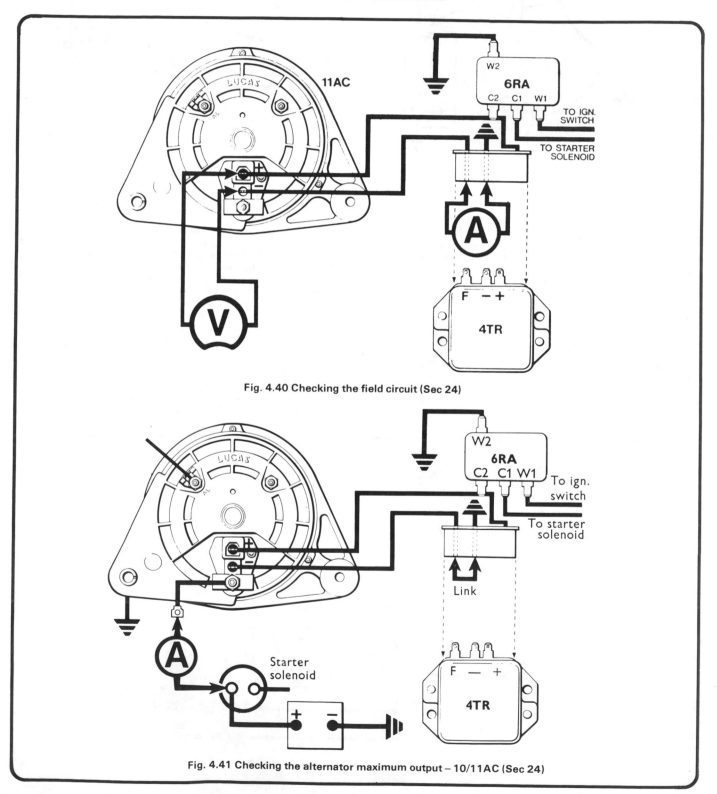

Fig. 4.40 Checking the field circuit (Sec 24)

Fig. 4.41 Checking the alternator maximum output – 10/11AC (Sec 24)

Test 4: Regulator setting measurement

The 4TR regulator is tested using a charged battery, and at normal operating temperature. It is necessary to see that the regulator is actually regulating by running the engine until the charge rate has dropped below 10 A and does not change with speed. Load the circuit with side (city) lamps and run the engine at 3000 rpm, connections according to Fig. 4.42. Voltage readings should be within the limits:

10/11AC Alternators	Voltage regulator setting
12 volt system	13.9 to 14.3 volts
24 volt system	27.9 to 28.3 volts

Test 5: Warning light control 3AW

If the alternator is charging normally, but the warning light does not work, the first thing to check is the bulb itself. Assuming the bulb is good, check the voltage to earth at the alternator AL terminal. This should be between 6 and 8 volts for a 12 volt system, or 14 to 15 volts for a 24 volt system, with 1500 rpm engine speed. An abnormal AL reading points to a faulty rectifier diode. Next check the 3AW unit by taking off the E and WL terminals and bridging them together (Fig. 4.43). With the ignition on the warning light bulb should glow. If this is so, then the 3AW unit is faulty.

25 Direct current dynamo

1 The dc dynamo has been in service with motor vehicles for many years, but has now been superseded by the alternator. Nevertheless, many vehicles still on the roads use the dynamo, and an understanding of its operation and servicing is essential.

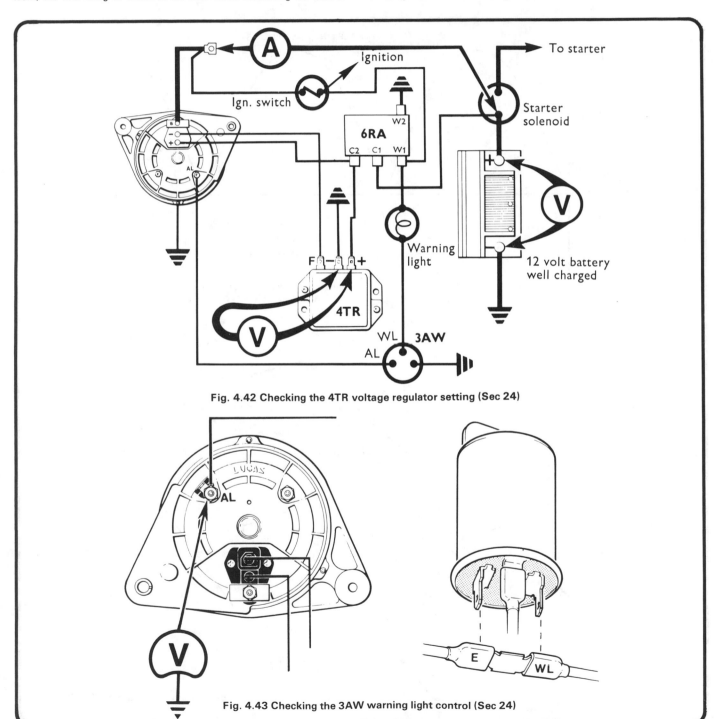

Fig. 4.42 Checking the 4TR voltage regulator setting (Sec 24)

Fig. 4.43 Checking the 3AW warning light control (Sec 24)

2   It is interesting to note that the dynamo armature conductors, in fact, have an alternating voltage generated in them while rotating under the magnetic poles, but the commutator acts as a form of rectifier, so that every time the voltage changes polarity the external leads are connected to the opposite conductors.

3   A closer look at this process (Fig. 4.44) shows a single loop of wire, the armature, rotating between N and S magnetic poles. It helps to imagine magnetic lines of force crossing from N to S; then with the armature coil being turned as shown the side 'a' is passing down through the magnetic lines (or 'flux' to use the engineering word) while side 'b' is going up through the magnetic flux. The voltages induced will add, so that the combined voltage will come out at the two commutator segments which rotate with the armature. Note the

current will flow out through the carbon brush B₁ round the external circuit and back in again at carbon brush B₂.

4   When the armature coil has passed through 90° so that sides 'a' and 'b' are at top and bottom of the magnetic flux field, ie halfway between the poles, then the brushes will just be connecting to the opposite commutator segment. As side 'b' starts to pass downwards under the N pole the generated voltage will now be in the opposite direction from when it was under the S pole; equally the voltage in coil side 'a' has changed. Because the connections to the brushes have changed the voltage appearing at the external load will be a sine wave, but with the negative half above the line, as shown (Fig. 4.44). Thus the voltage and current in the external load do not reverse, but come in the form of pulses which constitute a form of direct current and could be used for battery charging.

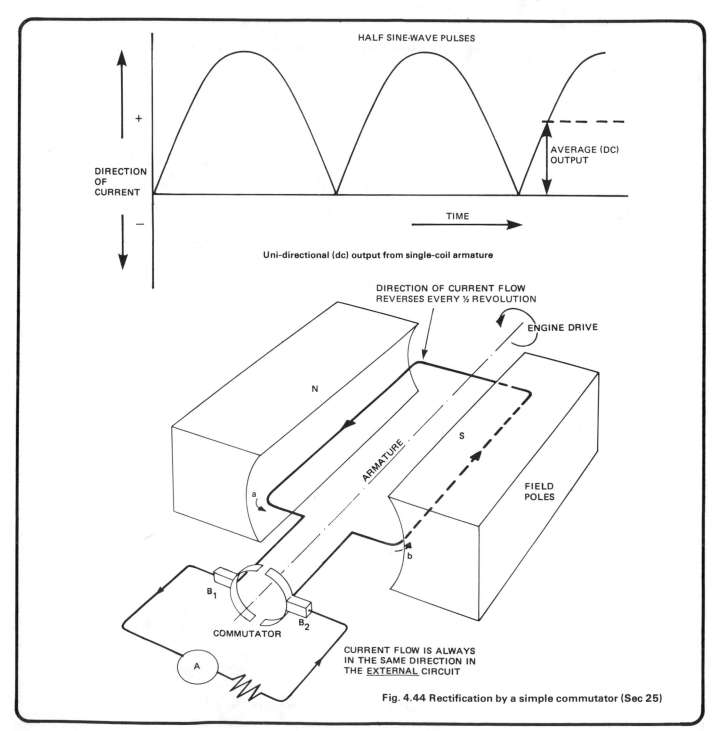

Fig. 4.44 Rectification by a simple commutator (Sec 25)

5   A practical direct current dynamo would use a number of coils connected to a commutator with the same number of segments; this way the magnetic field is utilised more effectively and the electrical output is improved. Additionally, the wave form of the resultant output voltage or current is smoother, as shown in Fig. 4.45.

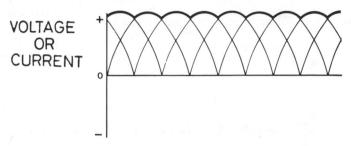

VOLTAGE OR CURRENT

Fig. 4.45 Multi-coil armature output (Sec 25)

6   A further substantial improvement comes by embedding the coils in slots of a laminated iron armature core mounted on a steel shaft (Fig. 4.46). This improvement in electrical output arises from the much stronger magnetic field using an iron armature, since the air gap is smaller.

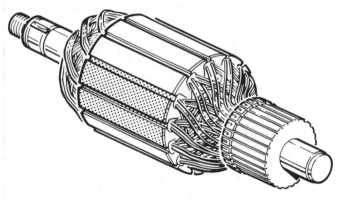

Fig. 4.46 Typical dynamo armature and commutator (Sec 25)

7   The iron core is made up of thin laminations insulated from each other. If the iron were solid, then it could be imagined as an infinite number of iron wires all short circuited to each other. Rotation in the magnetic field would induce voltages and currents in the iron and the result would be high circulating currents (called eddy currents) which would not only heat the iron considerably, but require high, wasted, drive power input.

8   The practical commutator (Fig. 4.47) consists of a number of copper segments arranged in cylindrical form and accurately machined for good contact with the carbon brushes. Each copper segment is insulated from the next by a material such as micanite, stennite or phenolic resin; since the copper will wear more quickly than the insulating material it is necessary to undercut the insulation (ie below

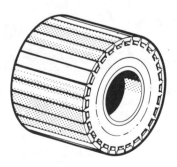

Fig. 4.47 Practical multi-segment commutator (Sec 25)

the copper level) during manufacture, and undercutting is sometimes required as a maintenance operation during the life of the dynamo. (See Section 36 of this Chapter).

9   The commutator assembly is pressed onto the armature shaft, and the armature conductors are soldered to the slots in the commutator segments. The brushes collect the dynamo current and are held in brush boxes, the commutator contact being ensured by pressure on the brushes from coiled springs (Fig. 4.48).

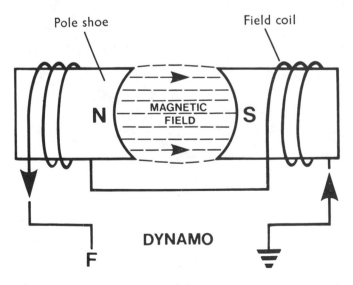

Fig. 4.48 Brush assembly (Sec 25)

10   In practice, permanent magnets are not used for vehicle dynamos; instead, electromagnets are employed. A coil of wire carrying direct current and wound round soft iron will produce a magnetic field around the iron similar to that of a permanent magnet, but with the great advantage that the strength of the magnetic field can be controlled by the amount of current flowing through the coil. Such electromagnets are used in dc dynamos, and the supply of the necessary current comes from the dynamo armature itself.

11   Fig. 4.49 shows a schematic of the pole arrangement. Actually the

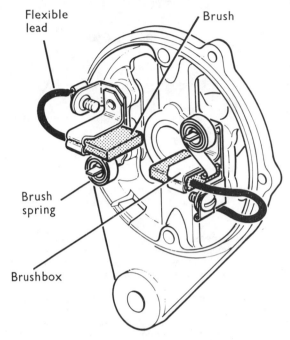

Fig. 4.49 Schematic diagram of electromagnetic poles (Sec 25)

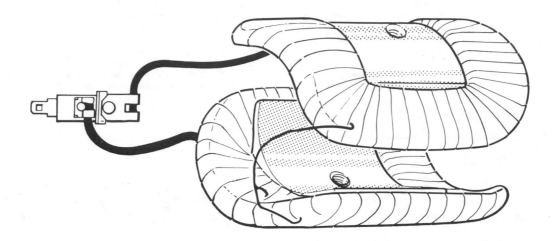

Fig. 4.50 Actual arrangement of pole shoes and coils (Sec 25)

coils are flattened and fit around the pole shoes as in Fig. 4.50, the latter being screwed tightly to the iron yoke (ie outer frame) of the dynamo.

12 The field coils consist of a pair of coils connected together in series. Each coil consists of several hundred turns of insulated copper wire which have been factory wound on a rectangular former. The final operation is to insulate the coils by means of cotton tape.

13 The yoke, pole shoes and armature frame are shown in Fig. 4.51. This shows the path of field magnetic flux; the armature conductors are located in the slots. Note that the steel yoke is part of the magnetic flux path and, observing that air gaps should be as small as possible to keep the flux high, the need for accurately and firmly fixed pole shoes is obvious, as is the need for good play-free armature shaft bearings. Fig. 4.52 shows the location and types of bearings often used in vehicle dc dynamos; some manufacturers employ ball-bearings at both ends.

14 The armature and field coils are connected in parallel (or shunt) and this type of assembly is known as a dc shunt dynamo. It is fortunate that the soft iron used in the magnetic circuit always retains a small amount of magnetisation even after coil current has ceased for the operation of the dc shunt dynamo depends upon this retention.

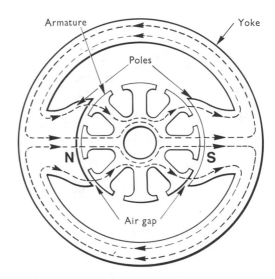

Fig. 4.51 The yoke forming part of the magnetic circuit (Sec 25)

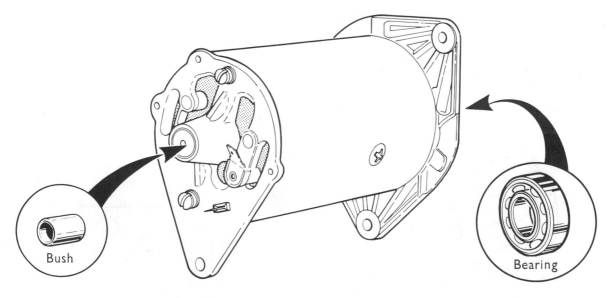

Fig. 4.52 Bearings for a dc dynamo (Sec 25)

15 Using symbols now, instead of drawing the dynamo in detail, we see in Fig. 4.53 the field and armature connected in parallel. As the armature rotates the conductors cut a weak magnetic field (the residual magnetism of the iron). A small voltage is generated (more correctly termed electromotive force – emf) in the armature and gives rise to a small current output, part of which will flow down through the field coils back to the armature. This strengthens the magnetic field, and so increases the generated emf in the armature; a higher field current flows which, in turn, raises the generated emf. The dynamo thus builds up to its working voltage.

16 It may occur to the reader that this process could go on indefinitely until the field coils burn out. This probably would happen were it not for the phenomenon of iron magnetic saturation. Iron can sustain only a certain maximum magnetic flux, however large the current in the electromagnet coils, and Fig. 4.54 shows what happens to the generated emf as the field current rises, (remembering that the emf varies directly with the magnetic flux). However, the final voltage of a direct current dynamo, left unchecked, would be far too high for charging a battery, and so some form of regulator is required. Incidentally, the shunt generator must always be driven in the correct direction, otherwise it will fail to start, for the initial generated current would tend to eliminate the residual magnetism.

17 The correct polarisation of the dynamo is thus vital, and when a replacement dynamo is fitted to a car it is necessary to ensure that the residual magnetisation of the iron is correct. To do this the dynamo field 'F' terminal is connected to the battery output lead for a few seconds with 'D' and 'F' leads removed.

18 Ventilation is important for the dynamo, since some heat will be generated internally. The usual arrangement is that the dynamo endplates will be slotted and a fan is built on to the driving pulley. The fan is of the centrifugal type and draws air through the dynamo (Fig. 4.55). Certain types of dynamos are totally enclosed, but are for special purposes, for example, in agriculture where dust levels can be high. In these machines the electrical power output is reduced to prevent overheating.

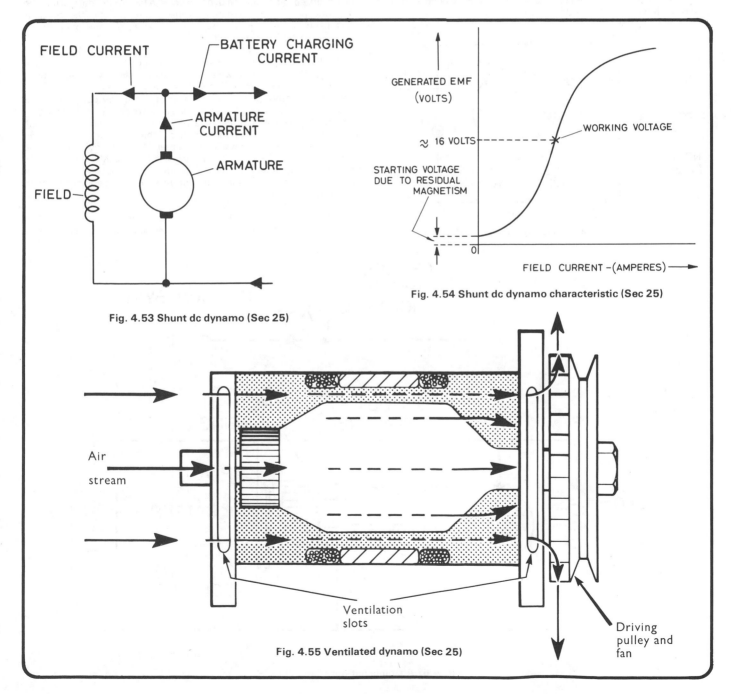

Fig. 4.53 Shunt dc dynamo (Sec 25)

Fig. 4.54 Shunt dc dynamo characteristic (Sec 25)

Fig. 4.55 Ventilated dynamo (Sec 25)

26 Battery charging

1   It is important to realise that the dynamo and battery both have terminal voltages in opposition (Fig. 4.56). In order to force current into the battery the dynamo voltage must be higher than that of the battery. This arrangement would be fairly simple to engineer, were it not for the fact that the battery voltage is not constant, but ranges from about 12 volts when low to nearly 16 volts when fully charged.

2   If the dynamo were regulated to give a constant voltage then the current flowing into a fully discharged battery might burn out the armature. For this reason a regulator used in conjunction with the dynamo is compensated to allow for the load demanded by the battery and auxiliary equipment on the vehicle.

3   It is worth thinking about what would happen when the dynamo voltage reduces below that of the battery; current would now flow from the battery to the dynamo which, if free, would turn as a motor. Clearly some device is needed to disconnect the dynamo from the battery as required – this device is the cut-out.

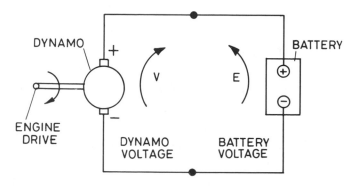

Fig. 4.56 Dynamo charging the battery (Sec 26)

27 The cut-out

1   The purpose of the cut-out is to connect the dynamo to the battery when the dynamo voltage rises above the battery voltage, ie at about 13 volts, and to disconnect it at tickover; the cut-out is an electromagnetic relay with a coil connected across the dynamo output terminal and earth. The coil is so designed that it will produce a level of magnetisation in the relay iron path sufficient to pull down a hinged plate (the armature) when the supply voltage to the coil reaches the pull-in voltage (Fig. 4.57). Note that when the engine is stationary and the ignition switch is on, the charge warning light will glow. As the engine runs up to speed, the generated voltage of the dynamo rises to approximately that of the battery, when the warning light will go out. The cut-out contacts close, connecting the dynamo and battery, but also shorting out the warning light.

2   The armature movement serves to close the cut-out contacts which connect the dynamo main output terminal to the battery. When the engine speed drops, the dynamo voltage falls to the point when the magnetic pull on the armature is insufficient to hold the contacts closed and they pull apart under spring pressure. The cut-out is thus a relay, or electromagnetic switch.

3   In Fig. 4.58, showing a practical cut-out, the bobbin has two windings. The main shunt winding consists of several hundred turns of enamelled copper wire and it is this coil which provides the main magnetic armature pull. A second winding of heavy copper wire, or strip, is in series with the contacts and carries the main charging current. As the contacts close, a heavy initial charging current will produce a magnetisation adding to that of the shunt coil and assists in closing the contacts firmly without chatter. When the dynamo voltage falls below that of the battery, at tickover for example, current flows the other way from the battery to dynamo. This gives rise to a magnetisation in opposition to that of the main shunt coil and helps to throw open the contacts cleanly.

4   Note also the leaf spring with an adjusting screw for setting the cut-in voltage of the cut-out. In practice this leaf spring consists of two

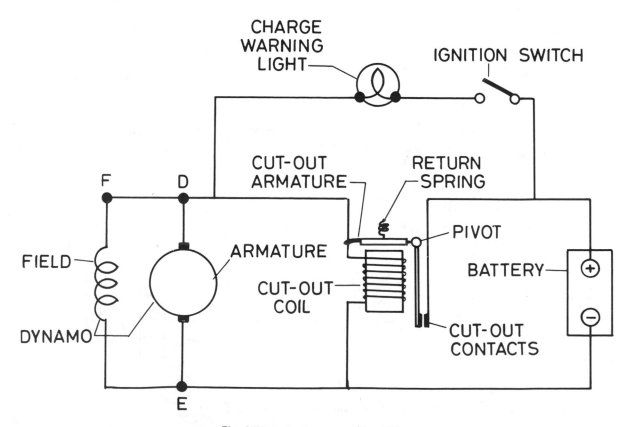

Fig. 4.57 A simple cut-out (Sec 27)

different metal strips riveted together and having differing expansion rates with heat; with change of temperature the spring will curve. As the temperature goes up, the shunt coil resistance will increase, and so a higher voltage will be required to pull in the armature; in compensation the bi-metal strip will bend away from the adjusting screw so that the spring load is reduced, thus tending to lower the cut-in voltage.

28 Regulator – dynamo circuit

1   If the dynamo voltage rises too high for battery charging requirements, the regulator unit opens the connection between field and armature and inserts a resistor. This lowers the field current and so reduces the dynamo generated voltage.

2   Fig. 4.59 shows the regulator, which has an electromagnetic relay like that of the cut-out. The magnetising (shunt) coil is connected between D and E, while the contacts are here shown mounted above the moving armature and are normally closed. When the armature pulls down, the contacts open and D and F are now joined through the resistor. Spring tension is controlled by the adjuster screw and, once again, the leaf spring is bi-metallic to compensate for temperature variation.

3   This regulator has a drawback in that a battery in a low state of charge will have a low terminal voltage. A heavy charge current would flow and could burn out the armature, so in practice compensation is provided, so that the difference between the regulator voltage and that of the battery is never great enough to cause dynamo damage.

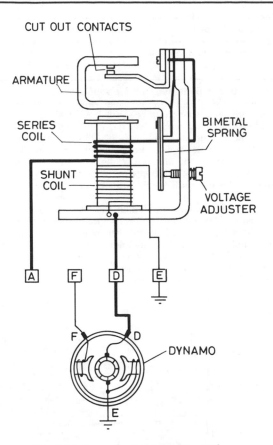

Fig. 4.58 A practical cut-out (Sec 27)

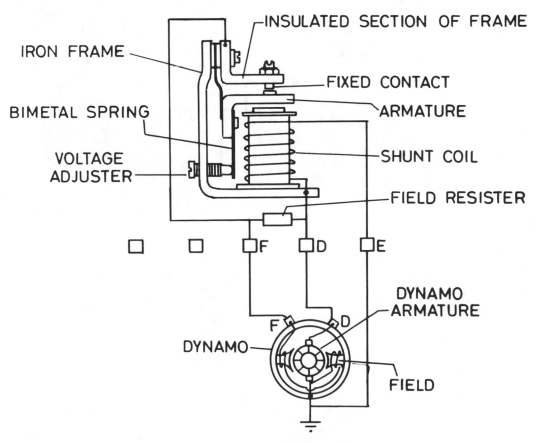

Fig. 4.59 Voltage regulator (Sec 28)

29 Compensated regulator

1   Fig. 4.60 shows an additional coil on the regulator bobbin, consisting of a few turns of thick wire or of flat strip. This series coil carries the load current and produces a magnetic field which aids that of the shunt voltage coil.

2   When a heavy load current flows the magnetic fields of the two coils add, giving a higher pull on the armature than that due to the shunt coil alone. The regulator contacts open at a lower voltage, and so the dynamo is operated at a variable voltage, according to the current flowing into the battery.

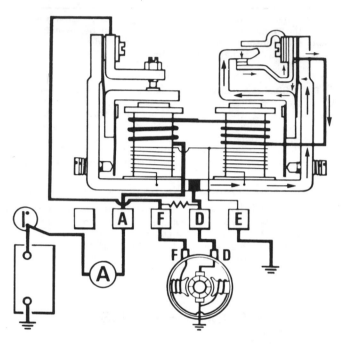

Fig. 4.60 Compensated voltage control (Sec 29)

30 Load compensation

1   The idea of a compensated regulator (Sec 29) is extended, so that extra series turns are added which carry currents to various vehicle loads, such as headlights. A battery in a low state of charge will suffer an additional terminal voltage fall when a load is switched on, and if this load current can be made to flow through a load coil such that the dynamo voltage is lowered with increased current, then additional protection is given (Fig. 4.61).

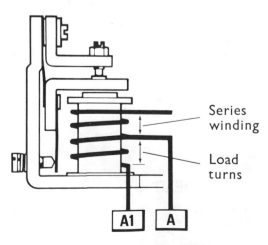

Fig. 4.61 Load turns (Sec 30)

2   The number of turns on both the compensation and load coils are made to suit the dynamo and vehicle loads, respectively, so control boxes cannot be interchanged without checking with the manufacturer's recommendations.

31 Complete compensated voltage regulator

1   The compensated voltage control box is shown in Fig. 4.62. Current flows out of dynamo terminal D to the metal frames of the cut-out and regulator units. After passing through the cut-out points it goes through the series coils on both bobbins and out to the A terminal for battery charging, and also out to the A1 terminal for lighting and ignition-switched loads. The circuit is completed, via the vehicle chassis, back to the earth brush of the dynamo.

2   This form of dynamo regulation has been used extensively for some years. There remains a disadvantage, however, in that the dynamo is not working to its full capacity for a proportion of the battery charging time. What is required is a maximum charge rate until charging is almost complete, thus ensuring the fastest possible battery recovery, and then to taper down gradually to a trickle charge. Such a requirement can be met with only slightly more complication in the current voltage regulator (Section 32).

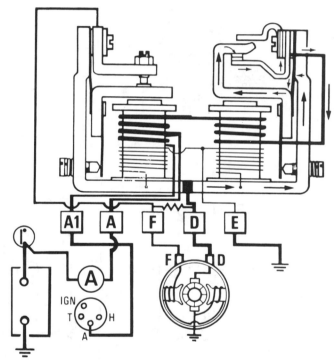

Fig. 4.62 The complete regulator (Sec 31)

32 Current voltage regulator

1   Reference to the graph (Fig. 4.63) shows that a compensated voltage regulator starts to charge a discharged battery at a high rate, but falls off quickly to a trickle level. Whilst this is happening the battery voltage rises slowly. The current voltage control regulator ensures that the battery is charged at a level rate by the current regulator until the battery voltage rises to a particular value, when the voltage regulator takes over and the charge rate drops off to a trickle. The unit consists of three parts:

   (1) The cut out
   (2) The current regulator, which allows full dynamo output until the line voltage reaches a set level
   (3) The voltage regulator, which assumes control of the dynamo for the final phase of charging when the current eventually drops to some 1 or 2 amperes

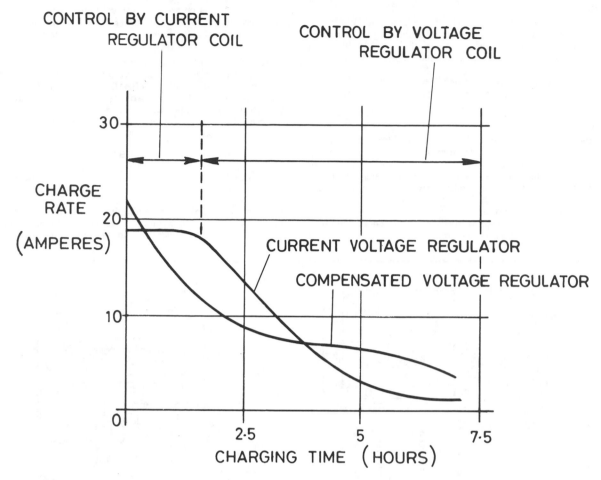

Fig. 4.63 Comparison of regulator performances (Sec 32)

2 Assuming the battery to be discharged initially, the dynamo voltage will rise with dynamo speed up to 12.75 to 13.25 volts when the cut-out contacts close. With further rise in dynamo speed the charging current, flowing through the heavy gauge wire or strip wound round the current regulator bobbin, will cause the contacts (3) to open (see Fig. 4.64). This breaks the link between D and F, and introduces the resistor R, so the dynamo voltage will fall because the field current drops. Note that at this stage the voltage regulator coil contacts are closed. The current to the battery also drops, allowing the contacts (3) to close again.

3 This process continues at a rate somewhere between 60 and 100 times per second, and so the dynamo current is limited to its rated maximum. Eventually, at about one-third full charge, the battery voltage will rise to the point where the voltage regulator armature is pulled in and thence vibrates. From this point it is the system **voltage** which is regulated, and not the current; the current regulator contacts stay closed for the remainder of the charging cycle because the coil current is insufficient to pull in the current regulator armature.

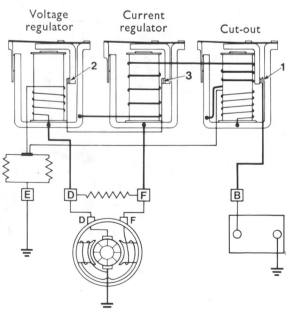

Fig. 4.64 Current voltage regulator (Sec 32)

33 Bucking coil

Some current voltage regulators have a few turns of thick wire wound over the voltage regulator bobbin to assist the magnetic pull of the shunt coil. The effect is to make the contacts break more rapidly, and also to increase the frequency of the vibration. For this reason it is sometimes called a frequency coil.

34 Dynamo system tests

Assuming that a fault exists in the system, it pays to follow a logical test procedure, unless the area of the fault is obvious.

Test 1: Check the battery
Use a hydrometer and heavy discharge test, as outlined in Section 24.

Test 2: Check belt tension

In the case of dynamos the belt should deflect about $\frac{1}{4}$ in to $\frac{3}{4}$ in with moderate finger pressure at the centre of the longest span. Note whether the belt is running at the bottom of the pulley V – if so, the belt must be renewed, and possibly the pulley also.

Test 3: Check for broken connections

Also check for possible corroded contacts between connectors and fuse carriers.

Test 4: Armature test

With the main dynamo output lead D removed from the regulator box, run up the engine to about 1500 rpm (see Fig. 4.65). The voltage from the D lead to earth should be between 1.5 and 3V, due to the field residual magnetism. If the reading is zero, or much lower than 1.5V, then either the lead or the dynamo armature circuit is faulty.

Test 5: Check dynamo field circuit

Disconnect the D and F leads at the dynamo. Connect an ammeter between D and F terminals of the dynamo, and a voltmeter from D to earth. Run up the engine until the voltmeter reads 12 volts when the field current should be of the order of 2 to 2.5 amperes. Remove the dynamo for field coil repair if the voltage is outside these limits.

Test 6: Zero load voltage setting

This checks the regulator voltage setting. For a compensated voltage box such as the Lucas RB106, take off the A and A1 leads and link them together. In the case of the current voltage regulator take off the two B leads and link them (Fig. 4.66). At 3000 rpm engine speed measure the voltage from the D terminal to earth. For Lucas boxes the voltage limits are:

Compensated voltage regulators	RB106, RB108	16 to 16.5 volts
Current voltage regulator	RB340	14.5 to 15.5 volts

Outside these limits, the regulators should be adjusted. Regulator boxes of most manufacturers have similar working voltages, and makers' information sheets should be consulted.

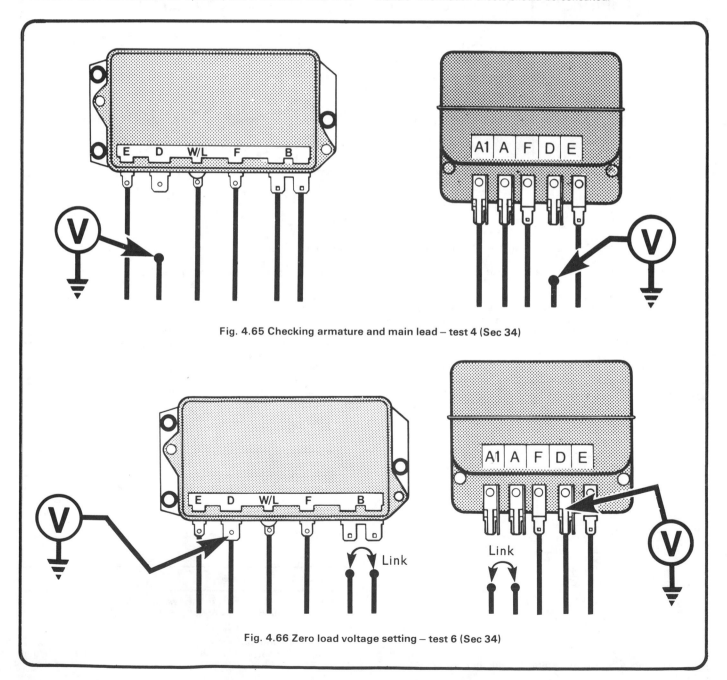

Fig. 4.65 Checking armature and main lead – test 4 (Sec 34)

Fig. 4.66 Zero load voltage setting – test 6 (Sec 34)

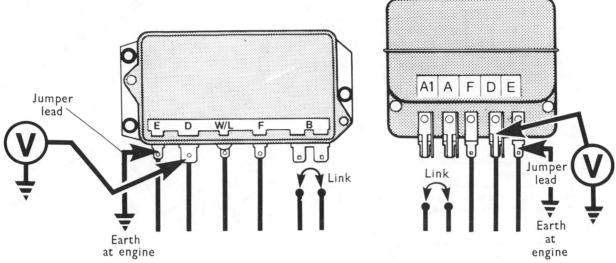

Fig. 4.67 Control box earthing – test 7 (Sec 34)

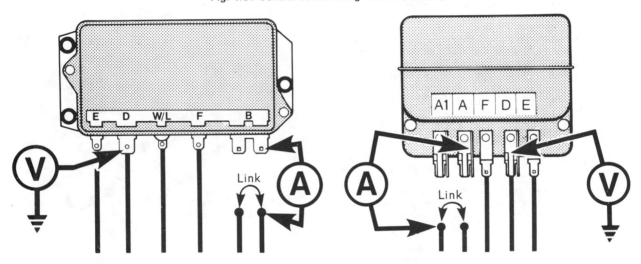

Fig. 4.68 Cut-in voltage – test 8 (Sec 34)

Test 7: Control box earth

Peculiar results occur if the earthing of the control box is faulty, examples being that the regulator works at the wrong voltage, or is incapable of adjustment. With the A, A1 or B leads bridged, as in Test 6, connect a jumper lead from the box earth terminal to an engine earth point (Fig. 4.67). If the box now regulates correctly, look for a corroded earth point. If the result is negative, renew the control box.

Test 8: Cut-in voltage

The box is connected as in Test 6, but with an ammeter between the A or B terminal and the bridged leads; a voltmeter is connected from terminal D to earth (Fig. 4.68). Start the engine, switch on headlights and raise the engine speed slowly. The cut-out contacts should close, indicated by ammeter charge, and the voltmeter should flick back to between 12.7 and 13.3 volts.

Test 9: Reverse current

Using the same connections as in Test 8, but with no voltmeter, run the engine up to about 3000 rpm and then slowly decrease the speed until the cut-out points open. At this point the reverse current should be 5A, dropping to zero at opening. If reverse current stays present down to tickover or standstill, the contacts are sticking and the control box should be serviced or renewed.

Test 10: Current regulator setting

For current voltage regulator boxes only, short out the voltage regulator contacts by bridging them with a suitable clip. Insert an ammeter between B terminal and the linked leads (Fig. 4.69), and run

up the engine to 3000 rpm. The ammeter should then show the full rated output current of the dynamo – typically of the order of 22 amperes. Reset the current regulator adjustment screw, if necessary. To check, leave the voltage contacts bridged and raise the engine speed from tickover to 3000 rpm, and recheck the current rating.

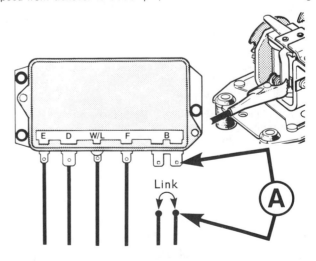

Fig. 4.69 Current regulator setting – test 10 (Sec 34)

35 Contacts

1   Contact cleaning is required occasionally, and it is important to use different methods for the regulator and cut-out contacts.

2   Regulator contacts are made of tungsten and should be cleaned with either a carborundum stone or silicon carbide paper. Cut-out contacts are silver and hence very soft. These should be cleaned with fine grade glass paper.

3   All contact dust should be removed with a cloth soaked in methylated spirits.

36 Dynamo – servicing notes

1   After a period of service, wear in moving and sliding parts requires removal of the dynamo for routine maintenance.

2   The commutator may become scored and grooved and the remedy depends on how badly it is affected. Sometimes all that is required is cleaning with petrol and the segment gaps scraped out. Possibly the commutator might need cleaning with a strip of fine glasspaper, but if it is burned away by arcing, then the armature must be mounted in a lathe and the commutator skimmed true.

3   With this last treatment, it is necessary to undercut the insulation between segments to a depth of about $\frac{1}{32}$ in (1 mm). Often a hacksaw blade with the teeth width reduced on a grinding wheel will be used for undercutting (Fig. 4.70). To complete the job care must be taken to remove any burr. Crypton market a machine for commutator undercutting (Fig. 4.71), a valuable piece of equipment for the large scale auto-electrical shop.

4   Brushes will throw carbon dust everywhere and this may be removed with petrol and a fine brush. It should not need stating that 'no smoking' is the rule, and work should be carried out in a well ventilated room. Brushes should be checked for adequate length and renewed if necessary. If new brushes are fitted, bed them in using a strip of fine glasspaper wrapped halfway round the commutator and rocking it back and forth a few times. This will profile the brush to the correct contour. Finally check for free brush movement in the brush carriers.

5   Bearing wear gives a rumbling noise and, if bad enough, may cause the armature to rub on the pole shoes, as evidenced by bright areas seen during inspection.

6   Removal of the bronze bush at the commutator end may be achieved by tapping it out with a suitable drift or, if it is reluctant, by cutting it lengthways and then drifting it out. The replacement bush should be soaked in oil for several hours (it is made of porous phosphor bronze) and then lightly tapped in place with a soft drift, preferably wood, or possibly pressed in ensuring suitable protection against damage. Regular oiling at 6000 mile intervals (Fig. 4.72) will prolong the life of this bearing bush considerably.

7   The bearing at the drive end lasts longer than the bush at the other end, but if it has to be renewed remove the fan/pulley either by leverage or using a puller, having first removed the shaft nut and washer.

8   With care the armature shaft can be tapped out from the bearing using a soft drift against the end of the shaft. Protection of the shaft thread is necessary by putting on the end nut; pressing out may be necessary if this method fails. After the bearing has been fitted, repack with high melting point grease.

9   The presence of solder thrown round the body of the dynamo may mean failure of the armature. It is worth resoldering the joints of the armature conductors and the commutator segments. A large capacity soldering iron will be needed and resin flux, **not spirit flux,** must be used. Indeed, spirit flux must never be used on electrical joints at all.

10 Failure of a field coil is usually shown by burn marks on the tape binding, and possibly by the coils having different resistance values.

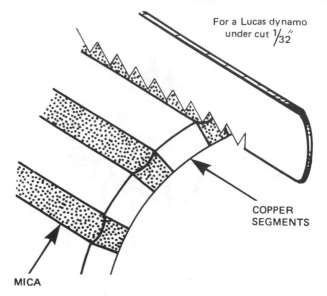

Fig. 4.70 Undercutting the commutator (Sec 36)

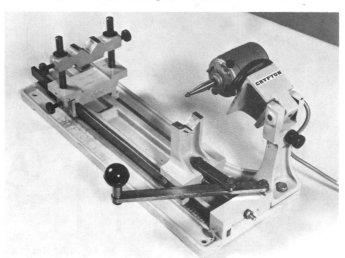

Fig. 4.71 Crypton commutator undercutting machine (Sec 36)

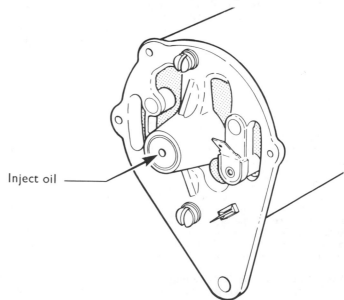

Fig. 4.72 Oiling the bronze bush in a dynamo (Sec 36)

Sometimes failure occurs due to shorting down to the metal frame and this again can be checked by a test meter on the ohms range. It is possible to rewind a field coil by counting turns off the old coil and rewinding as a copy. Retaping must be done with care so as not to occupy too much space, yet give protection.

11 Pole shoes are screwed very tightly to the dynamo yoke (body) and often need the use of an impact driver to loosen them. Take care to refit tightly, for a pole shoe working loose in service spells total failure of the dynamo. A pole screw machine is available commercially (Fig. 4.73). After reassembly, running the dynamo as a motor (join the field and dynamo terminals) will give a fair indication that everything is in order.

37 Dynamo to alternator conversion

1   While the dynamo is designed to power the original equipment of the vehicle, there will be a time when it cannot cope with added accessories. The best solution then is to remove the dynamo and substitute an alternator.

2   It is simpler to wire in an alternator having an integral electronic regulator, for then only two cables are required. It may be that the mounting and belt tension adjustment bracket will need to be changed or modified, and for some vehicles later models will have alternators fitted as original equipment so that brackets will be available.

3   Fig. 4.74 shows the changes in wiring. The dynamo control box may be left in place for the convenience of using certain blade terminals. In the example shown two B terminals strapped together internally remain connected to the battery via the live starter solenoid terminal and to the live terminal of the ignition switch.

4   Next, the charge warning lamp is disconnected from the regulator box (WL terminal in this example) and connected to the cable which has been taken off the regulator box F terminal. This field cable can now be connected at the alternator to the IND terminal. Alternatively a new cable can be used.

5   Similarly the D cable is disconnected both at the dynamo and the regulator D terminal. It is best not to re-use this, but to make up a fresh

Fig. 4.73 Crypton pole-screw machine (Sec 36)

cable to connect the alternator main output terminal + direct to the battery or the solenoid live terminal.

6   Manufacturers will supply an alternator and sometimes it may be possible to buy a conversion outfit with instructions, cables and alternator connectors. It is recommended that any cable joints are soldered to avoid possible trouble from corrosion at crimped joints.

7   Loading of the alternator will be higher as accessories are used, and so will the torque required at the alternator pulley. Correct tensioning of the drivebelt is important; too loose and slipping will occur, too tight and the alternator bearings will have a short life. Check tension according to Section 24 of this Chapter.

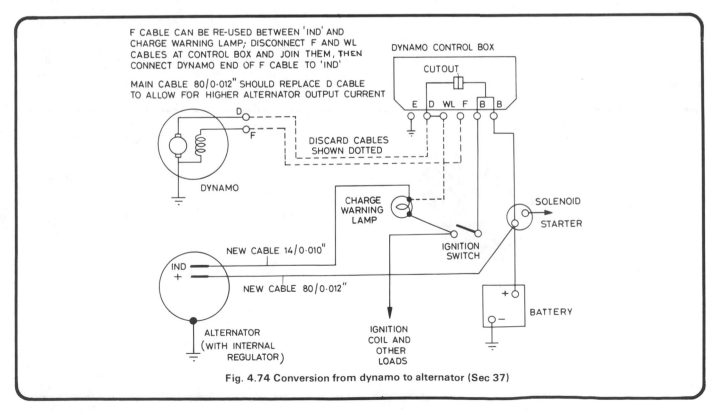

Fig. 4.74 Conversion from dynamo to alternator (Sec 37)

Chapter 5 Starter motors

Contents

1 Introduction

The early automobiles relied upon human power to turn over the engine until it fired. Every engine had a crankshaft dog into which a starting handle could be located, but the need for a starter motor soon became important. Engines became more powerful and difficult to swing over by hand, and many wrist injuries occurred because of kickback.

Starter motors work on direct current from the battery and are designed to give high torque at standstill and at low speeds. At the point of engaging with a 1500 cc engine the current may rise to 350 to 450 amperes, giving a shaft torque of the order of 15 lbf ft, ie the twisting effect of a 15 lb weight at a radius of 1 ft.

It follows that the minimum of unwanted resistance should be present in the battery-starter circuit, calling for thick cables, clean terminals and a battery with low internal resistance.

Direct current motors are classified according to how the field windings are connected to the armature. The series motor, in which the field winding and the armature are connected in series, has an ideal torque characteristic for engine starting, in that maximum torque occurs at standstill — just what is wanted to turn over an engine.

Fig. 5.2 shows an elementary dc series motor. The current will be high when the motor is loaded, so the field coils will consist of a few turns of thick copper or aluminium strip. Note that the magnetic field produced by a winding depends upon the number of turns of wire (or

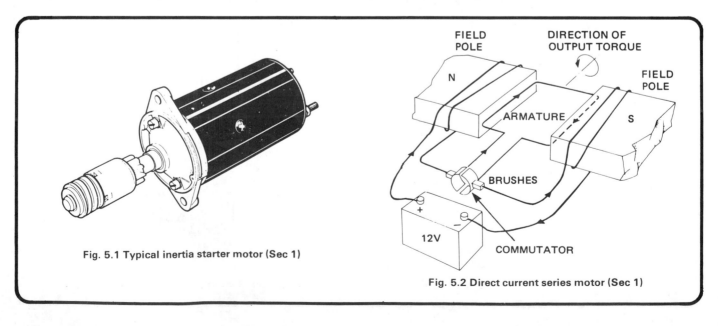

Fig. 5.1 Typical inertia starter motor (Sec 1)

Fig. 5.2 Direct current series motor (Sec 1)

strip) and the current, so if the current is high, as in a starter motor, only a few turns are needed for the field coils, and these will need to have low resistance to avoid excessive voltage drop (Fig. 5.3).

The principle of operation of the electric motor is closely related to that of the generator. Basically, the only real difference is that in the case of the generator the input is mechanical torque to turn the rotor, the output being electrical energy, whereas in the starter motor, electrical energy is put in and mechanical torque taken out at the shaft. Indeed, all dc generators can be made to run as motors simply by supplying direct current and, conversely, all dc motors can be made to act as generators.

For production of an output torque it is necessary to supply direct current to an armature situated in a magnetic field. There are three points to be noted:

(a) The magnetic field is produced by a current which flows through the field coils and then the armature. The poles are laminated iron sheet to give a stronger magnetic field, and for the same reason the armature conductors are in practice embedded in a laminated steel core. Fig. 5.4 shows a typical construction.

(b) In practice, many more coils are used in the armature than in the simple model of Fig. 5.2. This is so that the torque is more uniform over the complete rotation of the armature.

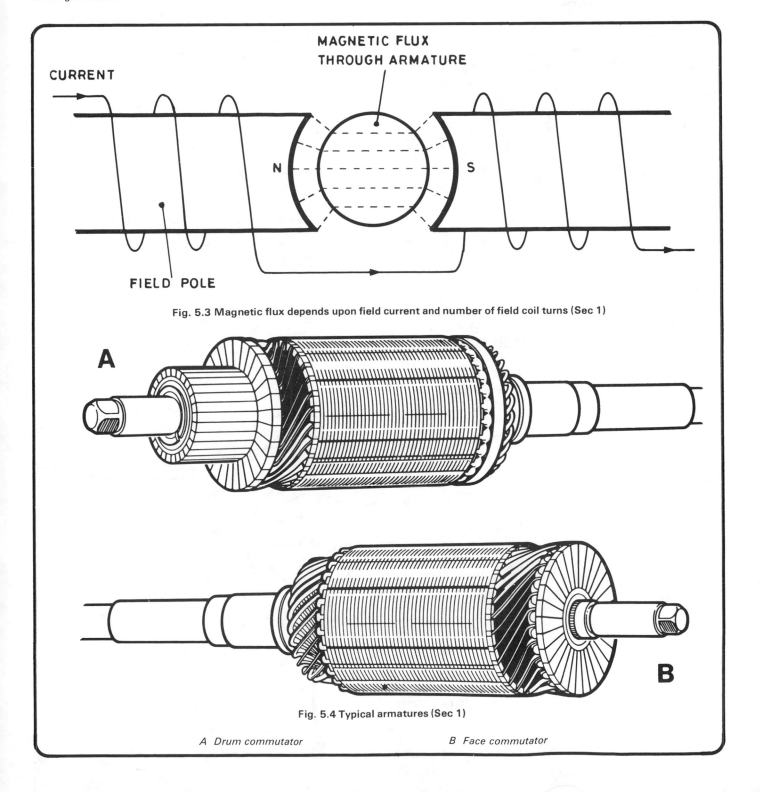

Fig. 5.3 Magnetic flux depends upon field current and number of field coil turns (Sec 1)

Fig. 5.4 Typical armatures (Sec 1)

A Drum commutator   *B Face commutator*

(c) In order to keep the armature coil current flowing in the same direction as it passes under a pole, it is necessary to reverse the connection every 180° in the simple model. This is achieved by splitting a ring into two parts as shown, where it is known as a commutator, the action being shown in more detail in Fig. 5.5.

Again, in practice, the commutator has a number of segments, or bars, but they perform the same function as in the simple model.

Finally, to see how an electric motor turns it must be remembered that:

(a) A wire carrying a current creates a magnetic field around it (Fig. 5.6).
(b) When such a current carrying conductor is located in another magnetic field, such as that set up by the field coils, then there will be an interaction.

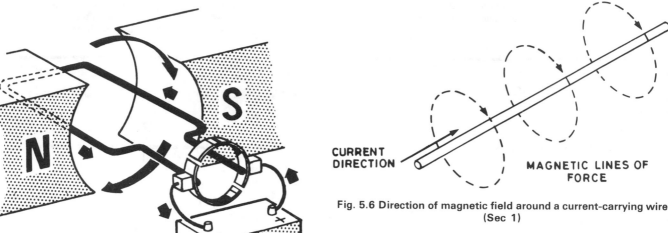

Fig. 5.5 An elementary dc motor (Sec 1)

Fig. 5.6 Direction of magnetic field around a current-carrying wire (Sec 1)

To work out this effect, image that magnetic lines of force behave like elastic threads, but tend to bow away from each other when acting in the same direction. Fig. 5.7 shows what happens when an armature conductor has current passed through it. The tendency is for the main pole flux lines to pull straight, and there is a resultant force on the conductor pushing it downwards.

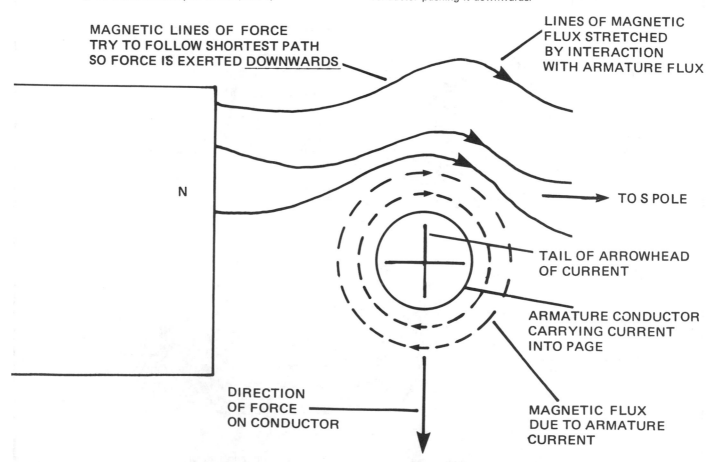

Fig. 5.7 Rule for working out the direction of motor rotation (Sec 1)

2 Speed and torque

1 When an electric motor armature is turning it should be remembered that the conductors of the armature are cutting through the magnetic field and will have a voltage (or back emf) generated in them. This is in no way connected with the fact that the rotation of the armature has been produced by a current supplied by a car battery, for the generated emf would be the same if the armature had been turned by an external mechanical drive.

2 This back emf, as the name suggests, is always in the opposite direction to an externally supplied voltage, in this case from the car battery, and its value is directly dependent upon the speed of rotation of the armature. Thus, in simple terms, an electric motor when switched on will speed up until the back emf is equal to the supply voltage, less a small amount to allow for the resistance volt-drop in the field, armature and brushes (Fig. 5.8).

3 Torque depends upon two factors, magnetic flux and armature current, and the series starter motor is ideal for producing a high starting torque for two reasons:

(a) When the starter key is turned the motor is at standstill. There is thus no back emf to limit the current, only internal

resistance voltage drop, and so the starting current is momentarily very high.

(b) This high current flows through the field coils which are in series with the armature, and so the magnetic flux is also high.

For these reasons, the series wound dc motor finds favour for starter applications and for vehicle traction work, eg fork lift trucks, because of excellent take-off characteristics.

4 Another characteristic of the series motor is that it will race up to high speeds off load. Do not leave a starter motor running light, or the armature may be damaged with windings flying out of place due to centrifugal force.

3 Power transmission

Power transmission takes place in two stages when the starter switch is operated. First there is a power flow from the battery to the starter motor, causing the motor armature to rotate; then there is the power flow from the armature to the vehicle engine, this being accomplished by the engagement of a pinion gear on the armature shaft with a geared ring on the engine flywheel (Figs. 5.9 and 5.10).

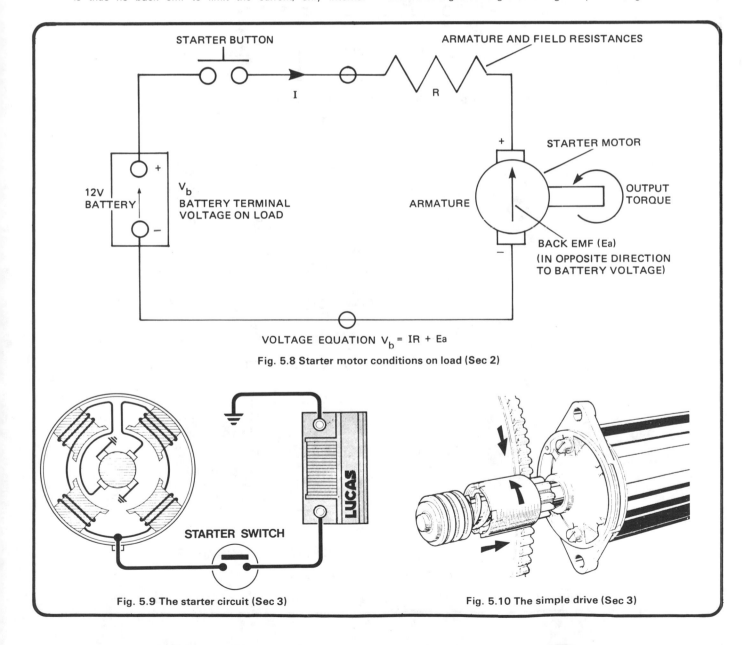

VOLTAGE EQUATION $V_b = IR + Ea$

Fig. 5.8 Starter motor conditions on load (Sec 2)

Fig. 5.9 The starter circuit (Sec 3)

Fig. 5.10 The simple drive (Sec 3)

4   Starter solenoid

1   Remembering that the starter takes a heavy current on load, it is essential to use thick cables from the battery and the shortest convenient cable route. For these reasons the switch is always remotely operated by a solenoid (or magnetic switch) which is a form of electromagnet. The solenoid coil (Fig. 5.11) takes a low current which is easily handled by the ignition key switch; the solenoid magnetic field pulls the iron plunger to the centre of the solenoid coil, and in so doing closes the heavy duty contacts of the starter switch.

2   There are two types of solenoid starter switch (Fig. 5.12).

(a)   The separate solenoid which may have a push button for manual operation, and is used with inertia drive mechanisms.

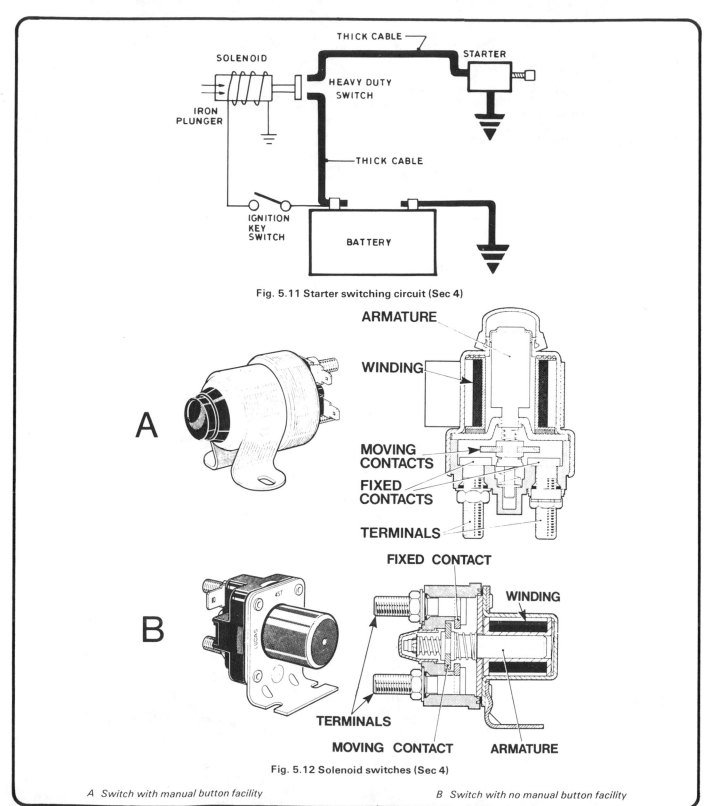

Fig. 5.11 Starter switching circuit (Sec 4)

Fig. 5.12 Solenoid switches (Sec 4)

A Switch with manual button facility   *B Switch with no manual button facility*

(b) The integral solenoid which is mounted on the starter body and carries out the functions of first engaging the pinion teeth with the flywheel gearing and then switching on the starter current. This is the pre-engaged starter motor (Fig. 5.13).

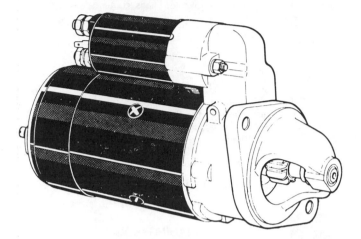

Fig. 5.13 Solenoid mounted on typical pre-engaged starter motor (Sec 4)

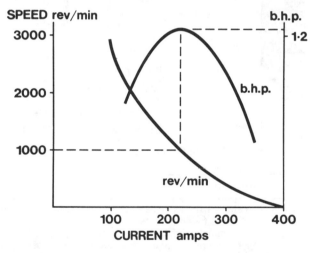

Fig. 5.14 Characteristic curves for speed and bhp (Sec 5)

5 Starter gear ratio

1 A graph showing the performance of a typical starter motor (Fig. 5.14) indicates that maximum power is occurring at about 1000 rpm. An engine should turn over at not less than 100 rpm for starting purposes, and so we derive the ratio:

$$\frac{\text{number of flywheel teeth}}{\text{number of pinion teeth}} \quad \frac{1000}{100} \quad = 10:1$$

Note that this would also be the factor which would be used to calculate the torque on the engine (Fig. 5.15):

If the torque of starter motor is 2 lbf ft and the above ratio is 10 :
Torque on the engine flywheel = 2 x 10
= 20 lbf ft.

Note: lbf equals the gravitational force on a mass of 1 lb at sea level; however, torque is usually read 'pounds-feet'.

6 Inertia drive mechanisms

1 The action of the inertia (or Bendix) drive is to throw the pinion along a coarse thread and into engagement with the flywheel gear. So long as the starter is driving the engine the pinion gear remains engaged, but when the engine fires and the flywheel rotates faster than the starter pinion, the pinion runs back down the screw thread and disengages (Fig. 5.16).

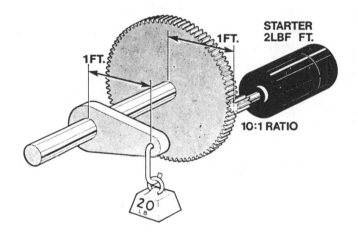

Fig. 5.15 Method of torque measurement (Sec 5)

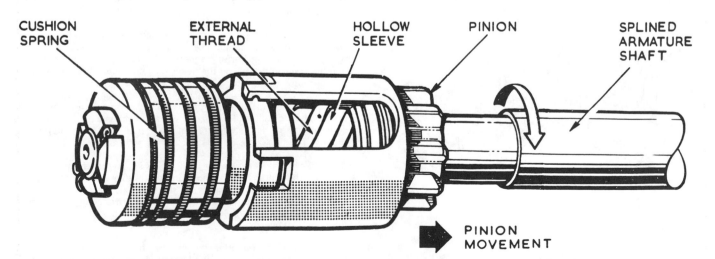

CUSHION SPRING   EXTERNAL THREAD   HOLLOW SLEEVE   PINION   SPLINED ARMATURE SHAFT

PINION MOVEMENT

Fig. 5.16 Inertia drive mechanism (Sec 6)

2   The speed of disengagement is often very high if the engine picks up readily, and so a spring is located at the shaft end to absorb the shock of pinion impact.

3   A fair variety of inertia drives are in use, including the Lucas S type, SB type, and Eclipse drive (Figs. 5.17, 5.18 and 5.19).

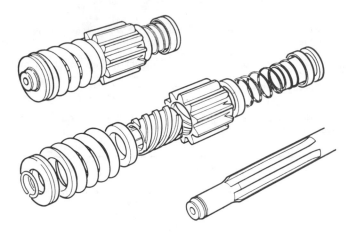

Fig. 5.17 'S' type drive (Sec 6)

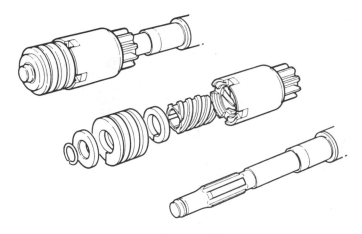

Fig. 5.18 'SB' type drive (Sec 6)

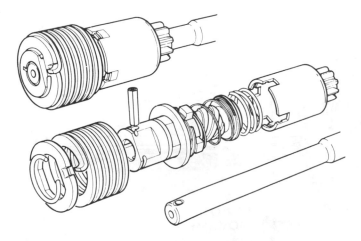

Fig. 5.19 Eclipse type drive (Sec 6)

7   Out-of-mesh clearance

1   The starter pinion must be set correctly in relation to the starter ring so that it will slide into engagement with the minimum of rotary movement. Out-of-mesh clearance is illustrated by Fig. 5.20 and should be within the limits shown for Lucas starters:

Drive type	Out-of-mesh clearance
All types except Eclipse	$\frac{1}{8}'' \pm \frac{1}{32}''$
Eclipse	$\frac{7}{32}''$ nominal

2   To check the clearance two measurements must be made:

   (a)   From the leading edge of the pinion to the fixing flange of the starter, distance A in the diagram.
   (b)   From the leading edge of the flywheel to the starter fixing flange (distance B).

   then Clearance = A – B

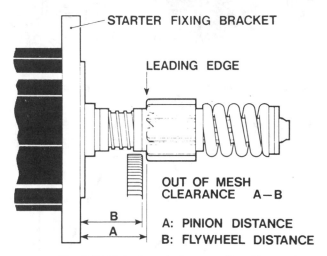

Fig. 5.20 Out-of-mesh clearance (Sec 7)

8   Pre-engaged starters

Pre-engaged starters (an example is shown in Fig. 5.21) are fitted to diesel engines and to an increasing number of petrol-engined vehicles. The main distinction from the inertia type is that the pinion is first fully engaged, at rest, with the flywheel gear ring before the starter motor current is switched on.

9   Solenoid operation

1   The solenoid has two windings which are connected in parallel (Fig. 5.22). When the ignition key switch is turned on, the heavy gauge winding creates a powerful magnetic field which pulls the iron plunger into the coil centre, closing the heavy duty contacts which connect the starter motor straight onto the battery.

2   It will be seen that when the contacts are closed, this closing coil is then short-circuited. The second winding acts as a hold-on coil with sufficient magnetic force to prevent the iron plunger from returning to the 'off' position.

3   When the driver releases the ignition key switch from the 'start' position, the voltage to the hold-on coil disappears and the plunger returns under spring pressure to the 'off' position, simultaneously opening the heavy duty contacts and so disconnecting the battery from the starter. As the plunger returns it withdraws the starter pinion from the flywheel.

4   An interesting variation on the straightforward operation of the solenoid starter occurs with the Lucas M50 machine. In this arrangement provision is made for only partial power to be applied to the drive

77

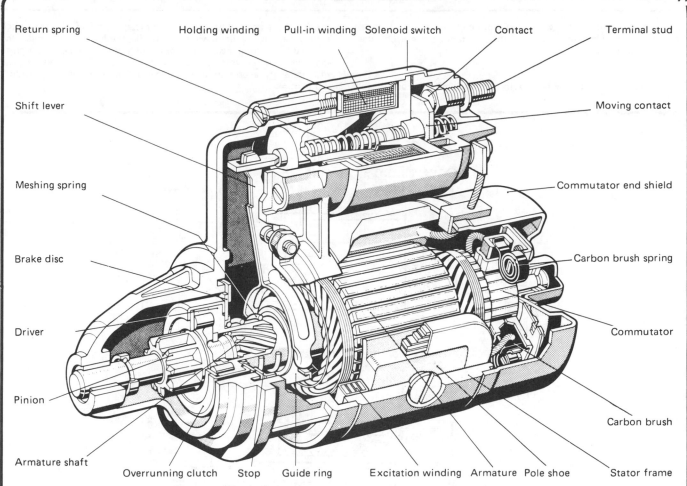

Return spring   Holding winding   Pull-in winding   Solenoid switch   Contact   Terminal stud

Shift lever   Moving contact

Meshing spring   Commutator end shield

Brake disc   Carbon brush spring

Driver   Commutator

Pinion   Carbon brush

Armature shaft

Overrunning clutch   Stop   Guide ring   Excitation winding   Armature   Pole shoe   Stator frame

Fig. 5.21 Cut-away view of a pre-engaged starter motor (Sec 8)

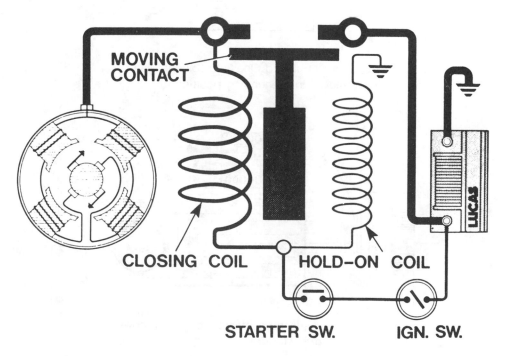

MOVING CONTACT

CLOSING COIL   HOLD-ON COIL

STARTER SW.   IGN. SW.

Fig. 5.22 Solenoid operated starter circuit (Sec 9)

for the short period of time when two teeth on the starter and starter ring may be in abutment — that is if the two teeth strike each other instead of meshing.

5   Fig. 5.23 shows that when tooth-to-tooth abutment occurs the solenoid closes one of two sets of contacts, the effect being to switch in only part of the field winding. As the teeth slide into mesh the solenoid travel continues to the point where the second contacts close and switch in all the field and hence give full drive power. The arrangement prevents tooth damage and jarring in the case of tooth abutment.

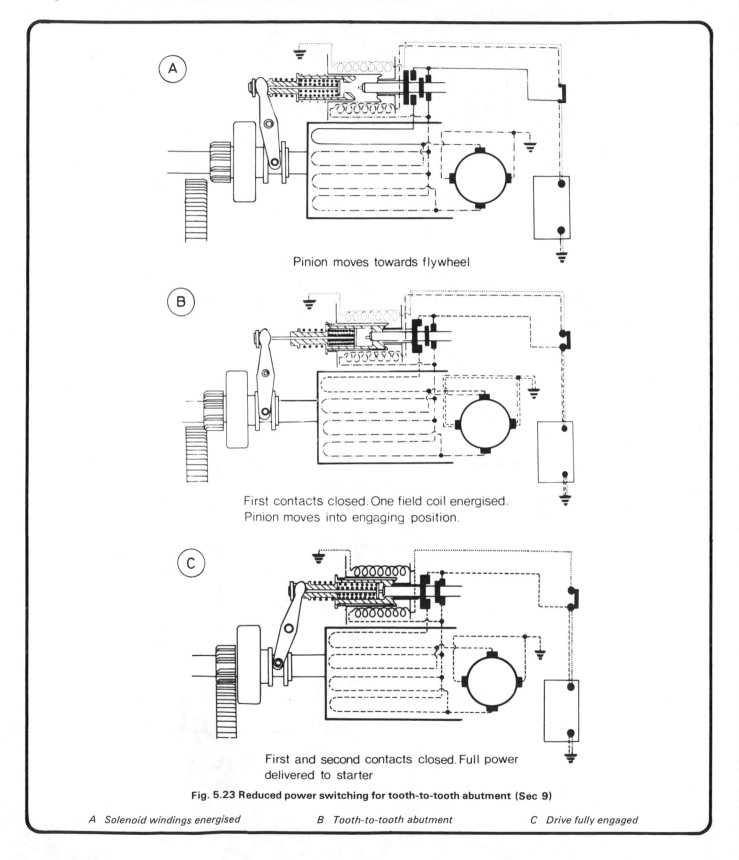

Ⓐ Pinion moves towards flywheel

Ⓑ First contacts closed. One field coil energised.
Pinion moves into engaging position.

Ⓒ First and second contacts closed. Full power delivered to starter

Fig. 5.23 Reduced power switching for tooth-to-tooth abutment (Sec 9)

A Solenoid windings energised   B Tooth-to-tooth abutment   C Drive fully engaged

10 Clutches

1   When the engine fires it will quickly run up to a speed so that it is then the starter which is driven. Severe overspeed will cause starter failure, usually due to armature conductors dislodging under centrifugal force.

2   In order to prevent this happening, pre-engaged starters are fitted with a clutch which will transmit torque in one direction only. Such a device will also give protection to the starter in the event of backfire. Most common are roller overrunning clutches, as shown in Fig. 5.24.

3   The roller clutch typically has four or five rollers running in tapered tracks in the clutch outer member. In the free state springs push the rollers into the wide zone, permitting motion in one direction between inner and outer parts. Reversing the direction will run the rollers up to the narrow gap so that wedging takes place, and inner and outer sections are locked together.

4   One manufacturer also utilizes a plate clutch which will slip in the forward drive direction at two or three times full load torque, and in the reverse direction transmits no torque at all. Fig. 5.25 shows the drive consisting of a pinion on a helical splined sleeve and a barrel assembly which contains the clutch.

5   When the starter begins to rotate the moving member slides forward along the helix, compressing the clutch plates, so that torque is transmitted. If, for any reason, the pinion sticks in mesh with the flywheel and is driven by it, the moving member runs back down the helix, the clutch plates are de-compressed and the armature is protected. In the event of backfire, the clutch plates slip, the slipping torque being set during manufacture.

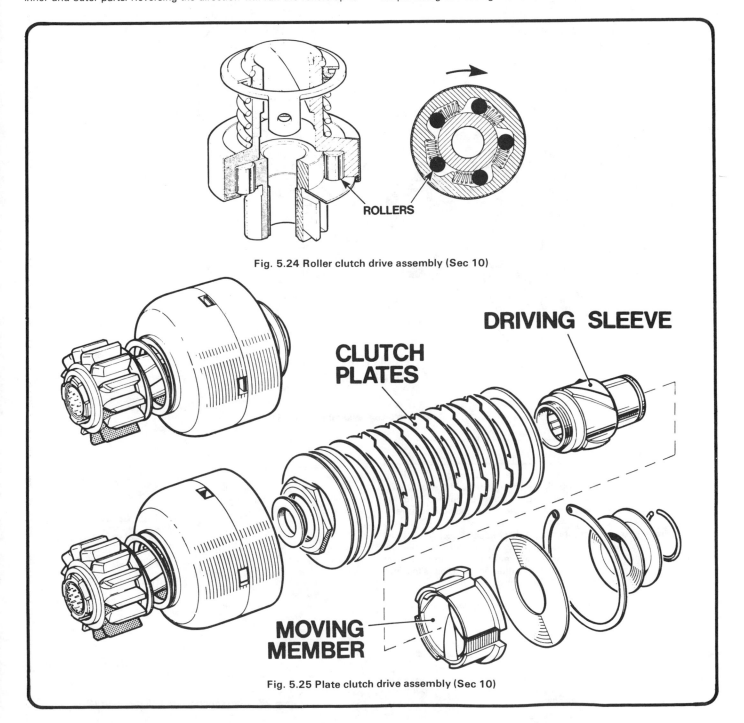

ROLLERS

Fig. 5.24 Roller clutch drive assembly (Sec 10)

CLUTCH PLATES

DRIVING SLEEVE

MOVING MEMBER

Fig. 5.25 Plate clutch drive assembly (Sec 10)

11 Armature brakes

1   Some starter motors have a brake fitted on the shaft, the purpose being:

   (a)   To slow down the armature rapidly when the starter switch is released
   (b)   To restrict the motor speed under light running conditions

2   Fig. 5.26 shows an assembly of the type fitted to certain Lucas starters. Two spring-loaded brake shoes are located on the armature shaft by a peg, and the shoes, therefore, rotate. Under centrifugal action the shoes fly out at high speeds and bear on the commutator end bracket stops, giving a braking effect.

1   A battery in a charged state is essential. Check by switching on the headlamps and noting if the brilliance is normal. If necessary test the acid with a hydrometer.

2   Check that all connectors are tight and there is no white electrolytic growth around a battery terminal. If there is a click and no operation when the starter is switched on by the ignition key, it is often due to a poor battery lug contact. Do not forget to check that the earth strap has a good connection to the body and the engine.

3   With drive in neutral and the ignition disconnected at the coil feed terminal, crank the engine if possible. Battery voltage should be of the order of 10 volts, and the engine should turn freely under normal temperature conditions. If the operation is sluggish it could be due to a worn out battery with high internal resistance, voltage loss in the cables, connectors or solenoids, or a faulty starter.

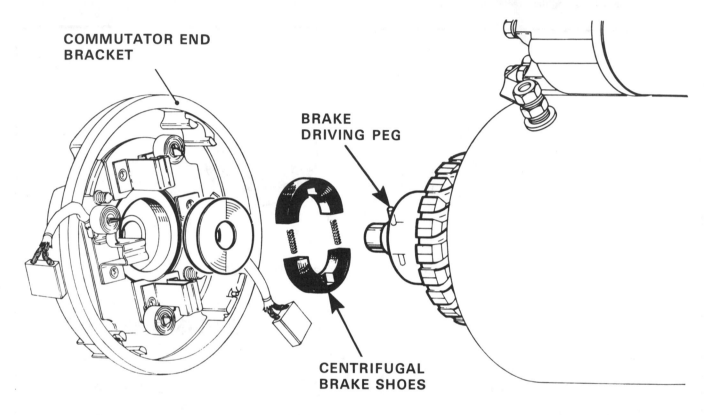

Fig. 5.26 Armature brake assembly (Sec 11)

12 Drive engagement

1   Reference to Fig. 5.27 shows the mechanism of pinion engagement. As the plunger is pulled into the solenoid the operating lever pivots on the centre pin, and the pinion is pushed into full engagement, when the solenoid contacts switch on the starter current.

2   Sometimes two teeth of pinion and flywheel strike each other as the pinion slides towards mesh. As the plunger goes into the solenoid, the operating plate compresses the engagement spring and the starter motor armature begins to rotate; the pinion tooth then slips into engagement under the pressure of the spring.

3   The purpose of the lost motion spring is to ensure that the main contacts open before the pinion is withdrawn from mesh with the flywheel.

13 Testing

If the starter is not working correctly, it is worth carrying out a few tests while the starter is still in place.

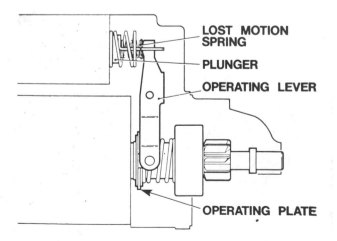

Fig. 5.27 Drive mechanism linkage (Sec 12)

4   If there is no drive, switch on the starter motor with the ignition key and listen for the click of the solenoid operation (inertia type) or, in the case of the pre-engaged type, listen for the motion of the solenoid plunger.

5   If some starter motor drive exists, in the case of the separate solenoid used with inertia type starters, check the voltage across the main (heavy current) terminals. Before switching, the voltage should be that of the battery, about 12 volts; at the instant of switching the volt-drop should be zero, but in any event not more than 0.25 volts. Any voltage across the terminals points to unwanted resistive volt-drop. Such solenoids are not repairable and should be replaced. **Note:** Some types have a manual pushbutton under a large rubber cover, or a smaller plastic button between the main terminals. This facility can be used as a get-home device if the solenoid winding fails, or as a means of starting the engine while undertaking maintenance without having to go into the car.

6   If the starter motor fails to turn, the headlamps remain bright and the solenoid operates, then the starter motor is faulty and must be removed (refer to Section 14 for repair procedures).

7   If the starter motor fails to turn and the headlights run dim, then the trouble could be a poor condition battery or a jammed motor pinion gear. There is also the possibility of the engine having seized up.

8   If the starter motor runs, but spins fast without engaging the flywheel, this could be the pinion stuck on the shaft (inertia type) or, in the case of the pre-engaged type, a fault in the solenoid or an overrun clutch failure. Another possibility is low battery voltage which in turn could point to a charging circuit fault.

9   If the starter motor runs and starts the engine but does not disengage when the engine fires there will be considerable noise from the starter. The fault could be a jammed pinion gear, or a sticking solenoid operating lever in the case of the pre-engaged type.

10 Should the engine start up correctly but whilst running it is possible to hear a metallic rattling or ringing, this could be a broken Bendix spring (inertia type).

11 If the engine starts, but upon starter pinion gear disengagement there is a sharp metallic ring or crunch, it is likely that the pinion buffer spring is damaged or possibly there is a damaged driveshaft.

12 Solenoid plunger chatter is often due to an open circuit hold-in winding in the solenoid. Another possibility is a low battery, since as it comes on starter cranking load, the voltage drops so low that the solenoid plunger pulls out. This is a cyclic phenomenon.

14 Fault finding and repair

Jammed starter
1   A starter motor pinion may sometimes stay in mesh with the flywheel, this often being a symptom of gear wear on either or both the pinion and starter ring. When this happens, rocking the car backwards and forwards in 3rd gear (ignition off) will often allow the pinion to return, or alternatively, use a spanner on the square shaft end of the starter. The symptom of a jammed starter is that the engine does not turn and lights will be dim. Take care here though, for a dirty battery connection has similar effects.

Brushes
2   When removing a starter motor from a vehicle, first disconnect the battery. Remove the cover over the brushes and raise them from their holders. Check for length and renew if less than $\frac{5}{16}''$ (8 mm) long.

Drives
3   The inertia drive should be examined next. Spring strength should be such that it is not possible to turn it on the shaft by hand – if in doubt renew the spring. Dirt on the drive can give rise to sticking, with the result of no or poor meshing between the pinion and flywheel.

4   Clean drives with petrol or methylated spirit and a brush, and operate the drive by hand until it runs freely. Take care with lubrication – the shaft may be lightly oiled, but the spiral grooves must run dry and clean. Good results have been reported by lightly rubbing the working surfaces with a soft lead pencil. Oil or grease here will attract road dust and result in malfunction.

Bearings
5   Bearing wear can occur, and this is confirmed if there is any sideways movement of the driveshaft. To replace bearings, the armature is removed and the old bearings tapped out with a drift. Graphite and bronze bush bearings can be obtained as replacements, and sometimes need to be soaked in oil before fitting.

Electrical tests
6   The armature and field coils are connected in series with current entering at the main terminal, flowing through the field coils, then entering the armature via brushes and out to the frame via earth brushes (Fig. 5.28).

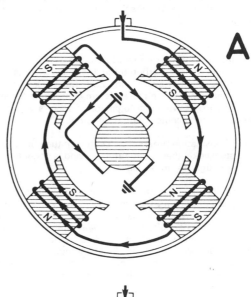

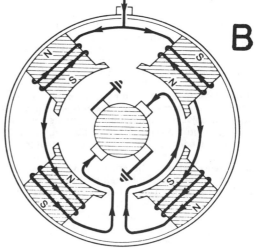

Fig. 5.28 Starter internal circuit (Sec 14)

A   Series field   *B   Series parallel field*

7   Field coils are of aluminium or copper strip, and should be checked for insulation to the frame. The brushes should be pulled back or removed from their holders, and an ohmmeter check from the main terminal to frame should read infinite, or very high. Alternatively, a battery and bulb may be used, in which case the bulb should not light.

Note: In Lucas face commutator starters, one end of the field winding is earthed; this part of the test procedure would need to be modified with this type, but the principles are the same.

8   If a coil breakdown is indicated, the pole shoes complete with surrounding field coils must be removed. Since the retaining screws will be very tight it is usual to employ an impact driver. Locate the fault by visual inspection for charred insulation. With care it may be possible to re-use the faulty coil by taping up the strip, and preferably varnishing with shellac.

Commutator

9   The commutator segments should be inspected carefully. Thrown solder blobs are an indication of overheating, and with care it is possible to re-solder the armature coils to the commutator, making sure that there is no accidental bridging of two commutator bars.

10   A commutator of the drum type may be cleaned with fine glasspaper (never emery cloth), but severe wear will require the commutator to be skimmed on a lathe. A face commutator should be cleaned only with methylated spirit, and never with any type of abrasive paper.

Armature

11   Sometimes an armature may be found wrecked because of overspeeding, this often occurring through a faulty engagement drive, or by leaving the ignition switch on 'start' too long. In these cases severe failure can occur when the armature conductors fly out of their grooves due to excessive centrifugal force; repairs are difficult, or impossible, and a replacement armature is needed.

12   Similarly, if insulation breaks down between the armature conductors and the steel yoke, then an armature rewind is generally not worth attempting, although not impossible.

13   Short circuits in an armature winding may be detected by a 'growler' (Fig. 5.29). Placing the armature in the V slot of the growler with its current on will produce alternating magnetic flux in the armature core. A short circuited coil has heavy current induced in it by transformer action and a steel bar (such as a hacksaw blade) held above the armature will vibrate noisily at the point of short circuit. It is worthwhile cleaning up the commutator bars and the coil ends nearest to the fault, but if no cure is produced, a replacement armature is required.

14   If no growler is available it is difficult to locate armature winding short-circuits by measurement, due to low resistance of the armature wires or strip. Visual evidence of burning is sometimes present, but direct measurement of resistance between commutator segments would require a highly sensitive ohmmeter.

15   A better check for shorted turns is to pass a current, say 10 amperes, through the armature via the brushes. Then measure the voltage between adjacent commutator segments with a low-range voltmeter using pointed probes. Any variations in volt-drop indicates short-circuited coils connected to the two commutator segments.

16   Insulation tests between the armature winding and the shaft or between the commutator and the shaft may be carried out using two probe leads in series with a 12 volt battery and a 6 watt bulb, or using

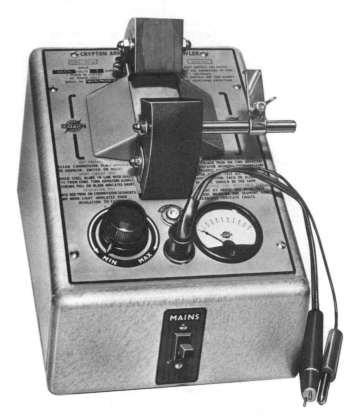

Fig. 5.29 The Crypton growler (Sec 14)

the ohm range of a test meter, if available (Fig. 5.30). There should be very high resistance between the armature winding or commutator and the shaft, so the bulb should not light – the ohms reading should be very high in this test.

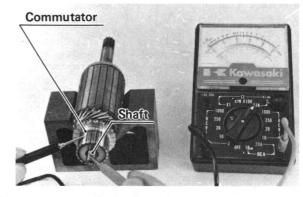

Fig. 5.30 Insulation test between commutator and shaft (Sec 14)

Chapter 6 Ignition principles

Contents

1 Spark requirement

1   Petrol engines of the two-stroke and four-stroke types require an electric spark at the plug electrodes at a precise point of the operation cycle. The timing of the spark should be such that the resultant pressure due to the burning gas should reach maximum just after the piston top-dead-centre position, so as to impart the maximum power to the crankshaft.

2   For a two-stroke cycle there will be one spark per revolution, but a four-stroke cycle needs one spark every two revolutions.

3   The sparking plug, invented by Lenoir in 1860, screws into the cylinder head and, when supplied with a high voltage pulse, will produce a spark across its electrodes, one of which is earthed to the engine head. The plug is by no means as simple as it looks and each

type has its own special application; fuller details are to be found in the sparking plug Chapter (Chapter 7).

2 Ignition advance

1   The pressure reached by the petrol vapour in the cylinder is achieved in two stages; first, due to the rising piston, (Fig. 6.1) the pressure may rise to something of the order of 70 to 100 lbf/sq in at the point of ignition, with the piston still on the up-stroke.

2   When the spark occurs, the vapour ignites and a pressure wave travels outward, the rate of propagation being accelerated by the turbulence of the vapour mixture. Thus the pressure rises to a peak far greater than that due to the piston alone, and Fig. 6.2 shows that there is a time delay T between spark point and pressure peak.

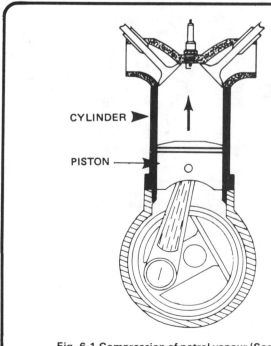

Fig. 6.1 Compression of petrol vapour (Sec 2)

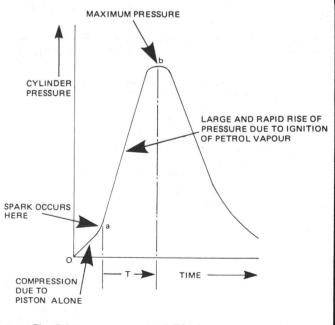

Fig. 6.2 Pressure rise and fall in the cylinder (Sec 2)

3   The spark is ideally timed in advance of top-dead-centre (TDC) to allow for this delay to ensure that the pressure peak is available for driving the piston downward at the best possible time. The point of ignition is typically some 30° to 45° before the piston top-dead-centre position when the engine is running at cruising speed.

4   It is obvious that one particular angle of ignition advance suits one engine speed only, so it is usual to incorporate a device to vary the ignition advance angle with speed.

3   Sparking

1   The plug voltage requirement may be anywhere within the range 5000 to 20 000 volts and depends upon several factors, including the mixture strength, the shape of the combustion chamber, the compression rate, the temperature, and the condition of the plug and its gap dimension.

2   Once the petrol vapour breaks down under the electric stress of the plug voltage, a high intensity spark travels from the negative centre electrode to the positive earth electrode. The spark temperature of several thousand degrees centigrade is sufficient to ignite the petrol vapour in the vicinity which then continues to burn by itself by the process of a travelling flame wave.

4   Ignition coil and battery system

1   C.F. Kettering of the Dayton Engineering Laboratories Company (Delco) is credited with the original patent relating to the battery ignition system, and his drawing (Fig. 6.3) dated 1908, shows that the method has changed little in three quarters of a century (Fig. 6.4).

2   Most cars have a 12 volt battery as the energy storage device and the power to supply the sparks comes from it. However, a high voltage is required, and so some means must be found to raise the battery voltage. The means of doing this is the ignition coil, which acts as a voltage transformer.

5   The ignition coil

1   Michael Faraday discovered the laws of electromagnetic induction in 1831 – the ignition coil is a direct application:

> When a wire and a magnetic field move relative to each other it is found that a voltage (or electromotive force) is generated in the wire.

This principle will be mentioned several times in this book, such is its importance in relation to car electrical equipment.

2   As stated in Chapter 1, Section 18, the voltage induced in the wire depends upon:

   (a)   the length of the wire in the magnetic field
   (b)   the relative rate at which wire and field move
   (c)   the strength of the magnetic field

The magnetic field could be produced by, say, a permanent bar magnet, but in the case of the ignition coil it is convenient to pass current from the battery through a primary coil, the result being a magnetic field which is similar in shape to that of a bar magnet field (Fig. 6.5).

3   Switching on the current results in the magnetic field spreading outwards, which in effect cuts the coils, generating an electromotive force in the opposite direction to that of the battery. Now if the current is switched off, the magnetic field collapses towards the centre of the coil – that is to say we have, in both cases, relative movement between the magnetic field and the wire, hence an induced voltage (Fig. 6.6). During the very short period of time over which the magnetic field reduces to zero the induced voltage which may be measured across the coil reaches up to 300 volts.

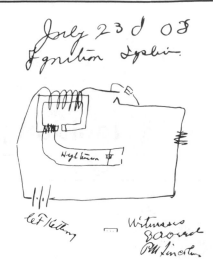

Fig. 6.3 Battery ignition system – patent sketch (Sec 14)

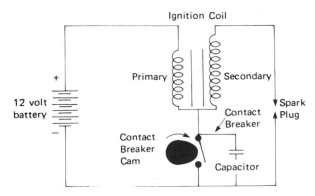

Fig. 6.4 Present day form of coil and battery circuit (Sec 4)

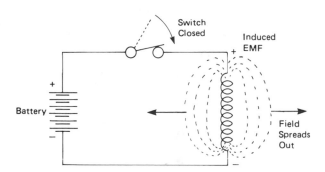

Fig. 6.5 Field build-up (Sec 5)

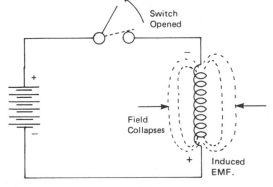

Fig. 6.6 Field collapse (Sec 5)

4   Note that this induced emf is not directly related to the 12 volt supply; the battery has simply been a means of creating the magnetic field. The switch is the means of rapidly altering the magnetic field so the coils are cut by magnetic force lines as the field either builds up or collapses.

5   Interesting though this result is, a much bigger voltage is required at the sparking plug. The solution is to wind another coil over the first, but insulated from it, the two coils being called primary and secondary windings. The secondary winding has thousands of turns and, because it is subjected to the same magnetic field changes, will have the same induced emf per turn as the primary. The result is a voltage sufficient to produce a spark at the plugs.

6   In practice the coils are wound over an iron core, and often the primary is wound on top of the secondary (Figs. 6.7 and 6.8).

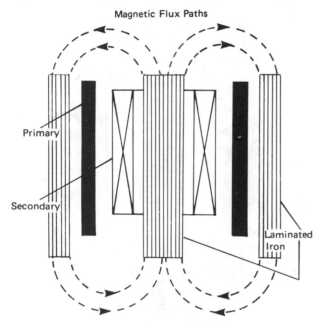

Fig. 6.7 Ignition coil windings and magnetic paths (Sec 5)

Fig. 6.8 Construction of the ignition coil (Sec 5)

6   The capacitor (condenser)

1   When the contact breaker (or switch) is opened, the primary current falls rapidly, so does the magnetic flux, and both primary and secondary windings will have an emf induced in them:

(a)   only as long as the current is charging
(b)   of a magnitude which depends on how fast the flux (and therefore the current) falls

2   At the moment of opening, the induced primary voltage will appear across the contact breaker points and current will jump the gap. This is seen as sparking at the points. It follows that the current does not drop to zero instantly, but remains, for a few millionths of a second, in the form of a spark. Looking again at (b) above, this will reduce the emf in the secondary – just where it is needed.

3   A capacitor connected across the contact breaker points provides an effective solution. This device is widely used in electrical equipment and is capable of storing electricity (more correctly one should say electric charge). Just as a bucket will hold a quantity of water, capable of being drained out again, so the capacitor holds electric charge. The amount of charge held depends (like the bucket) on certain dimensions, but also upon the applied voltage.

4   An interesting feature of the capacitor is that, as it fills up with electric charge, it develops a voltage across its terminals in opposition to the original voltage which drove the charge in. If the supply is disconnected the capacitor will retain the charge and the terminal voltage for a considerable period (Fig. 6.9).

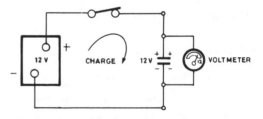

WITH SWITCH CLOSED, BATTERY CHARGES CAPACITOR LIKE A PUMP. CAPACITOR VOLTAGE BUILDS UP UNTIL, WHEN EQUAL TO BATTERY VOLTAGE, NO FURTHER CHARGE WILL FLOW.

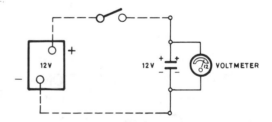

WHEN BATTERY IS DISCONNECTED BY OPENING SWITCH
CHARGE AND VOLTAGE ARE RETAINED.

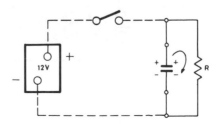

IF A RESISTOR IS CONNECTED ACROSS CAPACITOR, THE CHARGE DRAINS AWAY AND VOLTAGE FALLS. IF RESISTANCE IS HIGH, VOLTAGE FALLS SLOWLY AND VICE VERSA.

Fig. 6.9 Charge and voltage retention of a capacitor (Sec 6)

5   One point to note is that when charge (measured in coulombs) starts to flow down a wire the rate at which it moves is the current. Thus if 1 coulomb per second flows down a wire the current is said to be 1 ampere. Lastly, the measure of the charge handling ability of a capacitor is measured in **farads**. In practice the farad is an enormous quantity and the microfarad (μF) is used. A capacitor used in an ignition circuit (Fig. 6.10) has a capacitance of about 0.2 μF. (The microfarad is one millionth of a farad).

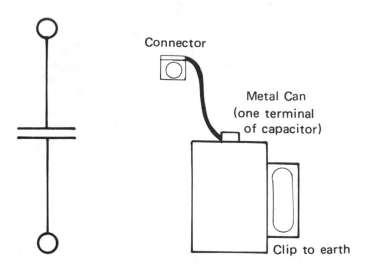

Fig. 6.10 The ignition capacitor – symbol and actual unit (Sec 6)

6   When the contacts are just opening, instead of a spark jumping the gap the charge will now flow into the capacitor which quickly develops a terminal voltage, so as to oppose any further charge flow. Thus the primary current drops to zero much more quickly than without the capacitor and from this there are two consequences:

(a)   The ignition coil secondary voltage will be higher
(b)   Because sparking does not occur at the contact breaker points, no metal erosion will take place

In practice, (b) is never completely fulfilled.

7   Ballasted ignition coil

1   When starting, the battery terminal voltage falls significantly, since cranking current for the starter motor can easily reach 300 amperes or more. This can have a serious effect on the ignition coil in very cold conditions when the engine is stiff to turn over.

2   Some systems use a special ignition coil designed to run in series with a ballast resistor (Fig. 6.11) in the primary circuit. When the ignition key is turned on to the start position, a contact in the solenoid plunger shorts out the resistor so the battery voltage is fully applied to the coil primary. As soon as the engine fires and the driver releases the ignition switch the resistor is again in series with the coil and the system works normally. This arrangement thus gives a boost to the ignition coil primary only when the starter motor is turning over (Fig. 6.12).

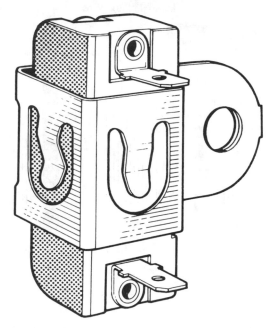

Fig. 6.11 A typical ballast resistor (Sec 7)

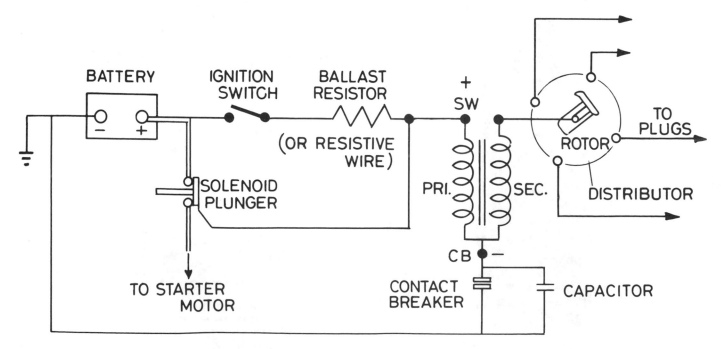

Fig. 6.12 A ballasted ignition circuit (Sec 7)

3   The ballast resistor has a resistance about equal to that of the coil primary, so when running normally, half the supply voltage appears across the coil and half across the resistor. It follows that the coil must be designed to work at a lower voltage than the system voltage. In some vehicles, a resistive wire going to the primary of the coil is used instead of a special ballast resistor.

4   There are several advantages of a ballasted system:

   (a) The cold starting performance is improved.
   (b) The primary winding of the coil has a lower inductance value (see next Section) giving a more rapid rise of current when the contacts close. It follows that the ballasted coil can be used at higher engine speeds.
   (c) Because half of the circuit resistance is outside the coil, the latter runs at a lower temperature giving an improved performance.

5   Note that on certain French vehicles, a temperature-dependent ballast resistor is used. This is made of semiconductor material that will have a low resistance when cold at switch-on, but increases in resistance when warmed by the ignition coil primary current. Thus at switch-on the whole of the supply voltage goes to the coil, but divides between the coil and the ballast resistor as the resistance of the latter rises.

8   Contact breaker assembly

1   The contact breaker points are opened by a cam mounted on the shaft of the distributor (see later). The cam runs at half engine speed for all four-stroke engines. The contact breaker assembly makes provision for positioning the capacitor and also for adjustment of the contact breaker gap — a factor vital to proper ignition system performance (Fig. 6.13).

2   The important feature of correct gap setting is to allow time for the primary coil current to build up again after the contacts close. All coils possess a feature called 'inductance' and the ignition coil is no exception. The effect of inductance is to slow down the build-up of

current in the coil in much the same way as the inertia of a flywheel retards the build-up of rotational speed from standstill.

3   It is important, therefore, that the points do not stay open too long or there will be insufficient close-time. A measure of this is the dwell angle (see Section 9) and is partly determined by the cam profile and adjustable by alteration of the maximum points gap. Setting the gap by feeler gauge is, in effect, to set the dwell but is a rudimentary method because of the possibility of 'piling' of one contact, and also because the static gap setting and the gap when the engine is running may be different due to distributor wear.

4   Some Leyland and Ford vehicles now are being fitted with a Lucas distributor which uses a one-piece sliding contact set (Fig. 6.14). The contact breaker heel has two small ribs in its base each side of the pivot post. Each rib rests on a ramp which is cut into a forked heel actuator which also is located on the contact breaker pivot.

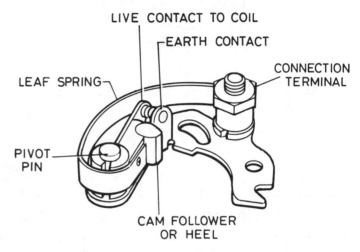

Fig. 6.13 One-piece contact breaker set (Sec 8)

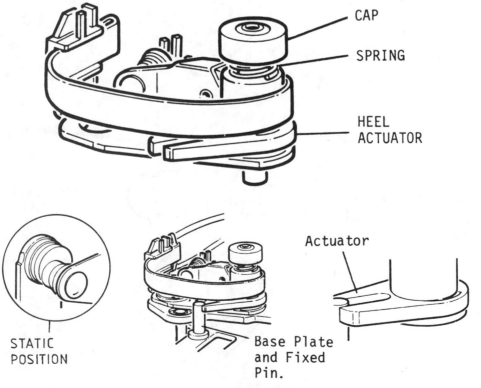

Fig. 6.14 Sliding contact set (Sec 8)

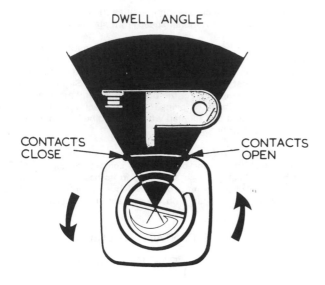

DWELL ANGLE

CONTACTS CLOSE

CONTACTS OPEN

ADJUSTMENT OF CONTACT GAP
ALTERS DWELL

5   When the vacuum unit rotates the bearing plate the heel ribs ride up the ramps, forcing the heel and the moving contact upward. The moving contact runs across the face of the larger fixed contact; this wiping action has a self-cleaning effect which reduces pitting and piling. The working life of the contact breaker is claimed to be 25 000 miles.

9   Dwell angle

1   Dwell angle is defined as the number of degrees of distributor cam rotation for which the contact breaker points remain closed during one ignition cycle. The setting of this angle is most important; moving the gap wider will reduce the dwell angle. Conversely, making the gap smaller will increase the dwell angle, the reason being that the contact breaker cam follower picks up on the cam earlier or later as the case may be (see Fig. 6.15).

2   Incorrect setting can have serious consequences, for if the dwell angle is too small the coil current cannot build up enough at high speeds and the ignition may cease to work. If the dwell angle is too large then contact burning may occur.

3   Both dwell angle and points gap should be within the maker's tolerances, and if both cannot be satisfied the distributor is faulty.

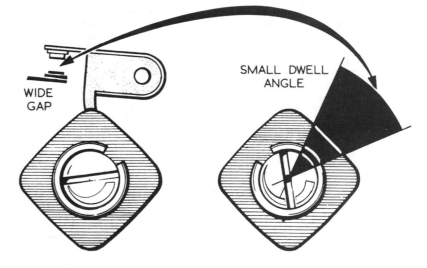

A wide gap results when the fixed point is adjusted too near cam centre (inwards). Later closing and earlier opening reduces dwell angle and advances ignition timing.

WIDE GAP

SMALL DWELL ANGLE

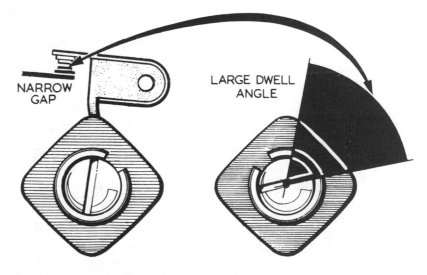

A narrow gap results when the fixed point is adjusted too far from cam centre (outwards). Earlier closing and later opening increases dwell angle and retards ignition timing.

NARROW GAP

LARGE DWELL ANGLE

Fig. 6.15 Illustrating dwell angle (Sec 9)

4   A total change in degrees of dwell angle is also equal to the ignition timing change which will result. Reference to Fig. 6.16 illustrates this. Assuming a change of 12° in the dwell angle, then the instant of points opening is changed by 6°, but 6° on the distributor cam is equal to 12° on the crankshaft.

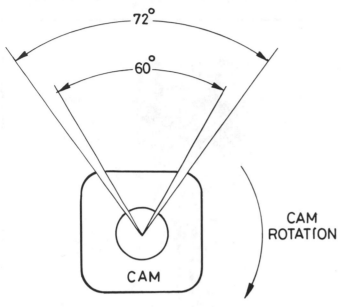

Fig. 6.16 Dwell angle change = ignition timing change (Sec 9)

5   Dwell cam be expressed as an angle (in degrees) or as a percentage; it is useful to be able to convert from one to the other. Example:

A four-lobe cam has four periods of 90° rotation and the points will open and close for a part of each period. In the case shown

in Fig. 6.17 the points are closed for 54° (the dwell angle) and open for 36°. The percentage dwell is:

$$\frac{54°}{90°} \times \frac{100}{} = 60\%$$

Converting back is straightforward: the dwell angle is:

$$\frac{60}{100} \times 90° = 54°$$

6   A dwell meter can be used to accurately measure dwell angle, but with some types of meter, care must be taken with interpretation of the scale reading, as one scale may be used for engines with differing numbers of cylinders. As an example, given a dwell percentage of 60% for single-cylinder, four-cylinder and six-cylinder engines, the following would apply:

Single-cylinder engine/one lobe cam – period 360°
Four-cylinder engine/four lobe cam – period 90°
Six-cylinder engine/six lobe cam – period 60°
The dwell angle readings would be:

Single-cylinder:	$\frac{60}{100}$	x 360°	= 216°
Four-cylinder:	$\frac{60}{100}$	x 90°	= 54°
Six-cylinder:	$\frac{60}{100}$	x 60°	= 36°

10 The distributor

1   As suggested by the name, the distributor passes the spark current to each plug in turn, but it is convenient to incorporate other functions as well. Four main actions are carried out by the distrbutor:

(a)   To pass the spark to each plug in the correct sequence
(b)   To make and break the ignition coil primary current
(c)   To arrange for the timing of the spark to be varied according to engine speed
(d)   To vary spark timing according to the engine load

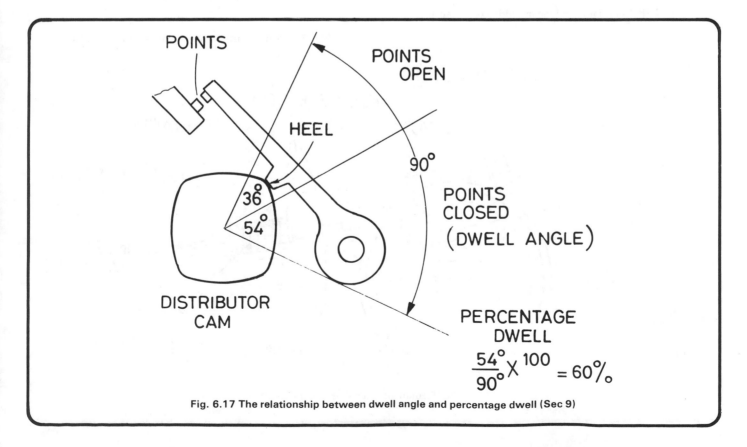

Fig. 6.17 The relationship between dwell angle and percentage dwell (Sec 9)

2   The distributor shaft runs at half the engine speed for a four-stroke engine and locates on the driving shaft by either an offset drive dog (Fig. 6.18) or by a gear (Fig. 6.19).

3   The contact points are mounted on a baseplate which is able to rotate round the cam over a limited range, this rotation being controlled by a vacuum unit (Fig. 6.20) which measures the degree of vacuum in the engine inlet manifold.

4   The heel of the moving contact is in contact with the cam which has the same number of rising lobes as the engine has cylinders. As the cam rotates the contacts are opened and closed alternately. The

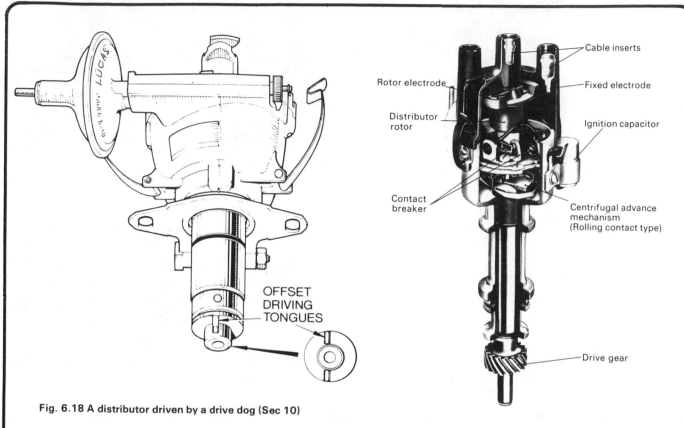

Fig. 6.18 A distributor driven by a drive dog (Sec 10)

Fig. 6.19 A distributor driven by drive gear (Sec 10)

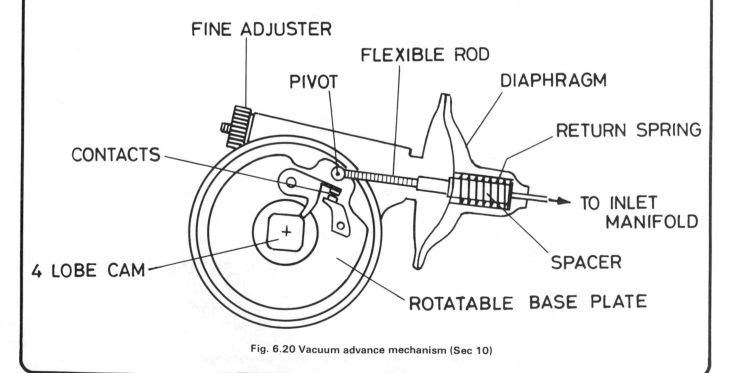

Fig. 6.20 Vacuum advance mechanism (Sec 10)

amount of opening of the contacts is determined partly by the rise of the cam lobe and also by the position of the fixed contact, which is adjustable and connected to earth.

5   The cover (Fig. 6.21) is moulded from high quality bakelite, and is intended to protect the distributor interior from dust and moisture, and also to provide pick-up electrodes which take the spark current from the rotor arm (Figs. 6.22 and 6.23) located at the top of the distributor shaft. From the cover, high tension (HT) leads go one to each plug, the centre lead being the HT input from the ignition coil. Connection is made to the brass electrode of the rotor arm by a small carbon brush or sometimes a spring loaded metal electrode.

6   Automatic ignition advance is achieved by employing two bob weights on springs (Fig. 6.24) which fly outwards under centrifugal force and twist the camshaft relative to the driveshaft of the distributor, according to engine speed, thus making the spark occur earlier with increasing speed.

Fig. 6.23 The distributor cover – interior view (Sec 10)

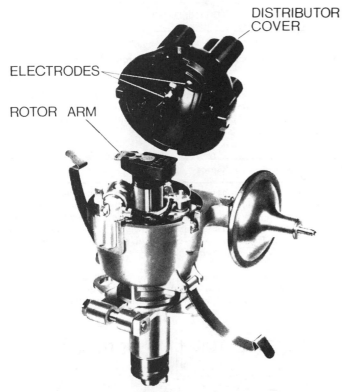

DISTRIBUTOR COVER

ELECTRODES

ROTOR ARM

Fig. 6.21 The distributor rotor arm and cover (Sec 10)

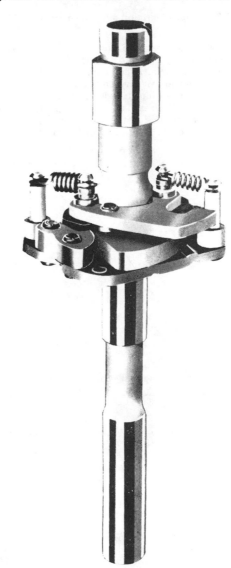

Fig. 6.22 A typical rotor arm (Sec 10)

Fig. 6.24 The auto-advance mechanism (Sec 10)

11 Ignition advance requirement

1   The amount of ignition advance required for a particular engine at any speed is found experimentally by the makers, the procedure being to set the engine speed then adjust the advance until maximum power is achieved. For a typical four-stroke engine the advance curve will look something like Fig. 6.25. Ideally the distributor should give a similar response, but in practice the shape of the actual advance curve is a compromise.

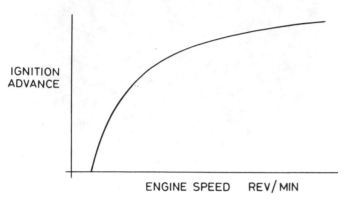

Fig. 6.25 A typical ignition advance curve (Sec 11)

2   The springs which hold back the advance mechanism bob weights have a linear characteristic, that is to say the extension is proportional to the force stretching them. Accordingly, a distributor using two springs of identical strength will give an advance characteristic which is straight – see Fig. 6.26 (the two lines showing the acceptable limits). Note that advance ceases at about 1800 rpm for the distributor shown (3600 rpm engine) due to the stop built into the cam which comes up against one of the fixed posts of the moving plate.

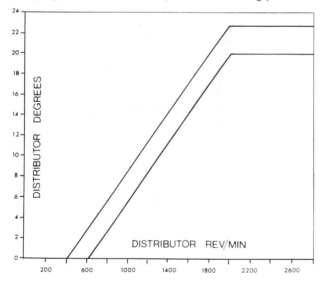

Fig. 6.26 Typical advance curve for an equal spring assembly (Sec 11)

3   A more complex curve is arranged by using two springs of different strengths, one of them also being initially loose by using an elongated loop at one end, so that it does not come into play until the bob weights are partly out in orbit. Fig. 6.27 shows the curve obtained from a distributor with a differential spring assembly.

4   As the speed of the distributor increases there is a rapid advance of about 9° at 400 rpm since only one spring is operating. The advance then increases more slowly until the maximum of 18° to 20° at 1350 rpm is reached. This characteristic is typical, but variations will occur for each engine design.

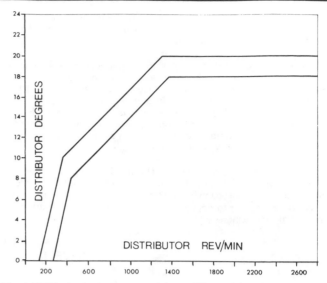

Fig. 6.27 Typical advance curve for a differential spring assembly (Sec 11)

5   The delay in operation of the second spring is obtained by, as stated, having an elongated loop at one end. The loop must not be altered or a different characteristic will result and the engine performance will be sluggish.

12 Vacuum ignition advance

1   Centrifugal advance adjusts spark timing for an increase in speed to allow time for air/fuel mixture to burn efficiently. However, when the vehicle is cruising under light load conditions, ie not hillclimbing, the fuel intake is reduced and the fuel charge will be at lower pressure at the spark point. These conditions result in a slower burning time and further ignition advance is required.

2   To achieve this, use is made of the fact that there will be a relatively high vacuum in the inlet manifold under light load and less vacuum under heavy load when the throttle is opened wider (Fig. 6.28).

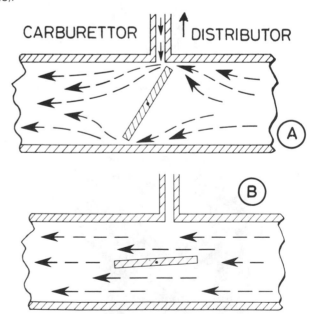

Fig. 6.28 Vacuum in the inlet manifold (Sec 12)

A Throttle partially open - high manifold vacuum
B Throttle fully open - negligible manifold vacuum

3   A hole in the inlet manifold near the throttle is connected by fine tubing to a vacuum advance unit which connects to a vacuum chamber and spring-loaded diaphragm. The diaphragm controls a linkage to the distributor baseplate on which the contact breaker set is mounted; when vacuum occurs the diaphragm pulls the baseplate and contacts in the opposite direction to the cam rotation, thus giving an earlier spark (Fig. 6.29). The vacuum advance will be determined by the strength of the spring (known as spring-rate) and the limit fixed by a spacer or slot in the diaphragm link. Initial setting-up of the distributor is by adjustment of the clamp unit at the base of the body; on some types a fine (micrometer) control is provided (Fig. 6.30).

4   Conditions under which the vacuum system comes into operation are worthy of note:

(a)   At tickover speed, the degree of vacuum in the inlet manifold is large, since the throttle butterfly is nearly closed. Vacuum advance does not occur, however, because the butterfly has not exposed the vacuum tapping hole.

(b)   When cruising on the flat, the engine is on light load and the throttle only partly open. The vacuum is still large and is transmitted to the diaphragm of the advance unit. Ignition advance occurs.

(c)   When the engine comes under heavy load the driver presses the accelerator pedal and opens the throttle. The vacuum is reduced considerably, allowing the vacuum unit spring to return the contact breaker baseplate to the original position. The degree of advance is then fixed only by the centrifugal advance mechanism.

5   An interesting method of vacuum-controlled ignition advance is used by Ducellier. As vacuum is applied, an eccentric moves the mobile contact pivot-point, thus having the effect of altering the opening and closing positions of the contacts (Fig. 6.31). Note that the contact points gap at the zero vacuum position and maximum vacuum position will differ according to the position of the cam when the initial adjustment was made.

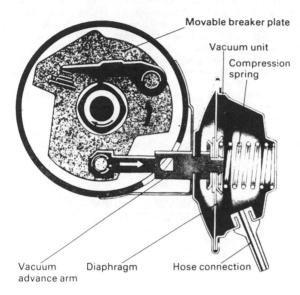

Movable breaker plate

Vacuum unit

Compression spring

Vacuum advance arm   **Diaphragm**   **Hose connection**

Fig. 6.29 A vacuum advance unit (Sec 12)

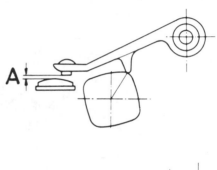

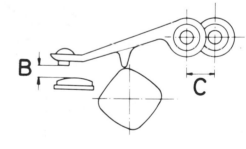

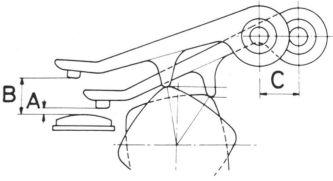

Fig. 6.31 Vacuum ignition advance by moving pivot post position (Sec 12)

A   Points gap at zero vacuum
B   Points gap at maximum vacuum
C   Movement due to eccentric

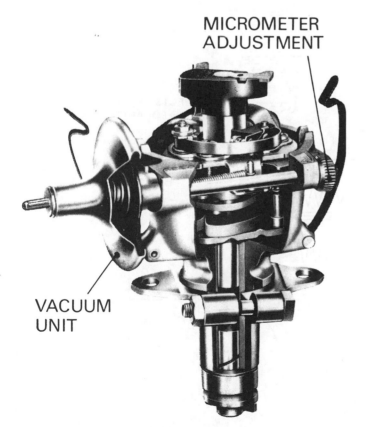

MICROMETER ADJUSTMENT

VACUUM UNIT

Fig. 6.30 Micrometer control assembly and vacuum unit (Sec 12)

13 Emission control vacuum unit

1   For those countries with emission control regulations, a double diaphragm unit is used with the distributor. Under idling or overrun conditions, pollution levels are kept low by running the engine with a degree of true retardation, past top-dead-centre.

2   Fig. 6.32 illustrates the principles in which, in addition to the main diaphragm, there is a ring diaphragm which pulls back the moving plate to give retardation. The figure uses the term 'early' meaning advance and 'late' meaning retardation.

3   To operate the two diaphragms, two separate vacuum lines are used. The advance line goes, as before, to a point near the throttle valve, but the retardation line goes to a position on the manifold nearer the inlet valves where a vacuum exists when the engine is running in neutral, or the vehicle is overrunning the engine such as in downhill work. The design is such that, on partial load conditions where a vacuum might exist in both diaphragm chambers, the resultant ignition timing is correct.

a   Adjustment in advanced position as far as Limit Stop A
b   Adjustment in true retarded position as far as Limit Stop B

14 Spark polarity

1   Ignition systems are designed to have negative polarity at the plug insulated electrode, and the earthed electrode positive. Electrons, which in part make up the spark, leave a metallic surface of negative polarity and jump to the + ve electrode. Electrons leave some metals more easily than others, and additionally will leave a surface more readily if it is at high temperature.

2   For these reasons the spark jumps from the centre electrode to earth, but there is also additional benefit from their arrangement. Over a long period the surface from which the sparks are emitted wears away because each spark actually conveys minute particles of metal with it. It is preferable to have the centre electrode wear away, rather than the earth electrode, especially when it comes to gap measurement by feeler gauge (Fig. 6.33). Reversed polarity can also require up to 40% higher spark voltage, and this can lead to misfiring.

3   An interesting case is that of the Citroën 2CV where both ends of the ignition coil secondary winding are brought out to the two sparking plugs, the engine being of the horizontally opposed twin type. From Fig. 6.34 it is seen that the secondary current (ie spark current) will flow through the two plugs, so there will be a wasted spark since only one cylinder will be ready to fire.

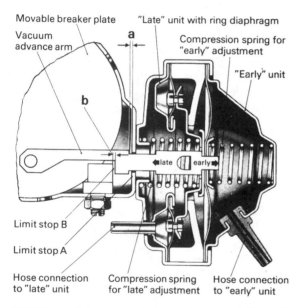

Fig. 6.32 The emission control advance/retard unit (Sec 13)

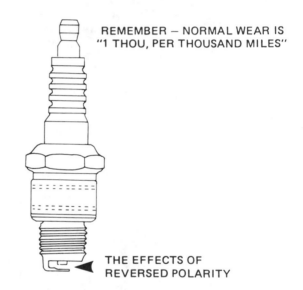

Fig. 6.33 Electrode erosion due to reversed polarity (Sec 14)

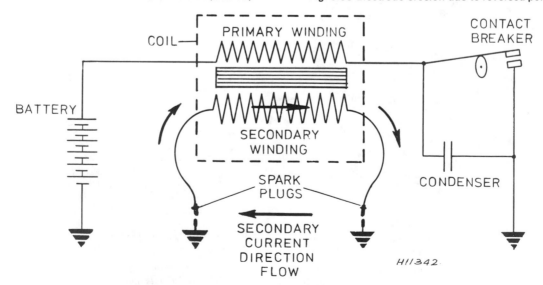

Fig. 6.34 Dual spark ignition as used in Citroën 2CV (Sec 14)

4   Only one of the plugs will be working with the preferred polarity and care must be taken to ensure that they are in good condition so as to avoid misfiring on the plug with reversed polarity. This arrangement is used as an economy measure, avoiding the use of either two ignition coils or a distributor.

15 Polarity test

1   A simple test for polarity uses a lead pencil interposed between the HT wire and the plug, as shown in Fig. 6.35.

2   The flare occurs between the pencil tip and the plug if polarity is correct, and between the HT lead and pencil tip if reversed.

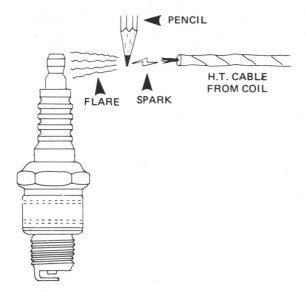

Fig. 6.35 Polarity test for coil connections (Sec 15)

16 Coil polarity

1   Modern vehicles usually use negative earth, but it is always worth checking the earth polarity of any vehicle under attention. Whichever terminal of the battery is connected to earth it is essential to arrange the spark to have the correct polarity at the plug.

2   Older Lucas coils have the low tension coils marked SW (to ignition switch) and CB (to contact breaker). Different versions of these coils were produced according to the earthing system. However, all that is necessary to change the spark polarity is to reverse the leads to the SW and CB terminals.

3   Modern ignition coils have the LT terminals marked + and -. The same coil can then be used for both positive and negative earth systems. The + coil terminal is connected to the contact breaker lead for a positive earth system and the - coil terminal to the contact breaker lead for a negative earth system.

17 Servicing notes

1   The present day coil ignition system is remarkably robust, requiring little maintenance except for some lubrication, adjustment for wear of the distributor's moving parts and regular cleaning.

2   Ignition coils are mounted on or near the engine and become soiled with use. It is important to keep them clean, particularly the insulation neck that holds the secondary cable outlet to the distributor. Dirt will encourage the surface passage of spark current to earth (tracking), as will wet conditions. On a damp morning it may pay to wipe down the ignition coil neck and the HT plug leads if starting difficulties are encountered; another effect of dirt or damp tracking on the coil neck is misfiring under acceleration load.

3   Coil connections can occasionally give trouble due to corrosion and possible looseness of the Lucar-type connectors.

4   Resetting the contact breaker is much the same operation for any make of distributor. The engine should be turned over, either by 'blipping' the starter switch, or manually with a spanner on the crankshaft pulley nut, until the cam follower heel is in the middle of one of the lobes and the points are open.

5   Examine the contacts for possible 'pitting and piling', the term used to describe the metal transfer which occurs due to sparking and arcing at the break point (Fig. 6.36). The pile should be removed with fine emery cloth, or dressed with a carborundum stick, but no attempt should be made to eliminate the pit, or crater, on the moving contact. Simple cleaning up of the remaining surface is all that is required – methylated spirit will do well.

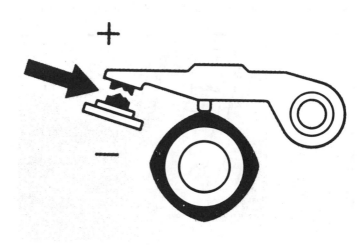

Fig. 6.36 Pitting and piling of contacts (Sec 17)

6   In general, the appearance of the contact surfaces gives an indication of the system condition, examples being:

(a)	Pitting and piling on clean contacts	– Normal condition; Contacts may be renewed
(b)	Uniform grey coating over the whole contact face	– Oxidisation due to low contact pressure (weak spring) or too small a gap
(c)	Severe burning or blued contacts	– Defective capacitor or ignition coil
(d)	Black burnt residue on and around contacts	– Oil, grease or dirt has become lodged between contacts

7   When the contacts are in order the gap may be measured with a feeler gauge according to the manufacturer's instructions. For most cars the gap will be between 0.35 and 0.5 mm – but check with the handbook. The stationary (fixed) contact is usually mounted on a plate which is locked in position by one or two screws. These are slackened until the movement of the fixed contact gives the correct gap and adjustment. The gap is correct when there is only a slight drag on the feeler gauge. Take care to retighten the locking screw(s), but undue force should be avoided.

8   A similar method of gap adjustment applies to Ford (Motorcraft), Bosch and Lucas contact breaker units. Hitachi distributors use an eccentric adjusting screw to achieve the same result, while Ducellier have the facility of an adjuster nut outside the distributor body. SEV Marchal are quite different, in that the points on some distributors come in a cassette which fits over the distributor shaft and cam, the adjustment being carried out with a 3mm Allen key through a hole in the distributor body.

9   As referred to earlier, it is preferable to set the points to give a particular dwell angle, and today the feeler gauge method is less favoured. Several inexpensive meters are now available for this purpose, further details being given in Chapter 14.

10   The cam face of the distributor should be given a smear (no more) of grease to reduce the cam follower wear.

11   Remove the rotor and apply two or three drops of clean engine oil to the top of the spindle (possibly a pad will be visible).

12   The centrifugal advance mechanism should be lubricated with a few drops of engine oil through the gap round the spindle at the contact breaker plate.

13   Finally the pivot post of the contact breaker should be given a light smear of grease or clean engine oil.

14   Over-generous application of oil and grease in the distributor can cause trouble due to the contacts becoming contaminated with flying lubrication.

15   HT leads are mostly of the push-in type, and proper seating into the distributor cap should be checked. Clean down the outer surface of the HT leads if they are soiled, if necessary with methylated spirit to remove stubborn grease.

16   Setting the ignition timing consists of adjusting the distributor so that the ignition spark occurs at the correct point in the cycle. There are two ways, static and dynamic (stroboscopic), and a few modern vehicles including Audi, certain Volkswagens, Datsun and Volvo can be timed only by stroboscopic means.

17   Engines have timing marks (Fig. 6.37) on either the crankshaft pulley or the flywheel, and these marks must be made to align with a fixed mark on the crankcase or the flywheel housing respectively. Most engines show at least two marks, one being the top-dead-centre position and the other the correct timing mark which may be several

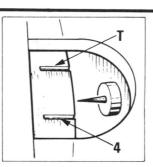

Fiat 127
Peg in flywheel visible through aperture in top of clutch housing.

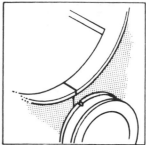

Honda Quintet
Hole in top of clutch housing. Marks on flywheel at 0° and 4° BTDC

Porsche 911
TDC mark on pulley. Line on fan shroud (joint face of crankcase).

Datsun (4 cyl. OHC & 6 cyl.)
Degree scale on timing cover.

Rolls Royce

Austin Morris Mini and Metro
6 pointers at 20°, 16°, 12°, 8°, 4° and 0° BTDC

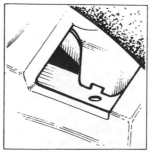

Daihatsu Charade
Hole in flywheel visible through aperture in top of clutch housing = 10° BTDC.

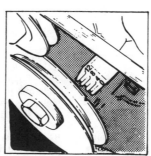

Ford Fiesta

Citroen CX
Remove spare wheel. Marks visible through hole in top of clutch housing

Fig. 6.37 Typical engine timing marks (Sec 17)

degrees before top-dead-centre. The difference between these two marks is usually the static ignition advance expressed in degrees.

18 Engines are mostly timed on No. 1 cylinder, but to be sure consult the handbook. No 1 cylinder is normally nearest the fan, but again some manufacturers call No 1 that cylinder nearest the flywheel. In the case of V8 engines the convention used for cylinder numbers must be checked in the handbook.

19 Static timing is carried out as follows:

(a) Check that the cylinder to be timed is approaching top-dead-centre on the compression stroke. Turn the crankshaft by a spanner on the pulley nut until compression can be felt by a thumb over the spark plug hole. Note that the distributor rotor is just passing the distributor cap electrode of No 1 cylinder.

(b) Line up the timing marks according to the handbook instructions.

(c) Switch on the ignition, having removed the distributor cap, and connect a 12 volt test lamp between the contact breaker terminal and earth.

(d) Slacken off the distributor clamp bolt so that the body can be swivelled, and turn it very slowly to the point where the test lamp is just lighting up, thus indicating that the contact breaker is just opening. Gently tighten up the clamp bolt and recheck. Rotate the engine crankshaft through two revolutions and check that the light-up point is still correct.

20 Dynamic timing is carried out with the engine running and uses a stroboscope lamp. This is actuated by No 1 spark plug, the lamp being connected onto the HT wiring to No 1 and giving a short duration flash of a few microseconds, but with high intensity.

21 Shining the flashing light onto the timing marks on the front pulley or flywheel, according to manufacture, will give an impression of the rotating mark being stationary. The marks should line up; if they do not, then the distributor body is moved round until they do. This operation is usually carried out at tickover of about 700 rpm, the vacuum advance being disconnected and the manifold pipe blocked, but the vehicle handbook should be consulted. Revving the engine should show the timing mark moving backwards against the direction of rotation, indicating that ignition advance occurs with increasing speed. The vacuum advance is reconnected once adjustments are completed. **WARNING**: *Avoid dangling leads, neckties or loose clothing near the fan or drivebelt.* For further details on stroboscopes refer to Chapter 14.

22 Sparking plugs are part of the high tension system and are dealt with in Chapter 7.

18 Testing

Test 1: Cable security
Check conditions for tightness and cleanliness. Push home HT leads in coil neck, onto plugs and into the distributor cap.

Test 2: Checking coil operation
HT sparking from the coil is checked by pulling out the centre HT lead to the distributor cap. Hold it with insulated pliers close to earth (6 mm or $\frac{1}{4}$''), crank the engine and look for regular, healthy sparks. If this is satisfactory, any fault present is likely to lie in the distributor, plugs, fuel supply or ignition timing.

Test 3: Contact breaker
If no sparking at Test 2, look at contact breaker condition and gap. Check for bad surfaces and reset gap, if necessary.

Test 4: Coil voltage to earth
Assuming the contacts are working satisfactorily, measure the voltage to earth at the LT feed terminal of the coil with the contacts closed. For ballasted coils the voltage should be approx 6 volts, but should be equal to the battery voltage for non-ballasted coils.

Test 5: Ballasted coil check
For ballasted coils only, put a temporary earth (a lead with two clips) on to the negative terminal (ie that going to the contact breaker). Measure the voltage at the + coil terminal and then crank the engine. The voltage should rise due to the action of the solenoid in shorting out the ballast resistor. If there is no increase, check the lead going from the coil to the solenoid ignition terminal.

Test 6: Check for faulty distributor or coil
Check the voltage at the coil -ve terminal with the contact breaker points open. The reading should be battery voltage. If, however, the voltage is zero, disconnect the LT lead to the distributor. Voltage should now rise to battery voltage, this indicating trouble in the distributor LT parts. If the voltage does not rise, the indication is a faulty coil and this should be replaced.

Test 7: Distributor
Assuming Test 6 showed a probable distributor LT fault, check the coil-distributor lead, then look for reasons for a short circuit to earth of the insulated contact. This can often be due to incorrect assembly of the contact breaker set after service, particularly with older vehicles where fabric insulation or plastic washers were used.

Test 8: Check for faulty capacitor
With the coil HT lead held close to earth, flick the contacts open and note if sparking is present and healthy. If not, next check the capacitor.

Test 9: Checking capacitor operation
Checking the capacitor is best done by substituting a test capacitor. It is good practice to have a spare available with clips already affixed to give rapid connections. If there is then no spark, or it is weak, replace the coil.

Test 10: High tension system
Assuming a good spark, if the engine still fails to start, further checks on the HT side are necessary. First check the rotor arm by holding the coil HT lead about 3 mm away from the brass insert on the top of the rotor arm. Flick the contacts open a few times. If a spark jumps more than once then the rotor arm insulation has broken down.

Test 11: Distributor cap
The distributor cap can sometimes break down, usually due to surface tracking or a crack in the body. The fault can be invisible and substitution is needed for a definite identification of the trouble.

Test 12: HT leads
Unlikely, but still worth checking, is the possibility of one or more of the HT cables being open circuit. Check with an ohmmeter or by substitution, remembering that the internal connection may be highly resistive (up to 20 000 ohms) for radio interference suppression purposes.

Chapter 7 Sparking plugs

Contents

1 Introduction

In principle the sparking plug is a simple device for bridging a high voltage into the cylinder space and providing a pair of electrodes for the spark to jump across. The reality is that years of development were necessary to produce the efficient plug in use today and the many different operating conditions of modern engines mean that a careful choice of plug is essential.

2 Component parts

The three main components of a plug are the insulator, shell and electrodes (Fig. 7.1).

Insulator

The job of the insulator is to ensure that the high voltage pulse will not leak to earth within the plug body. It also has an effect on the 'heat range' of the plug. Essentials are:

(a) Excellent insulating properties
(b) Resistant to thermal shock
(c) Resistant to the effects of fuel additives
(d) Mechanically strong enough for removal and fitting
(e) Tough enough to withstand abrasive cleaning action of plug cleaning methods

To meet these requirements, aluminium oxide is generally used.

Shell

Made of steel, the shell consists of a small plug of round section which is fed through a powerful press where the body is completely formed, apart from the screw thread. The thread, which is normally 14 mm diameter with a 1.5 mm pitch, is turned on an automatic lathe.

Electrodes

The electrode materials are vital to correct plug operation for they must have good electrical properties for spark emission, must stand up to extremes of temperature and be resistant to chemical corrosion. Nickel alloy is the most common material used and the alloying composition of a particular plug brand may be variable according to the particular engine application. Special quality plugs use more precious metals including alloys of silver, platinum, palladium or even gold. Note that the earthed electrode is welded to the plug shell.

Plug seals

Two gas-tight seals are necessary, one between the insulator and the outer body shell, and the other between the insulator and the centre electrode. The plug illustrated shows dry powder 'Sillment' seals while plugs of different manufacture have various forms of caulking rings which are crimped in position by high pressure and by heat shrinking. Whilst the arrangements of sealing are simple in concept, development has been in progress for many years to find materials that will remain gas-tight yet heat conductive, will stand extremes of temperature and have the correct thermal expansion characteristic.

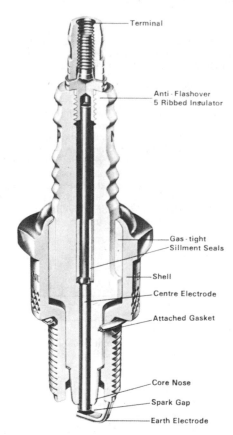

Fig. 7.1 Cross-section of a sparking plug (Sec 2)

Terminal

Anti-Flashover
5 Ribbed Insulator

Gas-tight
Sillment Seals

Shell

Centre Electrode

Attached Gasket

Core Nose

Spark Gap

Earth Electrode

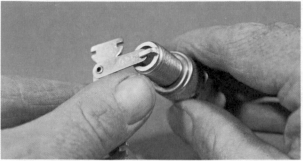

Measuring plug gap. A feeler gauge of the correct size (see ignition system specifications) should have a slight 'drag' when slid between the electrodes. Adjust gap if necessary

Adjusting plug gap. The plug gap is adjusted by bending the earth electrode inwards, or outwards, as necessary until the correct clearance is obtained. Note the use of the correct tool

Normal. Grey-brown deposits, lightly coated core nose. Gap increasing by around 0.001 in (0.025 mm) per 1000 miles (1600 km). Plugs ideally suited to engine, and engine in good condition

Carbon fouling. Dry, black, sooty deposits. Will cause weak spark and eventually misfire. Fault: over-rich fuel mixture. Check: carburettor mixture settings, float level and jet sizes; choke operation and cleanliness of air filter. Plugs can be re-used after cleaning

Oil fouling. Wet, oily deposits. Will cause weak spark and eventually misfire. Fault: worn bores/piston rings or valve guides; sometimes occurs (temporarily) during running-in period. Plugs can be re-used after thorough cleaning

Overheating. Electrodes have glazed appearance, core nose very white – few deposits. Fault: plug overheating. Check: plug value, ignition timing, fuel octane rating (too low) and fuel mixture (too weak). Discard plugs and cure fault immediately

Electrode damage. Electrodes burned away; core nose has burned, glazed appearance. Fault: pre-ignition. Check: as for 'Overheating' but may be more severe. Discard plugs and remedy fault before piston or valve damage occurs

Split core nose (may appear initially as a crack). Damage is self-evident, but cracks will only show after cleaning. Fault: pre-ignition or wrong gap-setting technique. Check: ignition timing, cooling system, fuel octane rating (too low) and fuel mixture (too weak). Discard plugs, rectify fault immediately

3   Heat range

1   The firing end of a sparking plug must operate between the temperature limits of 400°C and 800°C approximately. Below 400°C the plug cannot burn off the carbon deposits generated by combustion, and much above 800°C there is increasing oxide fouling and electrode burning. At 950°C the plug tip becomes so incandescent that premature igniting of the petrol vapour occurs – pre-ignition – resulting in damage to the piston and the plugs itself (Figs. 7.2, 7.3 and 7.4).

Fig. 7.2 Pre-ignition damage to plug (Sec 3)

Fig. 7.3 Piston crown holed by pre-ignition (Sec 3)

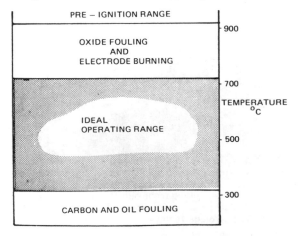

Fig. 7.4 Plug operating temperatures (Sec 3)

2   Heat flow from the plug has been measured by manufacturers with some accuracy and it is known that some 91% is transmitted via the screw thread and gasket to the engine body with the remaining 9% lost by radiation and convection from the plug shell and the exposed insulator (Fig. 7.5).

3   The figures do not take into account the cooling effect of the fresh inflowing vapour, but do give an informative picture. It is clear, for instance, that correct fitting and tightening down is vital, since the attached gasket is responsible for nearly half of the heat transmission – failure to maintain good seating contact could result in an overheated plug.

4   Clearly no one plug can be correct for all operating conditions and some manufacturers distinguish between plug choice for round-town work or for sustained motorway travel. Most important dimensions of a sparking plug are at the bottom end, and Fig. 7.6 shows vital statistics that **must** be correct.

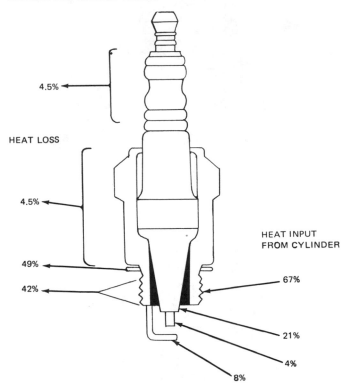

Fig. 7.5 Heat flow in a sparking plug (Sec 3)

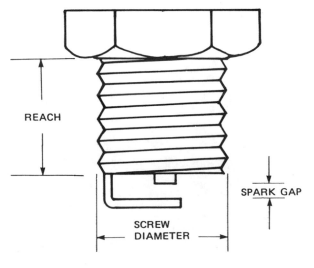

Fig. 7.6 Vital dimensions of a sparking plug (Sec 3)

5   It is essential for correct plug tip temperatures that the electrodes should **just** project into the cylinder. If the plug reach is too short, the spark is shielded from the petrol vapour, and bad misfiring will result and be accompanied by carbon build-up; too long, and the electrodes will run hot and there is also the chance that the screw threads of cylinder and plug may be damaged by overheating (Fig. 7.7).

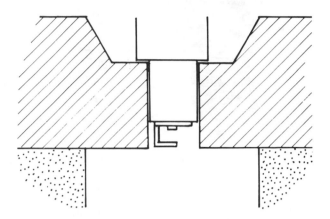

Fig. 7.7a Reach too short (Sec 3)

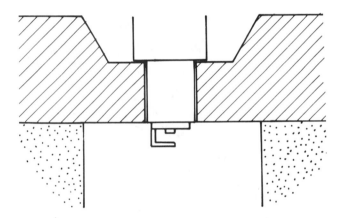

Fig. 7.7b Reach correct (Sec 3)

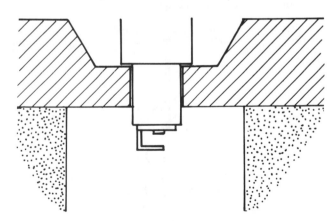

Fig. 7.7c Reach too long (Sec 3)

6   Plugs dissipate heat from the centre electrode via the nose of the insulator surrounding it; a short insulator will pass heat to the steel shell more readily than a nose insulator which is relatively long and thin (Fig. 7.8).

7   A high compression engine generally has hot operating conditions, and so a plug with best heat dissipation would be required. Conversely,

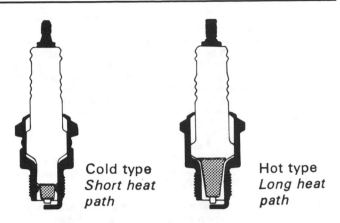

Cold type
Short heat path

Hot type
Long heat path

Fig. 7.8 Hot and cold sparking plugs (Sec 3)

a low compression engine has lower combustion chamber temperature and so a hotter grade of plug would be chosen so that the plug tip temperature could be maintained above the oil fouling level (Fig. 7.4). The rule is, therefore,

A hot engine uses a cold plug
A cold engine uses a hot plug

Note that sometimes hot plugs are referred to as 'soft' and cold plugs as 'hard'.

4   Plug examination

The state of a used spark plug tells much of conditions in the engine, and some typical examples are shown in the colour chart.

5   Ignition timing

1   It is said that incorrect ignition timing has the greatest single effect on plug temperatures. Well known to mechanics is the fact that advancing the timing may produce a small power increase, but what is sometimes not appreciated is the accompanying large increase in plug operating temperature (Fig. 7.9).

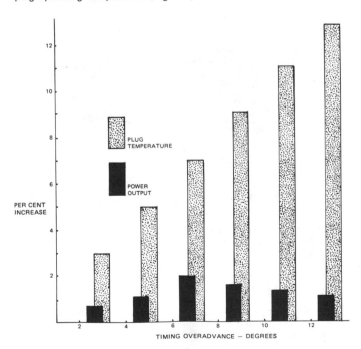

Fig. 7.9 Effects of ignition advance (Sec 5)

6   Plug servicing

1   Plugs need checking regularly and ideally should be examined by an electronics diagnostic unit. Failing this, faults may be shown up on a combined cleaning/testing machine, where air pressure and normal sparking voltage will be applied to the plug. A mirror system shows the electrodes, and when working the spark should jump at the correct point with no erratic wandering.

2   Plug cleaning may be carried out by hand, but workshops commonly use a bead or sand blast machine for this purpose. It is most important to blow away all traces of sand with compressed air after cleaning and for this reason the bead cleaner is preferred, although care must be taken also to remove all beads.

3   Cleaning manually is best carried out with a fine wire brush, going over external thread, plug tip and earth electrode **carefully.** A harsh abrasive brush may damage the plug and in any event check that no 'whiskers' from the wire brush remain in the plug. Finally clean the insulator with a methylated spirits soaked rag to prevent spark tracking paths from developing.

4   It is a horrifying thought that many mechanics do not seem to notice the grit or rust particles around the seat when removing a plug. Undo the plug a few turns and blow away the grit with compressed air or a fine brush. This is most important, because foreign matter entering the cylinder can be disastrous to the life of the engine.

5   Refitting is also important, especially to alloy head engines where the plug hole thread can be easily damaged by overtightening. First smear a trace of grease on to the plug thread and screw the plug in to be finger tight, making sure that the seating in the engine is clean.

6   With the gasket seat type of plug, tighten up by a maximum of one quarter turn with a plug spanner. Note that further tightening does not improve the seating property of the gasket (Fig. 7.10).

Fig. 7.10 Installing a gasket seat plug (Sec 6)

7   Taper seat plugs require special care. If this type of plug is overtightened, it may be difficult or impossible to remove it. Gentle tightening with a plug spanner not more than one sixteenth of a turn is required, or better still, use a torque spanner set to between 8 and 12 lbf ft (Fig. 7.11). Plug torque spanners pre-set to the correct loading are available, an example being the Champion CT 483 set.

8   Gap resetting should be carried out with a combination tool with electrode adjuster and feeler gauge, such as that made by Champion or Bosch.

9   The gap must be checked carefully, using a feeler gauge which

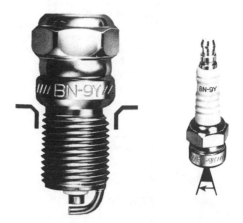

Fig. 7.11 Installing a taper seat plug (Sec 6)

should pass through the electrodes with a slight drag. Flat feeler gauges can sometimes give a misleading figure if electrode erosion has occurred, and for this reason the round wire gauge of the Bosch set may be preferred (Fig. 7.12).

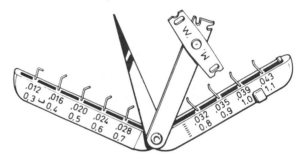

Fig. 7.12 Bosch spark plug gauge (Sec 6)

7   Surface gap plugs

1   This type of plug has been introduced for use with certain high energy capacitor discharge ignition (CDI) systems in order to combat fouling problems without overheating.

2   The spark is fired across the surface between the centre electrode (which protrudes very little) and the body shell. The discharge runs

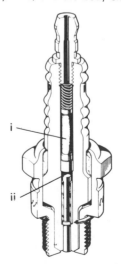

Fig. 7.13 Surface gap plug (Sec 7)

(i) inductive suppressor   *(ii) auxiliary gap*

across the surface in the form of a sudden flash and produces good burning characteristics. Fig. 7.13 shows one example of a surface-discharge plug in which an inductive suppressor and an auxiliary spark gap are built into the path between the top connector and the centre electrode.

8 Diesel glow plugs

1 The diesel engine does not require a sparking plug to ignite the fuel, since this is achieved by compressing air in the cylinder to give the required temperature for ignition when the fuel oil is injected by nozzle.

2 However, it is advantageous for cold start conditions to heat either the air in the engine intake manifold, or the fuel-air mixture in the combustion chamber.

3 Glow plugs (Fig. 7.14) have a built-in electric resistance coil which is energised from the battery. Once the engine is running the electrical supply is automatically switched off.

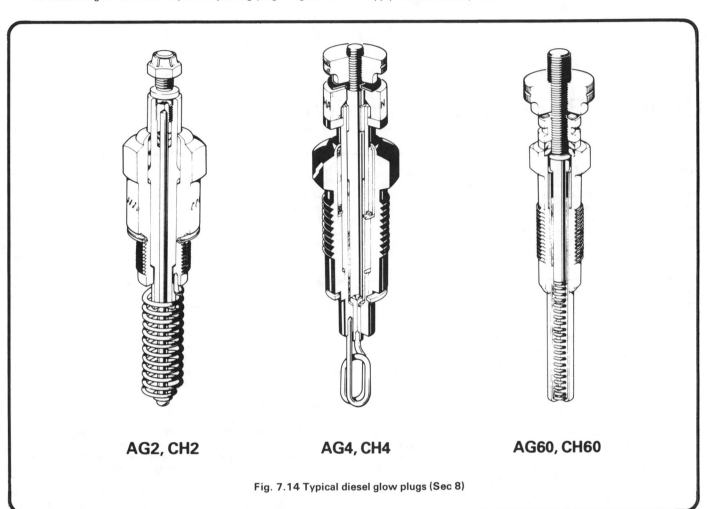

AG2, CH2   **AG4, CH4**   **AG60, CH60**

Fig. 7.14 Typical diesel glow plugs (Sec 8)

Chapter 8 Electronic ignition

Contents

1 Deficiencies of conventional ignition systems

1   Although the contact breaker plus coil and battery system has been in use for half a century at least, the shortcomings in performance and maintenance costs have long been appreciated. Mechanically, it is difficult to manufacture a cam, heel follower and spring mechanism which provide and maintain the required accuracies. Every few thousand miles it is necessary to reset the contacts to allow for heel wear; in addition the breaking of the coil primary current produces the effect of 'pitting and piling' because of metal transference with the spark.

2   It should be noted that to obtain enough energy for spark production (about 30 millijoules are required) the coil designer will allow as large a primary current as possible, consistent with reasonable life of the contact breaker points – but for long contact life the current should be small. The graph of Fig. 8.1 shows the general effect of break current on the life of points and that the designer does not have much latitude.

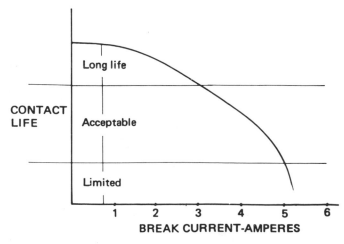

Fig. 8.1 Contact life versus break current (Sec 1)

3   At high speeds, the centrifugal force acting on the moving parts of the contact breaker assembly may be sufficient to cause the gap to increase beyond the design gap, due to flinging out when the heel loses contact with the cam.

4   The troubles mentioned above have always been present, but in recent years further problems have arisen due to developments in engine design. Compression ratios have increased from about 8.5:1 to 10.5:1 and maximum engine speeds have risen to about 22 000 rpm in certain racing cars and motorcycles. Limitations might now be summarized, therefore, as follows:

(a)   Plug fouling: for high compression ratios, petrol additives (lead salts) are used to prevent detonation. Unfortunately these additives appear to contribute to fouling of plugs.
(b)   Mechanical limitations of contact breakers are now severe.
(c)   The time taken for 30 millijoules of electrical energy to build up between sparks limits the rate to about 400 sparks per second, or time per spark 0.0025 second. This may be too low a spark rate for high-speed multi-cylinder engines.
(d)   To overcome fouling and the greater electrical load presented by a highly compressed vapour in the cylinder, higher spark voltages are required, ie ignition system voltages of 20 000 + in extreme cases.
(e)   Contact breaker points pitting and burning due to the high coil primary currents used.
(f)   Inaccuracy occurring at high speeds due to backlash and whip in the contact breaker drive mechanism.

It is not surprising that igniton system designers have looked for alternative methods, and the arrival of the transistor and allied semiconductor devices has provided several solutions to the problem.

2 Solid-state systems

1   'Solid-state' is a term meaning that all amplifying and switching components in a given circuit employ semiconductor devices, eg transistors, diodes, thyristors (SCR) etc, and not the obsolete vacuum valves (called tubes in the US) which were anything but solid!

2   It was the very fragility and bulk of electronic equipment before the advent of semiconductor devices that held back developments in automotive engineering, but gradually, from the mid-1960's, the position has changed. Now semiconductors are reliable, rugged and able to survive the harsh conditions in vehicle applications.

3   It would not be possible in a book of this size to delve far into semiconductor study, but an understanding of a few principles will help the mechanic considerably.

3   Types of electronic ignition circuits

1   At present there are three main types of ignition system using electronic techniques:

    (a)   Transistor-assisted contact coil ignition (TAC)
    (b)   Contactless transistor-driven coil ignition
    (c)   Capacitor discharge ignition (CDI)

2   Of these methods, (a) still uses a normal contact breaker unit, but this serves only to switch the transistor on or off, and since the current through the contacts is very small, the life and maintenance periods are greatly improved. The presence of a mechanical contact breaker, however, is thought by many to be undesirable, and so this system really is only a partial solution towards the long-life, high-reliability system.

3   Method (b) uses some form of transducer to give a timed electrical signal to the ignition circuit when the spark is required. It approaches the ideal situation since there is an excellent sparking performance

coupled with a negligible maintenance requirement, and it is competitive with system (c).

4   Some regard the CDI system as the best, but developments continue. It is certain, however, that the spark energy given by CDI is high enough to make fouled plugs work and to give adequate sparks under adverse conditions which would defeat conventional ignition circuits completely.

4   Transistor-assisted contact (TAC) ignition

1   It is sometimes daunting to sort out a complex electronic circuit, but much simplified if a few rules about transistors are remembered. For these purposes the transistor may be regarded as a switch (Fig. 8.2).

2   Current will flow through the transistor from the emitter to the collector if a small current is allowed to flow in the base lead. Break this tiny base current and the main current flow from emitter to collector ceases abruptly; in other words the base current controls the emitter-collector current.

3   The control current in the base must be made to flow back to the emitter, but it is only about 2% of the main emitter-collector current. It is also a requirement that for transistors of p-n-p construction the emitter is + relative to base (and negative for n-p-n).

4   Imagine now that the load shown in Fig. 8.3 was the primary of an ignition coil and the switch in the base-emitter path was the contact breaker of an ignition system. We then have the ingredients for a transistor-assisted contact breaker system.

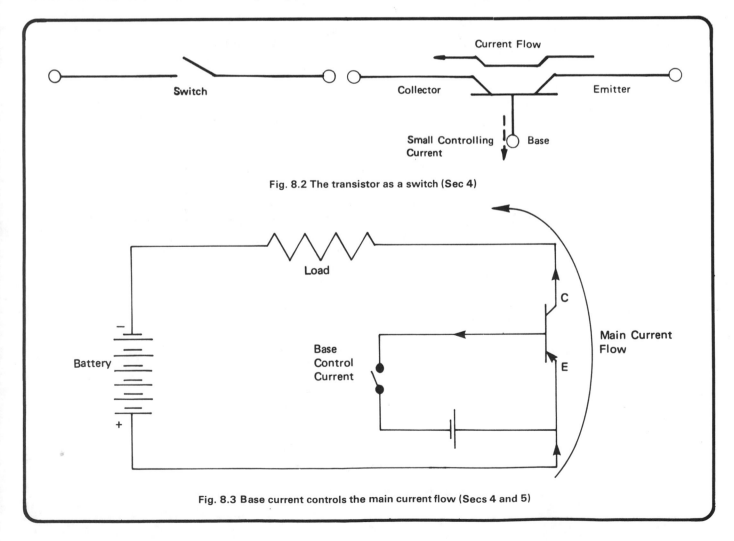

Fig. 8.2 The transistor as a switch (Sec 4)

Fig. 8.3 Base current controls the main current flow (Secs 4 and 5)

5   Suppose the collector current flowing through the ignition coil primary were, for example, 5 amperes; we no longer have to break this with a contact breaker with all the attendant pitting and piling troubles. Instead, the contact breaker has to deal with base current only, amounting to about 2% of 5 amperes, ie 100 milliamperes. Contact life is greatly extended, and because the base path is shielded from the inductive transient voltages generated in the ignition coil, there is no longer any need for a capacitor across the contacts. On the debit side, it is undesirable that a mechanical contact breaker should be used at all.

6   Most transistor-driven circuits use a special ignition coil, and a standard coil should not be used without checking the manufacturer's instructions.

7   A major limitation of contact breakers used in the conventional (Kettering) system is the amount of current which can be broken without excessive pitting and piling; now the energy stored in the coil depends on both the current I and the inductance L:

$$\text{Energy stored } W = \tfrac{1}{2}LI^2 \text{ joules}$$

This figure is generally reckoned to be 0.030 joules, and keeping I low to meet contact life requirements means that the inductance L has to be large enough to reach the energy storage figure.

8   Inductance L, however, is also a factor which determines the transient voltage surges generated by the coil when the primary current is broken; in the early 1960's, when transistor ignition developments first took place, transient voltages using standard coils were sufficiently high to destroy transistors of that time.

9   Although it is possible to use a conventional coil (with adequate surge protection) now that transistors have improved, engineers have take the opportunity to re-design ignition coils to match the electronic components. Reducing L means reducing the number of turns of wire in the primary and so the **ratio** of secondary : primary turns has increased. Typical ratios are now 250 : 1 and even as high as 400 : 1.

10   Claims are made that a set of contacts in a transistor-assisted circuit will have a life of up to 100 000 miles, due to the reduction of point current. The ideal value of point current is not yet settled, but it is clear that points will last for long periods if the current is reduced below 0.75A.

11   The inductance of the ignition coil is important for reasons other than those outlined in the last paragraph. The property of inductance in an electrical circuit is analogous to the inertia of an engine flywheel. Just as a heavy flywheel takes time to reach its final speed, so direct current in an inductive circuit takes time to reach its maximum.

12   This rise-time of coil current after the contacts have closed has been a limiting factor to the maximum possible spark rate, since at high engine speeds the next spark was due before the current could rise to its maximum value. The reduced primary inductance of ignition coils driven by transistors has meant much improved performance, as shown by the typical graphs of Figs. 8.4 and 8.5. The retention of good sparking voltage at high engine speeds is required for efficiency and economy.

13   Sparking plugs collect deposits of carbon, petrol additives and lead on their electrodes, and in time form a leakage path for current, which can lead to a weak spark and possibly incomplete combustion, with resulting poor petrol economy and, therefore, increased pollution levels.

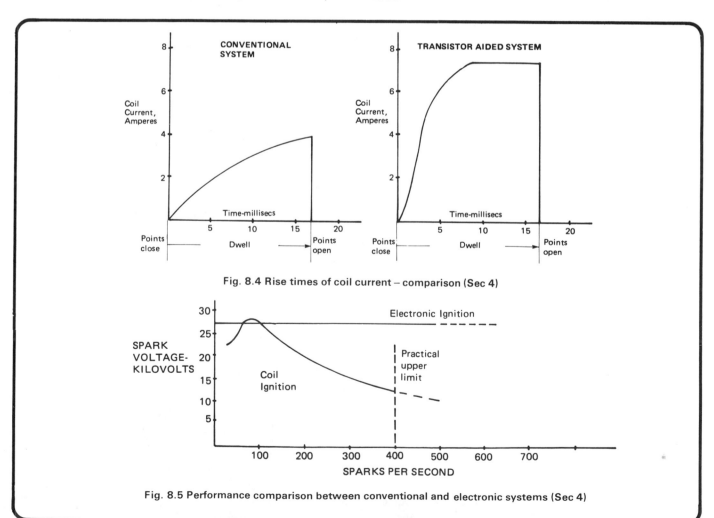

Fig. 8.4 Rise times of coil current – comparison (Sec 4)

Fig. 8.5 Performance comparison between conventional and electronic systems (Sec 4)

14 With accurate timing and a good spark voltage, most of these deposits burn away and the life of the sparking plug is reputed to be much higher – up to 30 000 miles compared with the maker's recommended replacement mileage of 10 000 miles when using conventional coil ignition.

5   Basic TAC ignition circuit

1   A drawback of the circuit of Fig. 8.3 is the need for a separate battery in the base control path. In practice the supply of current for both the base and collector branches is drawn from the same battery; all that is needed is a pair of resistors across the main battery supply, their resistances being calculated to make the centre tap correspond to the voltage required at the base. An illustration of this idea is given in the following working circuit, being a simple example of transistorised ignition.

2   The first approach to transistor ignition was to relieve the contact breaker of interrupting current in an inductive circuit. Fig. 8.6 shows a practical circuit using an ignition coil of 400 : 1 ratio. The transistor is protected from inductive transient voltages by the Zener diode connected across it; when the Zener conduction point is reached (56 volts) the transistor is effectively bridged by a low resistance path until the offending voltage disappears.

3   When the points are closed, R_2 and R_3 act as a voltage divider and thus bias the transistor so that it is switched on. Current flows round the main path of R_1, through diode D_1, the transistor (emitter to collector) and through the ignition coil primary back to the battery.

4   At break point, the chain R_2 and R_3 is broken and bias is removed from the transistor, causing it to switch off; a small current continues to flow through diode D_1 and R_4, the result being that the emitter is about 0.7 volts **negative** with respect to the base. This ensures abrupt cut-off of coil current, the effect of which is to generate a spark voltage in the secondary winding. The unit must be constructed on a heat sink, (an aluminium plate to disperse the heat) and can then be encapsulated in epoxy resin to give protection from damp.

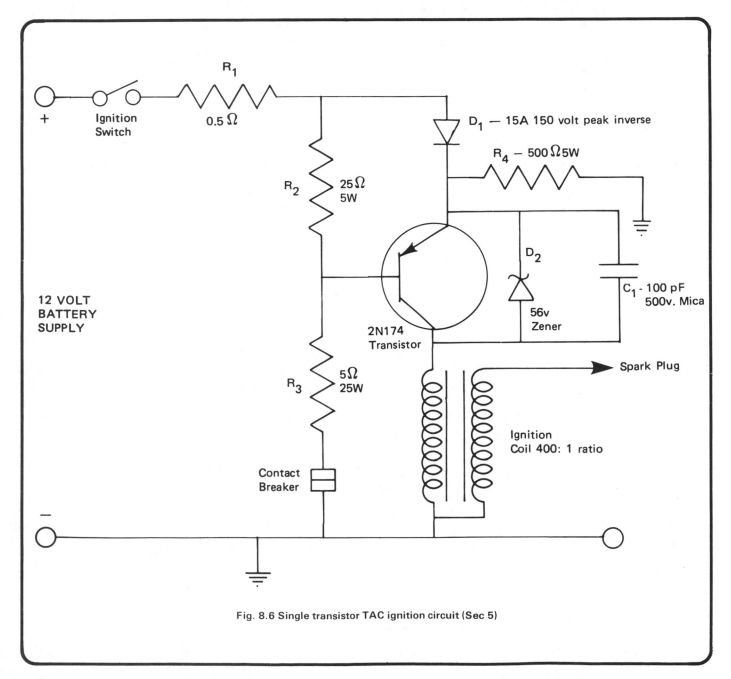

Fig. 8.6 Single transistor TAC ignition circuit (Sec 5)

6   TAC ignition – dual transistor method

1   It is usual to employ a second transistor in TAC circuits, its purpose being to drive the power transistor on and off. A TAC system is shown in Fig. 8.7.

2   The mode of operation is as follows:

(i)   Assume CB is open. A small current flows through R_2, R_3 and the base-emitter junction of transistor T_2
T_2 is therefore switched on
ie collector current is flowing.

(ii)   Since T_2 is conducting, the volt-drop from collector to emitter V_{ce} is small, so the input to transistor T_1 is short circuited, thus T_1 is switched off.

(iii)   Suppose the contact breaker points now close.
The base of T_2 is shorted to earth so T_2 is now switched off. Since no collector current flows down R_1 there can be little volt-drop, so the base of T_1 rises in voltage and T_1 is switched on with R_1 acting only as base current limiter.

(iv)   Finally, if the contacts now open, T_2 switches on and switches T_1 off very rapidly. This current break causes the field to collapse in the ignition coil and a spark is generated.

Note: The capacitor C_1 is to absorb transient voltages which appear across transistor T_1.

8   Contactless systems

1   TAC ignition is now little used outside the DIY market, but serves as an introduction to more sophisticated systems. A variety of devices (called transducers) exist to pick up some form of signal, which is then arranged to trigger off a spark at the plug with the aid of an electronic amplifier or electronic switch.

2   Transducers, or pick-ups, are based on one of the following:

(a)   Magnetic pick-up in which small magnets in a distributor rotor generate signal voltages in static coils spaced round the rotor.

(b)   Ferrite rods (ie small rods of high permeability magnetic material) set in a rotor which serve to disturb the magnetic balance of two coils wound on an iron core, and hence generate a signal voltage in them.

(c)   Optical pick-ups in which a photo-electric cell is illuminated by a light emitting diode until the light beam is interrupted by a projection on the rotor.

(d)   Infra-red beam interruption, but similar to (c) above.

(e)   Hall Effect: if a chip of semiconductor material has a current passed through it and is located in a magnetic field, then a voltage will appear across the chip at right angles (physically) to the current (Fig. 8.8). If a slotted metal vane is used in an ignition system to interrupt the magnetic field, then the voltage across the chip (the Hall voltage) changes and can be used to trigger off a transistorised ignition spark.

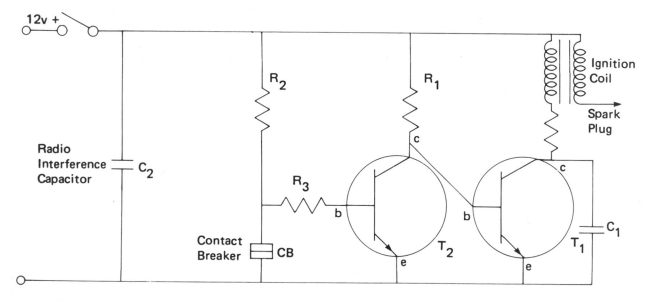

Fig. 8.7 Lucas TAC ignition circuit (Sec 6)

7   Limitations of TAC ignition

1   It is self evident that interruption of current by a mechanical contact breaker is a limitation; although TAC ignition gives a much improved life to the contacts, there is still the periodic re-setting of the points gap to be done due to heel wear. There remains the problem of contact bounce at high engine speeds and, for mass production, of cost-effectiveness. Better means of providing electronic ignition have finally relegated the TAC system towards obsolescence.

2   Transistor systems do have other disadvantages in that the contacts do not burn away any dust, dirt or oil which gets on them and this can lead to intermittent or total failure.

3   It is always a thought that in the event of roadside failure of any transistor ignition circuit, nothing can be done in the way of repairs, although some DIY sets can be switched back to the basic coil and battery circuit. It is assumed that, eventually, systems will be standardised for ready replacement.

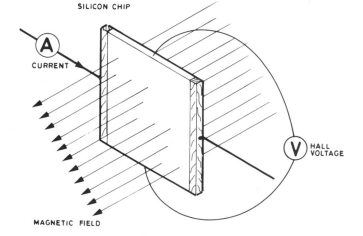

Fig. 8.8 Illustrating Hall Effect voltage (Sec 8)

3   In general, transistorised ignition systems come into two categories:

(a)   in which a power transistor is used to break the primary current in an ignition coil. These are inductive discharge systems, since the energy is stored in the magnetic field of the coil; the form of output to the sparking plug is like that of a conventional coil-ignition set.

(b)   in this second group, the energy is stored in a capacitor which is discharged abruptly through the primary winding of a special ignition coil. This is capacitive discharge ignition (CDI) and is characterised by an intense spark of short duration.

9   Inductive discharge systems

Lucas Opus ignition

1   This is fitted as original equipment to certain Aston Martin and Jaguar engines, and can give correct regular sparking from cranking speeds up to peak speeds for twelve-cylinder engines using only one distributor (Fig. 8.9).

2   A conventional centrifugal advance mechanism, a retard-type vacuum unit, distributor cap and HT rotor are fitted. In place of a contact breaker an electronic timing rotor and pick-up module are fitted. The timing rotor is a glass filled nylon disc housing small ferrite rods round the edge. The number of ferrite rods is the same as the number of engine cylinders. The timing rotor and the HT rotor are mounted on the same shaft, and therefore are subject to the centrifugal advance. An air gap separates the ferrite rods in the timing rotor from the ferrite core of the pick-up (Fig. 8.10).

3   The pick-up module is a precisely balanced transformer having two windings, a primary and a secondary. When the timing rotor turns, ferrite rods pass close to the ferrite core of the balanced transformer and upset the magnetic balance.

4   Within the amplifier unit, there is an oscillator producing an alternating output voltage which is applied to the pick-up module primary winding. In the balanced state only a small voltage is induced into the secondary winding and hence into the amplifier, but when a ferrite rod passes and upsets the balance a large voltage at oscillator frequency reaches the amplifier input.

5   The amplifier increases the voltage, then rectifies it, and this is used to switch the power transistor TR4 which supplies the ignition coil primary. When switching off occurs the sudden drop of ignition coil primary current gives rise to a spark voltage in the coil secondary which reaches the plugs via a conventional distributor rotor.

6   The ballast resistor unit seen in Fig. 8.9 is an encapsulated unit containing 4 resistors (3 in earlier versions). Resistors 2 and 3 give a satisfactory voltage to the ignition coil primary winding under starting and running conditions, resistor 2 being shorted out for starting. Resistors 1 and 4 supply the amplifer unit and tachometer respectively.

7   The ignition coil is special to the Opus system, (Lucas 13C12) having inhibited connectors (ie these cannot be connected the wrong way round) for LT terminals which are marked + and −.

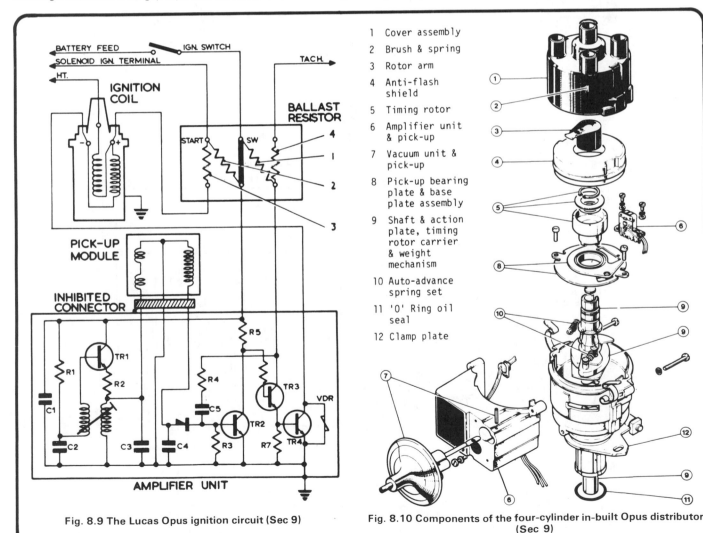

1   Cover assembly
2   Brush & spring
3   Rotor arm
4   Anti-flash shield
5   Timing rotor
6   Amplifier unit & pick-up
7   Vacuum unit & pick-up
8   Pick-up bearing plate & base plate assembly
9   Shaft & action plate, timing rotor carrier & weight mechanism
10   Auto-advance spring set
11   'O' Ring oil seal
12   Clamp plate

Fig. 8.9 The Lucas Opus ignition circuit (Sec 9)

Fig. 8.10 Components of the four-cylinder in-built Opus distributor (Sec 9)

Lumenition ignition system

8   This is an example of a transistorised switch unit which uses the interruption of an infra-red light beam to provide the spark-triggering signal. The light source lens is housed in the distributor instead of a normal contact breaker set and the light beam is broken by a segmented disc fitted on to the distributor cam (Fig. 8.11). A standard ignition coil is normally used.

Chrysler ignition system

9   Available for use on four, six and eight-cylinder engines, this is an inductive discharge arrangement in which a power transistor drives an ignition coil. The set comprises a distributor with centrifugal advance, vacuum advance, rotor and distributor cap. In place of the contact breaker there is a pick-up unit, and the rotor is a spiked wheel known as a reluctor. The number of spikes corresponds to the number of cylinders (Fig. 8.12).

10 The pick-up is a coil wound on a steel pole piece attached to a permanent magnet, thus in effect becoming an extension of the magnet. The reluctor teeth pass within 0.008 inch (0.2 mm) of the pole piece, and at the point of passing, the magnetic field increases rapidly (the magnetic reluctance of the path has been reduced). This generates a pulse voltage in the pick-up coil which is then passed on to the control unit to produce a spark.

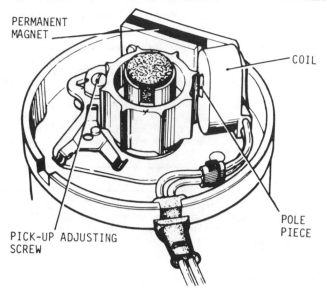

Fig. 8.12 The Chrysler ignition triggering assembly (Sec 9)

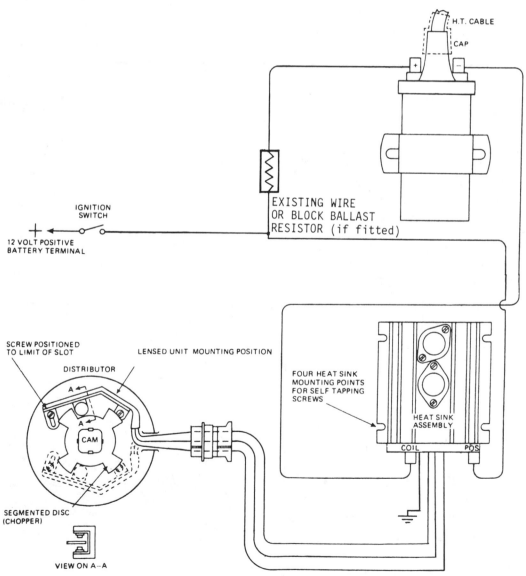

Fig. 8.11 Lumenition ignition system (Sec 9)

11 This system has two ballast resistors, one of 0.5 ohm in series with the ignition coil primary, this being shorted out under engine cranking conditions. The second ballast resistor is of 5 ohms resistance and is used to protect the control unit, the whole system being shown in Fig. 8.13. This unit is an example of a magnetic variable-reluctance transdencer.

Delco-Remy high energy ignition (HEI) system
12 This unusual arrangement, all built into a distributor unit (Fig. 8.14), is designed to be maintenance-free and to provide up to 35 kilovolts to supply larger gap spark plugs.

13 With pressure to reduce carbon monoxide (CO) levels in exhaust gases, designers have weakened fuel mixture. This has led to spark plug misfiring under adverse conditions and two basic causes have been found:

(a) To fire a spark plug on a weak mixture requires a considerably higher voltage than for rich mixtures.
(b) To ensure good regular combustion of weak mixtures, plug gaps have to be widened.

In some recent vehicles plug gaps of 0.060 inch (1.5 mm) have been specified. The Delco-Remy HEI system will deal with such conditions.

14 The pick-up assembly located around the distributor shaft contains a permanent magnet, a circular pole piece with internal teeth and a pick-up coil. A timer core which has teeth around its outer edge is fixed to the distributor shaft. When the teeth of the timer core, rotating inside the pick-up assembly, line up with the teeth of the pole piece, a voltage is induced in the pick-up coil because of the sudden rise of magnetic flux crossing the small gap between teeth (Fig. 8.15).

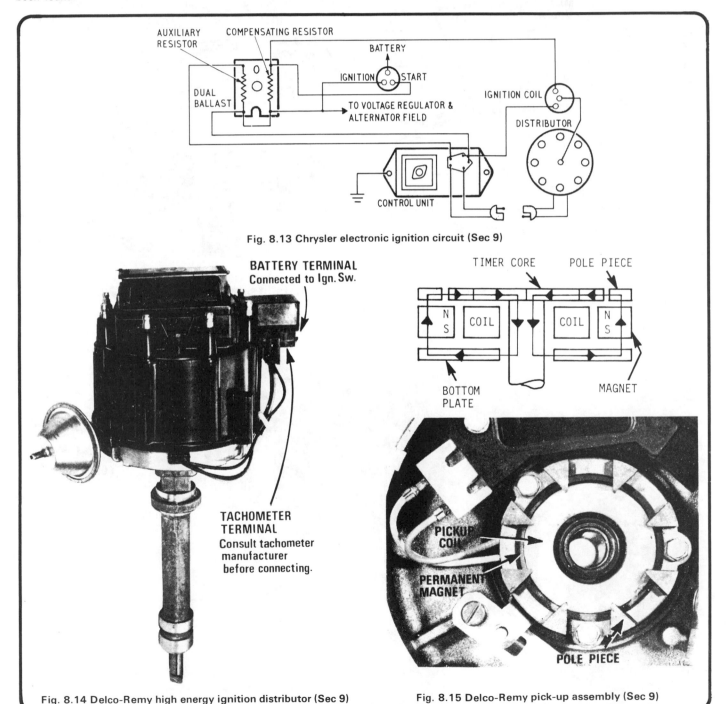

Fig. 8.13 Chrysler electronic ignition circuit (Sec 9)

Fig. 8.14 Delco-Remy high energy ignition distributor (Sec 9)

Fig. 8.15 Delco-Remy pick-up assembly (Sec 9)

15 This induced voltage sends a signal to the amplifier in the electronics module, cutting off the ignition coil primary current abruptly, and so delivering a high voltage to the secondary winding, hence to the spark plugs. The magnetic pick-up is connected to a conventional vacuum advance unit and a conventional centrifugal advance is also used.

16 Available spark voltages are compared with maximum required voltages for used spark plugs in Fig. 8.16, and Fig. 8.17 shows the main components of the HEI distributor.

Sparkrite SX2000

17 This is an example of an electronic conversion kit which uses mechanical contacts and retains the original ignition coil (Fig. 8.18). In this set, both capacitive and inductive energy is used for sparking, giving the characteristic long burn time of the inductive (ie standard ignition coil) system and the fast rise time of the capacitor discharge. An explanation of capacitor discharge appears later in this Chapter (Section 10).

18 The overall result is claimed to be successful ignition of weak mixtures under all load and speed conditions, but another advantage to drivers is that a switch to go back to conventional ignition is provided, most useful in the unlikely event of a failure in the electronics box.

19 Where diagnostic equipment is used (see Chapter 15) it is best with the Sparkrite set to carry out all tests and adjustments with the switch set to 'conventional' ignition. Once timing has been set correctly, switching over to the electronic section will give the same

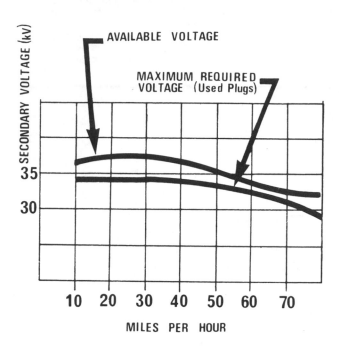

Fig. 8.16 HEI voltage and plug requirements (Sec 9)

Fig. 8.18 Sparkrite SX2000 ignition set (Sec 9)

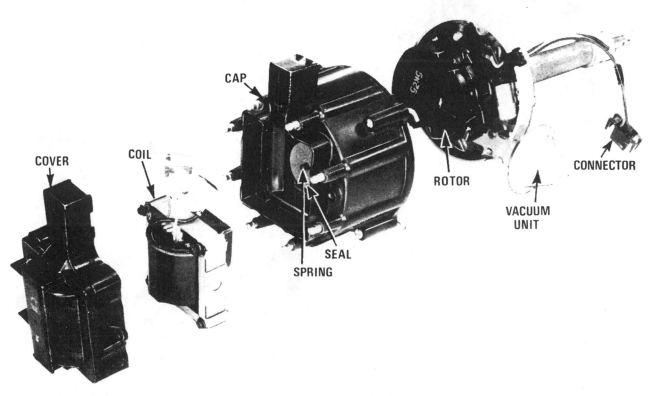

Fig. 8.17 Main components of the HEI distributor (Sec 9)

timing accuracy. Initial ionisation voltage at the plug tip is positive, and so readings of the spark voltage with the oscilloscope parade display will not be possible with the switch in the 'electronic' position.

Ford Escort breakerless ignition
20 Ford Escort 1.3 and 1.6 CVH models (front-wheel-drive) are fitted with a magnetically-triggered breakerless ignition set manufactured by Lucas and Bosch (Fig. 8.19). The electronic module is built into the distributor which is mounted horizontally on the end face of the cylinder head with direct drive from the camshaft end. It is stated that, because of improvements in the distributor drive design and in production timing method, timing adjustments during routine servicing will be unnecessary.

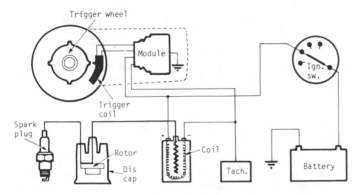

Fig. 8.19 Schematic diagram of the Ford Escort ignition system (Sec 9)

21 The distributor (Fig. 8.20) uses a conventional cap, resistor rotor arm and shaft-mounted trigger wheel. A trigger plate and pick-up coil replace the usual contact breaker and capacitor. Electronic plug-in modules (Fig. 8.21) are bolted onto the outer surface of the distributor which acts as a heat sink to keep down the module's temperature. The modules are manufactured by Bosch and AC Delco, and are interchangeable for both types of Bosch and Lucas distributors.

22 No ballast resistor is used, as the equivalent has been bult into the module circuitry. Dwell angle is variable with this system, in contrast to mechanical arrangements, and is determined by the module so cannot be altered.

23 Special high-output coils are made by Lucas and Bosch for the Ford system, the coils being interchangeable and identified by a red label. Tests have been carried out at up to 32 kilovolts.

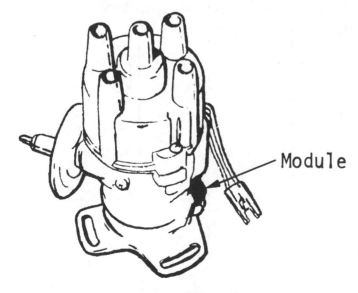

Fig. 8.20 Ford Escort horizontally mounted distributor (Sec 9)

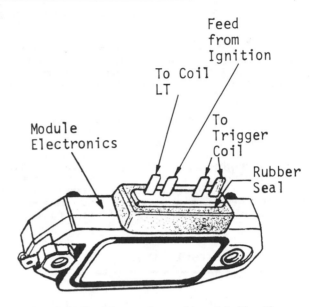

Fig. 8.21 Ford Escort electronic module (Sec 9)

10 Principles of capacitor discharge ignition (CDI)

1 Under ideal conditions less than 1 millijoule of energy will properly ignite the petrol/air mixture in the combustion chamber. The first part of the arc of perhaps only 1 microsecond duration ignites the mixture and the remainder of the spark contributes little or nothing. However, the practical condition is that the mixture may be wrong, or unevenly mixed, and it may be that the ignitable gas may not even have reached the plug electrodes at the time that the spark occurs. It is found that if the spark duration is made to last about 300 microseconds then the probability is that ignition will occur satisfactorily for all normal cylinder conditions.

2 A further desirable feature of the ideal spark in an engine is that the energy flow at the plug should reach a maximum in a very short period of time. This sudden rush of electrical energy will help to counteract plug fouling and may be regarded as a 'punch through' effect.

3 An ignition system which gives correct spark duration coupled with rapid rise of energy flow is the Capacitor Discharge Ignition system (CDI) (Fig. 8.22).

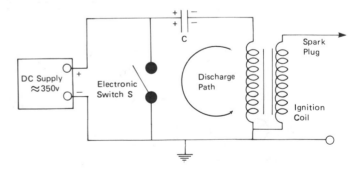

Fig. 8.22 Principle of capacitor discharge (Secs 10 and 11)

4 If we assume a dc supply is available to charge the capacitor C to about 350 volts with the polarity shown, then the working principle is that the energy of the capacitor is discharged rapidly through the coil primary at the precise time when a spark is required. The key to the problem is the switch S which, in practice, is a semiconductor device called a thyristor (or silicon controlled rectifier, SCR). The observant will be asking why the thyristor does not short circuit the dc supply — it does, but internal resistance of the supply limits the supply current

to negligible proportions compared with the capacitor discharge current.

5   Returning to the thyristor; this is a development of the transistor, being a 4-layer device having the property of blocking current flow until a control signal is applied to it. When the signal is applied to the thyristor it will allow current flow through it in much the same way as a switch.

6   The thyristor is, in fact, an electrical switch which may be switched on and off with only a very small current signal and may control very large currents to a load – in this case an ignition coil. Not only is the switch-on gate current very small compared with the main current flow through the thyristor, but it need last for only a brief period. Once the thyristor is switched on, no further gate current is required, and the only way of stopping the main current is to reduce the supply voltage below a certain level. After switching off, the thyristor behaves like an open circuited switch and is thus a highly efficient on-off device (Fig. 8.23).

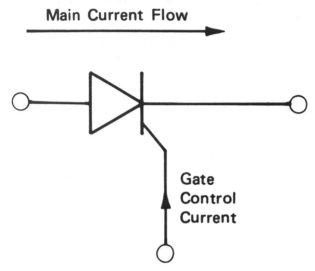

Fig. 8.23 Thyristor symbol – silicon controlled rectifier (SCR) (Sec 10)

7   The CDI system is thought to be superior to most inductive electronic ignition sets because the rise time of the spark voltage is some 10 times faster. The advantages of fast rise time are:

(a)   leakage of charge in the HT side become unimportant because there is insufficient time for current to drain away before the spark pulse is completed, ie the shunt (parallel) resistive paths due to carbon, damp, etc are of negligible effect.
(b)   the rapidity of the capacitor discharge 'punches' through accumulations on dirty sparking plugs and as a result service periods for plugs will be much longer.

There is, however, a view that rise times can be too quick in some cases to ignite lean mixtures reliably.

8   Triggering of the spark can be by a variety of means including contacts, magnetic, and Hall Effect. Even weak trigger pulses can set off the thyristor, however, and so contact breaker systems must include some provision to eliminate spurious operations due to 'contact bounce', an effect which will occur at higher speeds. Every contact breaker triggered system has to include a blocking device to stop bounce pulses.

9   Breakerless pulse triggering arrangements with CDI meet all present day ignition requirements, being able to produce 40 000 sparks per minute with no difficulty.

10   Battery-operated CDI systems have means of converting the vehicle 12 volts supply up to the 350 to 400 volts required to charge the ignition capacitor, but small engines used in motorcycles, mowers, chain saws, etc can produce this supply directly by a magneto-generator.

11   Magneto-generator CDI system

1   By way of illustration an example from present motorcycle technology shows how a simple CDI system can be made. Looking at Fig. 8.22 there is a need for a supply of 300 to 400 volts dc to charge the capacitor. In the lightweight motorcycle, one solution is to use a special winding on a flywheel magneto (Fig. 8.24).

2   As the magnets rotate, a pole passes the ignition charge-coil, which generates a current through the rectifier R_1. This charges up the

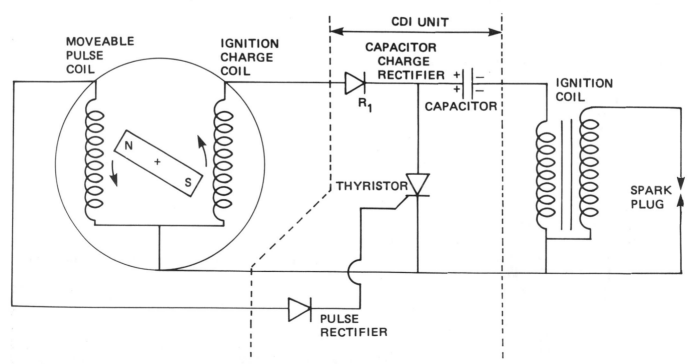

Fig. 8.24 Simplified CDI circuit using a flywheel generator (Sec 11)

capacitor to a voltage of, say, 350 volts; the magnet rotates further and generates a pulse of electrical energy in a 'pulse coil'. The coil is moveable round the stator so that timing may be adjusted. The energy pulse passes through the rectifier R_2 to the gate of the thyristor, whereupon the thyristor conducts and the stored electrical energy in the capacitor gives a high, short-duration current through the ignition coil primary. The secondary voltage produces a plug spark in which the 'rise time' is extremely short, a condition which will make the plug work well even though it may have an incorrect gap or be partly fouled. One may think of this sudden discharge as punching a way through the plug fouling salt deposits. Note the absence of a contact breaker in this form of CDI.

3   Hitachi, Femsa and Motoplat have marketed a range of flywheel electronic ignition systems which have certain common features; sparking will begin at speeds from 200 rpm to 500 rpm, depending on the make, and all depend on good electrical connections between the engine, the electronics boxes (usually housing the ignition coil and CDI components) and the generator.

4   Most units should produce a spark of 5 to 6 mm long in air and it is important that the engine is never stopped by pulling off the HT lead. Furthermore, the systems should not be run with sparks longer than 8 mm under test, or there may be trouble with internal insulation.

5   Where the ignition is for twin cylinders it is important to test with both plugs connected. Finally, mechanics should remember that CDI systems generate a lot of energy and are **DANGEROUS**.

12 Battery CDI system

1   In order to charge the capacitor to the operating voltage, typically 350V dc, a transistor oscillator is used, followed by a rectifier to convert the alternating voltage output of the oscillator back to dc. The whole unit is known as a converter (Fig. 8.25).

2   Such an oscillator is made up of one or more transistors connected to a small transformer which feeds back energy froom the transistor amplifier output to the input, so that, being self-feeding, oscillations of a sine wave form will be generated. The transformer which is used for passing back this energy also has a third winding which steps up the alternating voltage to be suitable for feeding the capacitor C after rectification (Fig. 8.26).

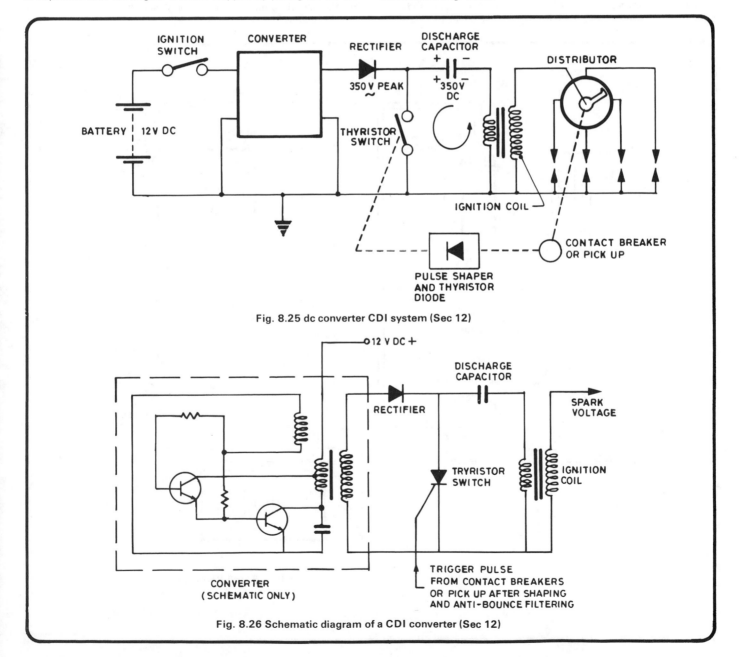

Fig. 8.25 dc converter CDI system (Sec 12)

Fig. 8.26 Schematic diagram of a CDI converter (Sec 12)

3   The frequency of the oscillations is determined mainly by inductance and capacitance values used in the oscillatory circuit. To use low frequencies would require large sizes of oscillator coil and capacitors, and high frequencies might give rise to radiation and conduction interference with radio and other equipment. In practice the operational frequency may be at the top end of the audio range and sometimes the oscillator can be heard.

4   As a general rule radio interference suppression is built into CDI units, and the use of additional capacitors in the ignition coil will result in damage to the CDI. *No radio interference capacitors should, therefore, be used with CDI.*

13 Mobelec CDI system

1   This is a kit using the existing distributor cam on which an adaptor is fitted as part of the triggering system. The triggerhead fits in Lucas four and six-cylinder distributors and can be made to fit others; the fitting is to the distributor baseplate after contact points and capacitor have been removed.

2   Fig. 8.27 shows the layout of the Mobelec CDI system, and from it the gap between the triggerhead sensor and cam lobe peak is seen.

It is important that contact does not occur between the sensor tip and the lobe, due to the sensitivity of the sensor tip.

3   In order to achieve rapid discharge through the ignition coil primary, a specially designed ignition coil is supplied. This will have low primary inductance, but with a higher turns ratio than a conventional coil. Such coils are not interchangeable.

14 Bosch BHKZ system CDI

1   This is an original equipment CDI system (Fig. 8.28) supplied to several manufacturers including Porsche and NSU. The contact breaker is retained in this case, but a special low inductance coil is supplied having a primary resistance of only 0.5 ohm.

2   Extremely rapid rise time is claimed for this CDI unit, having the advantages of clearing fouled plugs and achieving good damp starting performance because the spark is completed before leakage path current has time to be effective.

3   The manufacturers stress that no test connections of any sort must be applied to the low tension terminal of the ignition coil – even after ignition has been switched off.

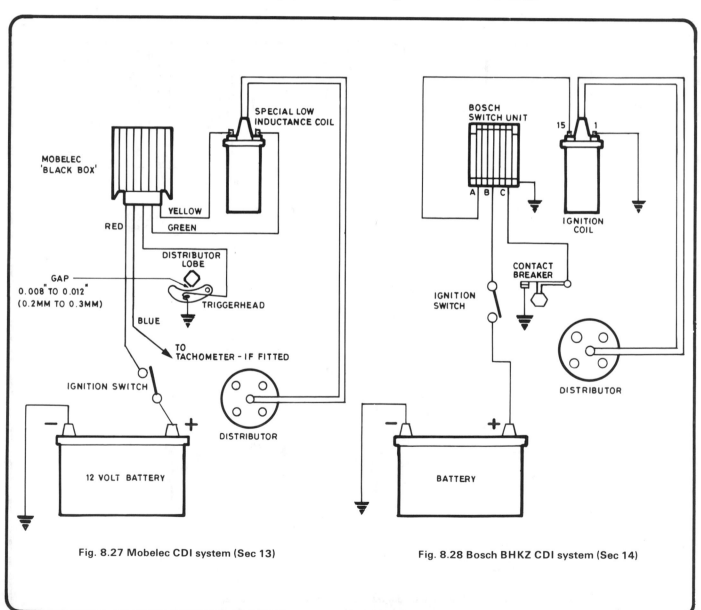

Fig. 8.27 Mobelec CDI system (Sec 13)   Fig. 8.28 Bosch BHKZ CDI system (Sec 14)

Chapter 9 Lighting

Contents

1 Lighting arrangements

1   In most countries the local regulations will specify that a motor vehicle must have two forward-facing lights, two red lights at the rear, two red reflectors at the rear, and the number plate at the rear should be illuminated. In France the forward-facing lights are coloured yellow, but in most other cases the light is white.

2   In the UK such obligatory front lamps must be fitted at the same height and, if the bulbs are over 7 watts, must be capable of being dipped to avoid dazzle to oncoming vehicle drivers. In the case of the modern four-headlamp system only two lamps need to be capable of being dipped, but a control must be arranged to switch off the other two under dipped conditions.

3   Headlamps must have bulbs of at least 30 watts power rating, both of a pair to be of the same size and light colour. In addition, a pair shall be mounted at the same height and set equidistant from the centre-line of the car.

4   Rear lights will have bulbs of 5 watts rating as a minimum, with similar requirements on the symmetry of installation. Usually the rear light has a lens built into the unit to give a red reflection as a safety precaution in the event of bulb failure.

5   Stop-lights are usually housed in the rear light units and each gives a red light of 21 watts rating.

6   At the front and rear, amber flashing lamps are mounted as turn indicators, and repeater flasher lamps are often mounted on the side of the front wings. Main flasher lamps are each of 21 watts rating.

7   Readers seeking a full treatment of lighting and other regulations relating to vehicles in Britain are referred to Kitchen's Road Transport Law (Butterworths).

8   Lamps are always connected in parallel across the battery supply so that the total current drawn is the sum of all the lamp currents when switched on. A typical arrangement is shown in Fig. 9.1, being part of the Vauxhall Chevette wiring diagram.

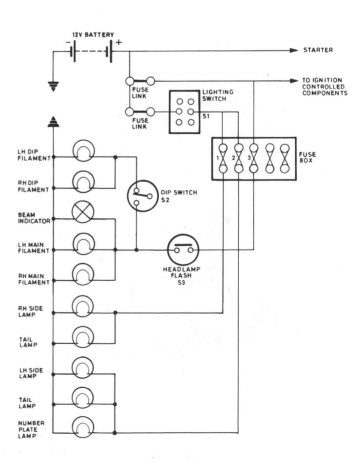

Fig. 9.1 A typical lighting circuit (Sec 1)

9   Main protection is given by fuse links, and lighting control by means of the double pole switch S1. Dipswitch (dim switch – US), S2, routes the supply to either the main beam filaments or the dip beam filaments. Provision is made for the driver to flash on the main beams by means of the spring-loaded switch S3.

10 Side and tail lamps are supplied through fuses 1 and 2, and it should be noted that double fusing will avoid both left and right-hand lamps being lost in the event of a circuit failure in one of them.

2   Bulbs

1   The filament of an automobile bulb is generally made of tungsten, and is heated by electric current from the vehicle to a temperature of about 2300°C.

2   Early bulbs had filaments working in a near vacuum, but many today are gas-filled. This gives greater light efficiency and since inert gases are used, eg argon, there is no reaction between the gas and the filament. Filaments are wound in the form of a tight spiral to give better efficiency, since there will be less heat loss due to convection in the gas filling.

3   Headlamp bulbs usually house two filaments, one for main beam and one for dipped (meeting) beam (see Figs. 9.2, 9.3 and 9.4). The two usual arrangements for the dipped beam filament are:

(a)   offset filament – in which the filament is set above and to one side of the focal point of the associated reflector.
(b)   shielded filament – here the dip filament is covered with a small shield which deflects the light to one side of the

reflector only. The shield has an effect on the main beam in that the centre of the parallel rays is missing. Also, on dip, only one half of the reflector is utilised and projects light downwards.

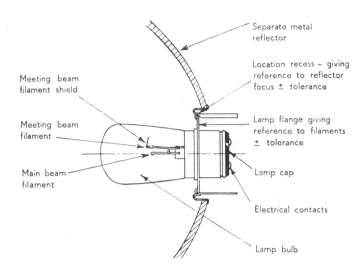

Fig. 9.2 Prefocus bulb located in the reflector (Sec 2)

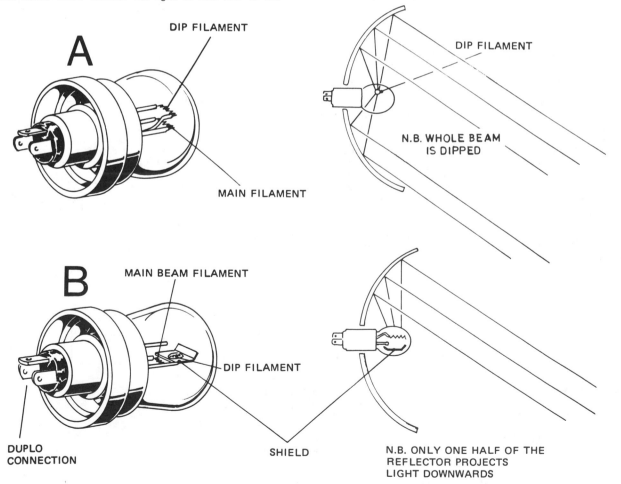

Fig. 9.3 Headlamp bulbs (Sec 2)

A   Offset dip filament   *B   Shield dip filament*

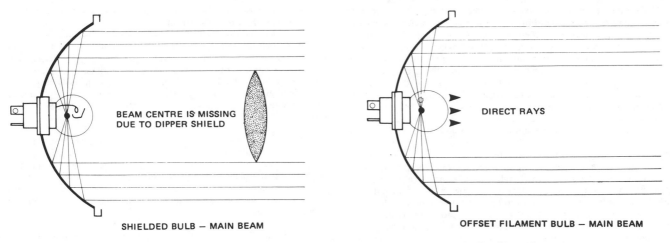

SHIELDED BULB — MAIN BEAM   OFFSET FILAMENT BULB — MAIN BEAM

Fig. 9.4 Main beam patterns for shielded and offset filament bulbs (Sec 2)

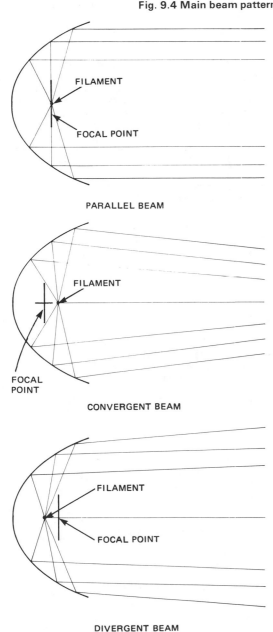

PARALLEL BEAM

CONVERGENT BEAM

DIVERGENT BEAM

Fig. 9.5 Filament location should be at the focal point of the reflector (Sec 3)

3 Disadavantages of a separate bulb and reflector

1   The makeup of the main and dipped beams is primarily dependent upon the filament position relative to the focal point of the reflector, and for many years road vehicles used the prefocus bulb in which the filaments were welded in place with precision.

2   Even the close tolerances to which this design could be made were too wide for proper beam control. To them should be added the tolerances between the lamp seating in the reflector and the focal point (Fig. 9.5). Additionally, about 20% of light from the filament is lost due to obscuration by the bulb and cap; also in service the evaporated tungsten from the filament settles on the upper surface of the bulb, and although the total light from the lamp is reduced by only 10% to 15% at halflife (about two years, say) the obscuration presented to a large section of the reflector is of serious consequence and the beam is disturbed (Fig. 9.6).

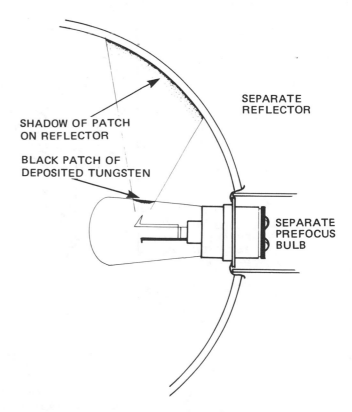

Fig. 9.6 Obscuration due to lamp blackening (Sec 3)

3   Finally, due to oxidation and the effects of dust and dirt, the reflector loses efficiency so that after four years service the beam intensity may be reduced to about 60% of the original value. Most of the troubles mentioned occur because in the design, the reflector and bulb were considered as separate entities. When combined into a single sealed beam unit a considerable improvement is obtained.

4   Service life and output of bulbs

1   Bosch give figures for the estimated life of vehicle bulbs based on an operating voltage of 13.5V under charging conditions, or 6.75V for a nominal 6 volt system. It is interesting that while household bulbs are estimated to have a life of only 1000 hours, headlamp bulbs have a life of only 100 hours, and small bulbs an estimated 200 hours. This applies to conventional plug-in filament bulbs, and not to halogen sealed beam units; the reason for the relatively low working life takes into account vibration and, in some vehicles, large differences may occur because of variations in type of service and springing/body construction.

Applied voltage (V)	11.48	12.15	12.83	13.5	14.18	14.85	15.2
Applied voltage (%)	85	90	95	100	105	110	120
Relative light output (%)	53	67	83	100	120	145	200
Relative life expectancy (%)	1000	440	210	100	50	28	6

This shows the importance of maintaining a steady system voltage, this being determined by the voltage regulator.

5   Tungsten-halogen type bulbs

1   In the last decade, a new form of bulb has found wide use and is now fitted as standard in many vehicles. The tungsten-halogen bulb goes under various other names, ie quartz-iodine, quartz-halogen or tungsten-iodine, but all are really the same thing, namely a bulb giving a much higher illumination and longer life than a conventional type. Several considerations determine the high efficiency, shape and life of tungsten-halogen lamps.

2   The normal wearing-out of a conventional filament bulb is due to the evaporation of tungsten from the filament surface (for a mental picture of evaporation think of steam coming from the surface of water). As the filament temperature is raised then evaporation increases rapidly and not only does the filament become thinner but the tungsten vapour also blackens the inside of the bulb and illumination decreases.

3   It is found that if one of a group of chemical elements known as halogens is added in precise quantity to the normal inert gas filling of a bulb, great improvements are possible in terms of life and illumination. (Halogens are elements that compound themselves to form salts)

4   When tungsten vapour leaves the filament surface it works its way towards the glass envelope. Between the filament and the glass there exists a temperature gradient; when the tungsten atoms reach the zone of about 1450°C the halogen combines with tungsten to form tungsten halides (Fig 9.7) and these diffuse back to the region of the filament without the glass-blackening effect taking place.

5   As the filament is approached the temperature rises again towards 2000°C (the surface temperature) and the tungsten halides break up

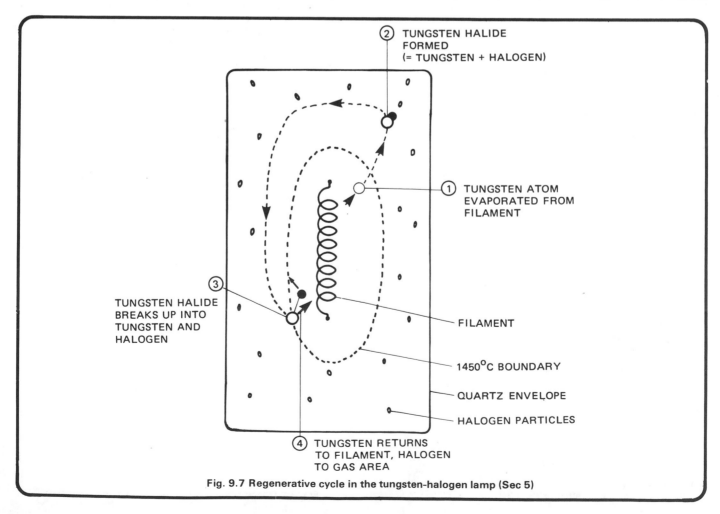

Fig. 9.7 Regenerative cycle in the tungsten-halogen lamp (Sec 5)

again into tungsten and halogen at the 1450° boundary. The halogen goes back to the gaseous area whilst the tungsten atoms return to the filament, although some surround the filament and tend to reduce evaporation. Because evaporation is thus reduced it is possible to have a hotter filament and so there is a corresponding increase in illumination; also because the filament is being constantly replenished with tungsten atoms it has a very long life and, as stated, because the tungsten atoms do not reach the glass there is no blackening of the inner surface.

6   One final point — the usual halogen is presently iodine, and the tungsten-halogen formed with it is gaseous only above 250°C. For this reason the bulb must be small so as to stay hot, and so not only are the bulbs much smaller in volume but also they are made of quartz to withstand the temperature. Because quartz is stronger than normal bulb glass, designers increase the gas pressure which in turn reduces the amount of evaporation.

7   The increase in gas pressure and the halogen cycle of returning tungsten to the filament produces a lamp of high luminous power which is almost constant throughout the life of the lamp.

8   Two disadvantages should be noted:

(i)   the bulb should not be handled because the salt from body perspiration will stain the quartz: should the bulb be accidentally touched it may be wiped carefully, whilst cold, with methylated spirit and allowed to dry before use again.

(ii)   life is reduced rapidly if the quartz bulb and the gas filling are not maintained at the correct working temperature. A low supply voltage results not only in a drop in luminous power but also a serious fall in service life.

6   Sealed beam light units

1   In earlier days of motoring, headlamp bulbs, front glass and reflectors were separate components. Ensuring that the bulb filament was exactly at the focal point of the reflector was chancy and the light intensity fell off quite quickly due to dirt and dust on the reflector surface.

2   Later came the light unit — the front glass and aluminized reflector were combined in a single assembly. The bulb was of the prefocus type giving a good focus location, but still dust and dirt would eventually find a way on to the reflector surface.

3   Current designs are of the sealed beam type. Fig. 9.8 shows a cross-section through a lamp which is totally sealed and has two accurately located filaments, but no separate bulb.

4   Lenses are cast into the front glass of headlamps to produce correct lighting patterns on the road for both main and dip beams. Fig. 9.9 shows optical means of obtaining beam spread and vertical deflection.

5   For a single central filament the beam emerging from a parabolic reflector is approximately tubular. However, this gives no side-spread to the kerb or road centre-line and the upper part of the beam would be largely wasted illuminating the sky.

6   The refracting prisms (ie light bending prisms) shown in Fig. 9.9 can give any desired configuration of the beam because the borosilicate glass is thick (3 to 5 mm) and hence is ideal for moulding into prisms during manufacture. Reflector surfaces in sealed beam

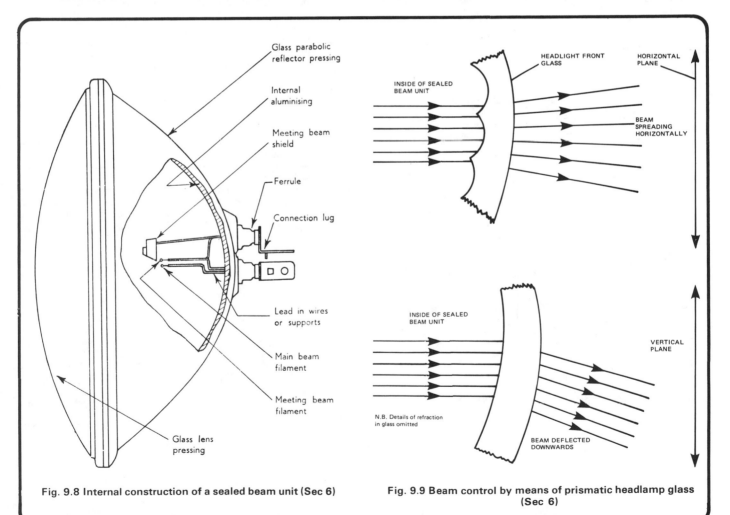

Fig. 9.8 Internal construction of a sealed beam unit (Sec 6)

Fig. 9.9 Beam control by means of prismatic headlamp glass (Sec 6)

units are evaporated aluminium and are protected throughout the life of the lamp by an inert gas filling.

7 The unit suffers little from tungsten evaporation because it is spread over such a large reflector area, unlike the case of the bulb. Light is maintained at greater than 98% of the initial figure throughout the estimated five year life compared with 58% for a separate light bulb headlamp.

8 Tungsten-halogen lamp designs were soon incorporated into sealed beam units, originally with one filament only, but in 1966 a means was found of incorporating both main and dip beam filaments.

7 European headlamps

1 An asymmetric bulb is used in European headlamps and is characterised by the flat shield which deflects light down and sideways when on dip. Deflection to left or right is obtained by having two possible locations of the bulb in the reflector neck.

2 One result of this form of light dipping is the rather sharp cut-off of the beam with possible trouble if the vehicle has a large rear load, causing the beam to rise. In addition, little light is available to the driver to see beyond this cut-off line.

8 The four headlamp system

1 To design an efficient lamp for both main and dip beams is difficult and at best is a compromise. In order to maximise light output and aiming efficiency, a system of four headlights is now in common use (Fig. 9.10).

Fig. 9.10 The four headlamp system (Sec 8)

2 The lamps are mounted either in a line horizontally, or in two pairs one above the other; they may be rather smaller (146 mm diameter) than those used in two headlamp vehicles where the diameter is typically 170 mm.

3 The inner headlamps each contain only one filament and these two provide the greater part of the main beam. The outer headlamps each have a filament located precisely at the focal point and will give a good dip beam without compromise. In addition the outer lamps have a second filament which is slightly off the focal point and below the dip filament. These are on when the main beam is required.

4 Thus, when main beam is on, the inner lamps are operating together with the lower filaments of the outer lamps. On dip, the outer lamps work alone with the inner lamps switched off.

9 Beam setting

1 Setting of headlamp beams is ideally carried out with a beam setting meter which is available commercially. It is possible to check the distribution of light from the headlamps separately with the vehicle on a flat road at night, the main requirements being:

(a) no dazzle at the statutory height of 1.068 metres (3.5 ft) at a distance of 7.6 metres (25 ft) in front of the lamp when on dip
(b) adequate illumination to the front of the vehicle and to the road nearside consistent with (a)
(c) main beam to be straight in front of the vehicle and to give optimum penetration and road surface illumination

2 An ideal diagram showing the desired settings for a two headlamp vehicle is given in Fig. 9.11. The vehicle should be level and with the usual driver and passenger loading. One headlamp is covered or disconnected, the other lamp being adjusted by means of adjusting screws built into the reflector frame and which screw into steel pads on the inner frame, this being firmly attached to the car body.

10 Double bulb headlamps

1 Marchal produce a highly efficient headlamp containing two bulbs (either conventional or tunsten-halogen) each having a separate reflector. The result is that both bulbs can be focused with accuracy. Both round and rectangular versions are available and can also give white or yellow light.

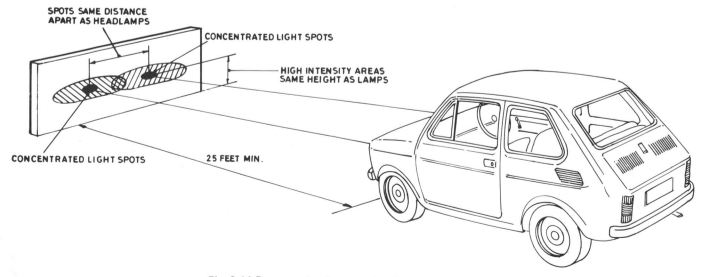

Fig. 9.11 Beam setting for a two headlamp system (Sec 9)

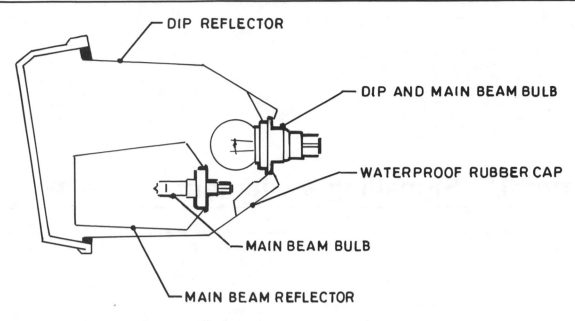

DIP REFLECTOR

DIP AND MAIN BEAM BULB

WATERPROOF RUBBER CAP

MAIN BEAM BULB

MAIN BEAM REFLECTOR

Fig. 9.12 A double bulb twin reflector headlamp (Sec 10)

11 Rear lamps

1   Two red reflectors and two red lamps are required for a car and are specified to meet the SI 1971 standard No 694. It is usual to incorporate bulbs not exceeding 6 watts.

2   Tail and stop-lamps are usually combined in the same fitting of moulded glass or plastic; 21 watts being standard for stop-lamps.

3   Red rear foglamps of 21 watts with an area not exceeding 100 sq cm result in a high intensity warning; such lamps are now popular but can give rise to distressing dazzle if used under normal night driving conditions.

4   Reversing lights are often built into the rear light fitting and are usually operated by a gearbox switch which closes automatically on engaging reverse gear; 21 watt bulbs are generally used. It is illegal to have the reversing light on whilst driving forwards as is possible if the switch is manually operated. Consequently separate manual switching is permissible only if there is a warning device which is visible (or audible) to the driver.

Chapter 10 Signalling equipment

Contents

1 Direction indicators

1   The flasher unit makes and breaks the current flow to the front and rear amber indicator lamps at a frequency of between 60 and 120 flashes per minute. Different countries legislate for a variety of wattages, but in the UK 21 watt lamps are used.

2   Most modern flasher units have only two terminals (Fig. 10.1) which are connected to the flasher lamps to either left or right,

according to the direction of the indicator switch. An obsolescent type has three terminals, the third being connected to a dashboard warning lamp, Fig. 10.2.

3   Note that the two-terminal flasher set has the warning lamp connected across the indicator switch. The current passed by the lamp is too small to operate the 'off' pair of indicator lamps, but the latter provide an earth path for the warning light.

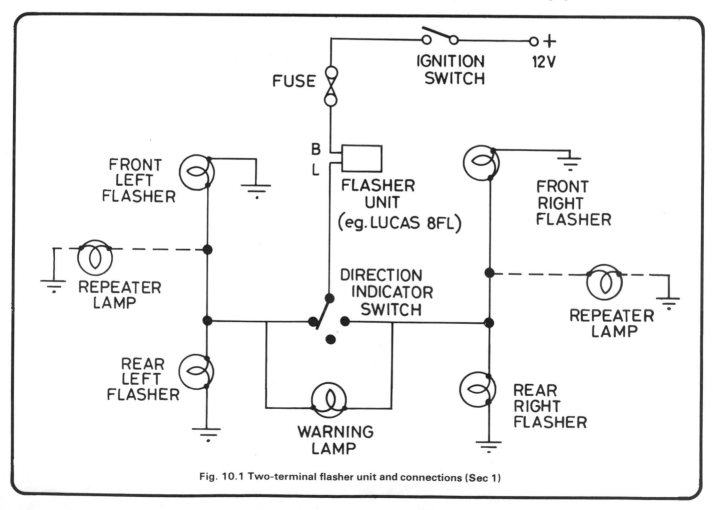

Fig. 10.1 Two-terminal flasher unit and connections (Sec 1)

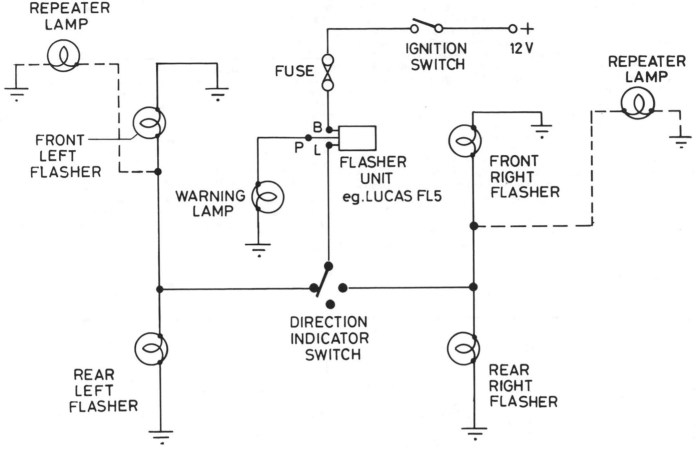

Fig. 10.2 Three-terminal flasher unit and connections (Sec 1)

2 Flasher relays

Vane type

1 Most common is the two-terminal 'clicker' type of flasher unit, having now almost entirely replaced the older hot-wire three-terminal model.

2 Fig. 10.3 shows its construction. A vane or diaphragm of spring steel is normally in the 'bent' position shown and held in place by a taut metal resistive ribbon. When the flashers are switched on the resistance ribbon, which carries the lamp current, expands and allows the spring steel diaphragm to snap straight with an audible click. This also opens the main contacts, cutting off the heater current, the heater cools and at a particular point the spring steel bends suddenly back to its original shape with another click.

3 This flasher has only two terminals. If one bulb fails the click action usually stops, the pilot light and remaining lamp stay on but do not flash.

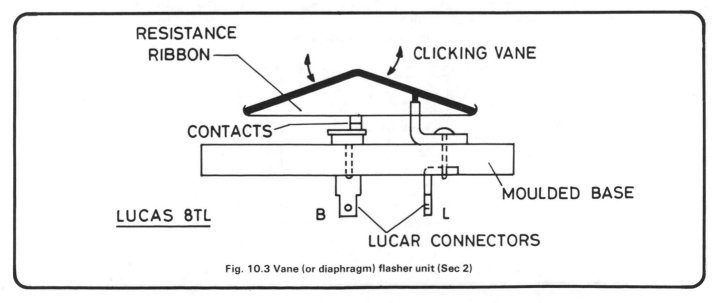

Fig. 10.3 Vane (or diaphragm) flasher unit (Sec 2)

Hot-wire type

4 The hot-wire flasher is still found on some vehicles, and is illustrated in Fig. 10.4. When the direction indicator switch is on current flows through the heater wire and the coil. As the heater wire expands, the main armature moves under spring tension to close the main contacts. During heating the limiting resistance prevents lighting of the indicator lamps, but when the contacts close this resistance is short-circuited and connects the indicator lamps straight on to the 12 volt supply via the coil.

5 The higher current in the coil then magnetises the iron core and attracts the armature so that the contacts close firmly. This magnetism also attracts the secondary armature so as to close the pilot light contacts.

6 As the short circuited heater wire cools, it contracts and the contacts open. The magnetism drops to a low value and the main and secondary armatures return to original positions.

7 If an indicator lamp fails the current drawn is lower and the flashing frequency will rise. Additionally it may be that the secondary armature will not close at all, so no dashboard warning light will come on.

Electronic types

8 Several manufacturers have employed the integrated circuit (as a chip) to produce an electronically operated flasher unit. Lucas and Hella offer units which give a stable flashing rate irrespective of supply voltage, and independent of directional or hazard signalling.

3 Capacitor type flasher relay

1 This type depends upon the charge and discharge of a capacitor and uses an iron cored solenoid with an attracted armature. In this case the solenoid has two windings, one of which has about 4000 turns of thin wire and the other 400 turns of thicker wire wound over the first. Before looking at the circuit, however, it is important to understand that the magnetic flux produced in an iron core depends on:

(a) the current in amperes
(b) the number of turns of wire

ie magnetic flux is proportional to ampere x turns, usually just written ampere-turns. Thus the magnetic flux (or field) produced by 1000 turns of wire with 0.1 amperes (= 100 ampere-turns) is the same as 100 turns of wire with a current of 1.0 ampere (also = 100 ampere-turns).

2 One last point; if the direction of the currents spiralling round the coils (Fig. 10.5) are in the **same** direction, the magnetic fluxes **ADD**, but if in the **opposite** direction they **CANCEL**.

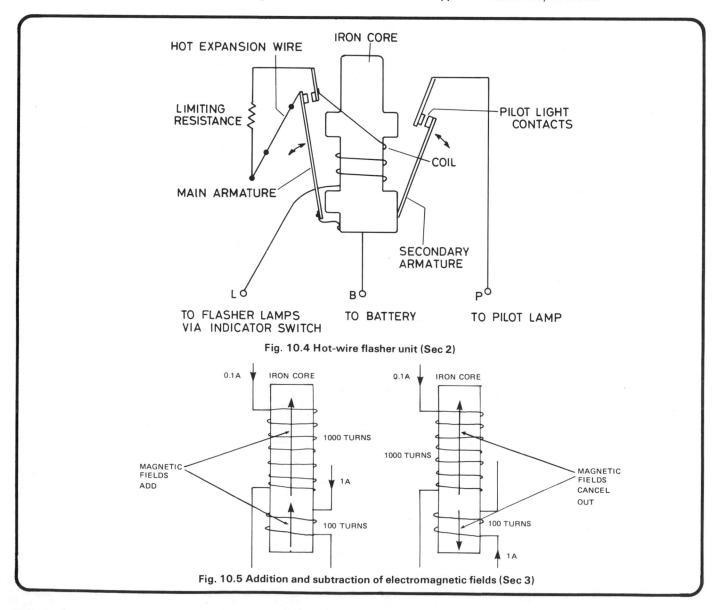

Fig. 10.4 Hot-wire flasher unit (Sec 2)

Fig. 10.5 Addition and subtraction of electromagnetic fields (Sec 3)

3   The unit is remarkably small (Fig. 10.6) and has two flying leads, the third terminal being the enclosing can which is earthed to the vehicle frame.

4   Referring to the whole circuit, Fig. 10.7 shows the relay solenoid with two windings, the current coil A and the voltage coil B. Usually the term current coil means that it produces magnetic flux by a relatively high current flowing through a small number of turns, in this case about 400, as stated; in contrast a voltage coil is one which still actually produces flux by the current flowing in it, but has a high number of turns, and the attachment of the word 'voltage' simply means that it is connected across the supply voltage, whereas a current coil is connected in series and bears the main circuit current.

5   When the flasher switch is in the central position and the ignition is switched on, current flows down through voltage coil B to charge the capacitor. The + and - signs indicate the polarity of charge and the capacitor will remain charged to 12 volts ready for use when the flasher switch is operated.

6   When the flasher switch is moved to the left, current now flows from the battery, through the current coil A to the left-hand flasher lamps. Note that the pilot lamp will light because it is effectively earthed by the two right-hand flasher lamps, but they will not light because the small current flowing through the pilot lamp is insufficient.

7   The current through coil A attracts the armature to the core and the contacts open – current abruptly ceases. As the contacts open, however, the capacitor (which is charged up like a miniature battery) now discharges and its current flowing up through coils A and B will produce enough flux to keep the armature attracted and enough current to light the flasher lamps until the capacitor is discharged. At this point the magnetism disappears and the contacts close again. The time taken for this depends upon the capacitance (in microfarads) and the effective resistance to earth comprising coils B and A and the resistance of the two flasher lamps in parallel.

8   When the contacts close current flows from the battery downwards through coil A and upwards through coil B, thus cancelling the flux and allowing the contacts to stay closed and the flasher lamps to stay alight, now with battery current. The charging current through coil B does not last long, however, as the capacitor charges up. When it drops to a low figure the contacts open again due to the single magnetic flux produced by current in coil A.

9   When the contacts open, current in coil A and the lamp is cut off and the sequence repeats. The same happens if the flasher switch is operated to the right.

10 Working features of the capacitor-type relay flasher relay include:

(a)   The capacitor is always ready charged and the contacts closed so that signal lamp flash is given as the flasher switch is operated, with no delay.
(b)   The flashing rate is fairly accurate and does not vary greatly with changes in battery voltage.
(c)   The relay unit is rugged and not susceptible to vibration from the engine.
(d)   Failure of any of the indicator lamps causes the relay to stop and also the pilot lamp ceases flashing. Thus the driver has definite warning.

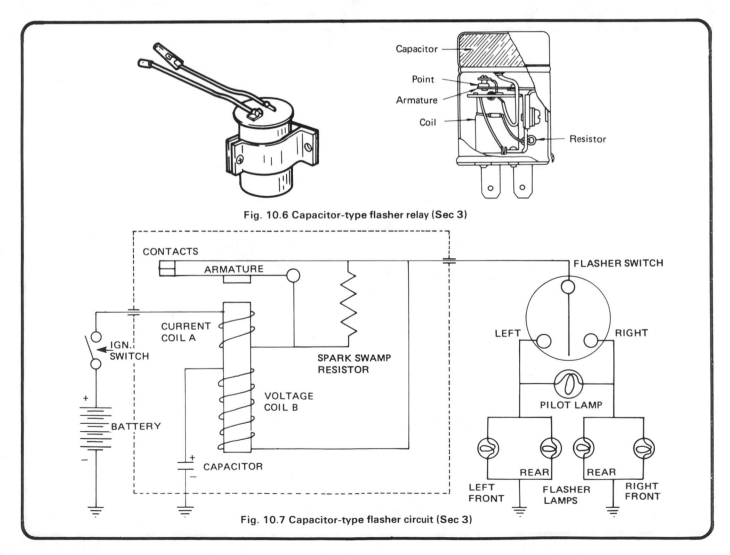

Fig. 10.6 Capacitor-type flasher relay (Sec 3)

Fig. 10.7 Capacitor-type flasher circuit (Sec 3)

4   Bi-metal type flasher relay

1   The principle of the bi-metal strip is based on the fact that metals expand at different rates when heated. If two such dissimilar metal strips are riveted or spot welded together then a rise in temperature will cause the bi-metal strip to bend (Fig. 10.8). Such movement is used in many ways to switch current or operate hydraulic valves in various branches of engineering, and in this case is used to switch flasher lamps on and off at a pre-determined rate.

2   The physical layout of Fig. 10.9 shows two bi-metal strips clamped at the lower ends and with a contact on each, normally apart, at the upper tips. Of the two coils, wound in heating resistance wire, the voltage coil has more turns and so higher resistance than the current coil which has few turns and carries the full flasher lamp current.

3   Fig. 10.10 shows the circuit with the direction switch in the neutral position. Note that the contacts are apart and that the voltage coil connects straight onto the battery. When the switch is operated, the voltage coil carries a current through the flasher lamp, which does not, however, light because of the high resistance of the voltage coil. However, enough current flows to bend the left bi-metal strip towards the right (Fig. 10.11).

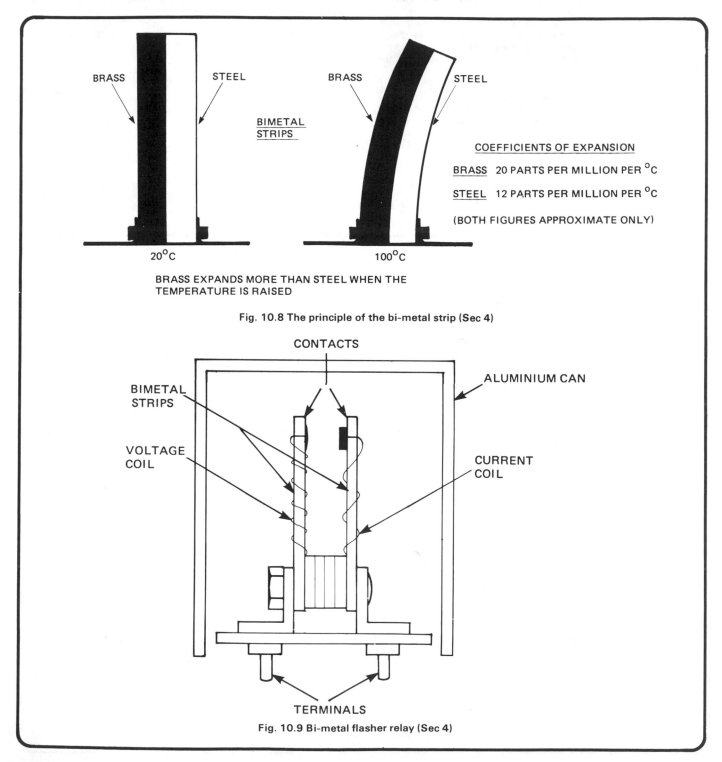

Fig. 10.8 The principle of the bi-metal strip (Sec 4)

Fig. 10.9 Bi-metal flasher relay (Sec 4)

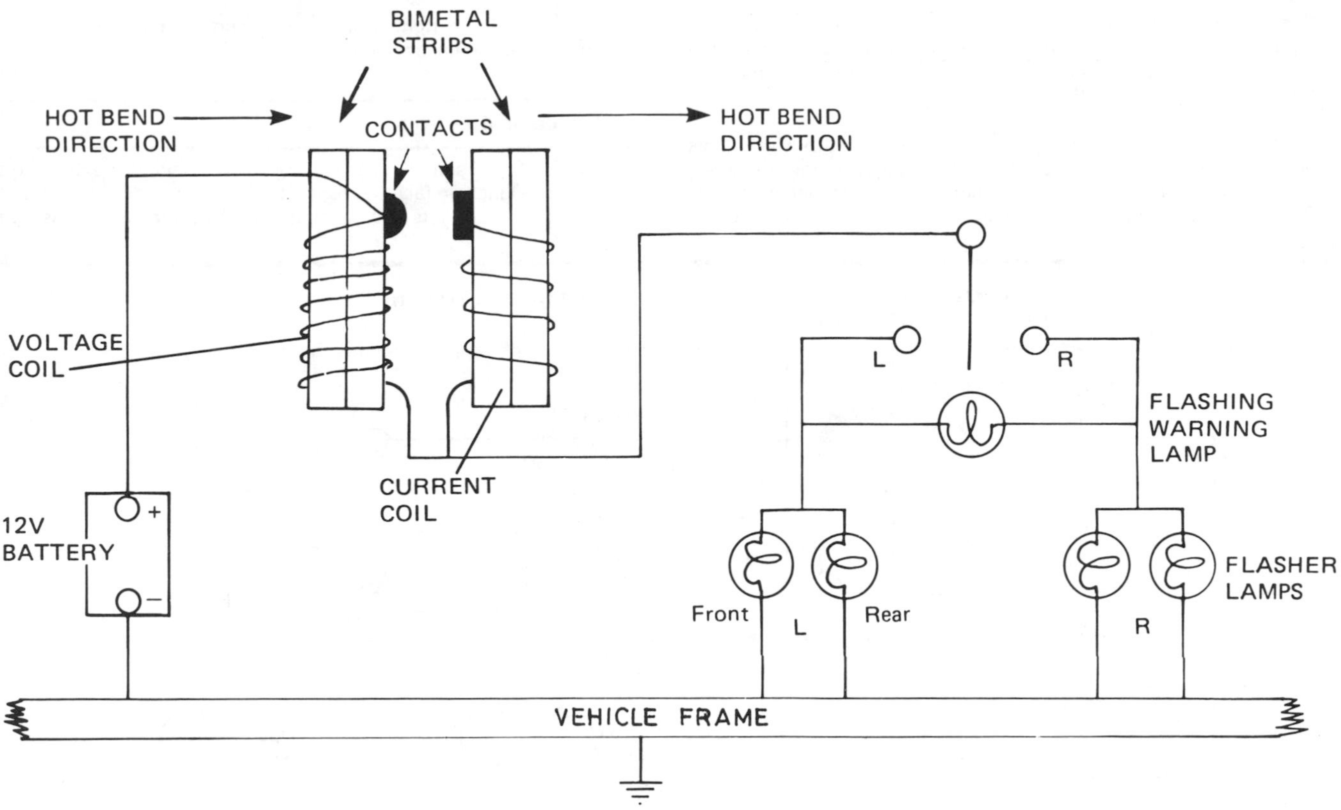

BIMETAL STRIPS

HOT BEND DIRECTION

CONTACTS

HOT BEND DIRECTION

VOLTAGE COIL

CURRENT COIL

12V BATTERY

FLASHING WARNING LAMP

L

R

Front   Rear

L

R

FLASHER LAMPS

VEHICLE FRAME

Fig. 10.10 Bi-metal flasher circuit (Sec 4)

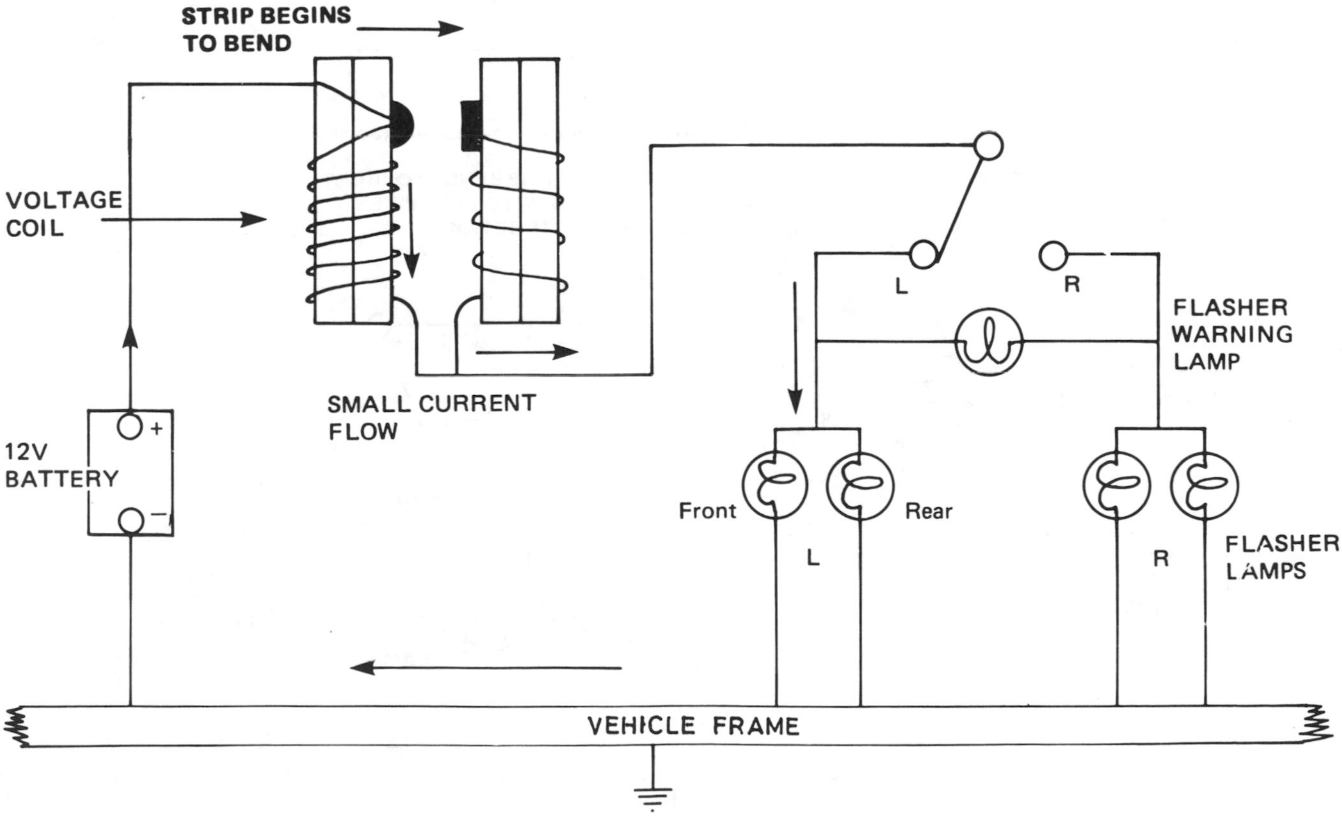

STRIP BEGINS TO BEND

VOLTAGE COIL

SMALL CURRENT FLOW

12V BATTERY

FLASHER WARNING LAMP

L

R

Front   Rear

L

R

FLASHER LAMPS

VEHICLE FRAME

Fig. 10.11 Switch closed – left-hand strip begins to bend (Sec 4)

4   At the point when the contacts close, the lamp current increases sharply because the voltage coil is now almost shorted out by the current coil which, remember, is of much lower resistance; the left-hand lamps light (Fig. 10.12).

5   The voltage coil no longer heats the left bi-metal strip which cools and begins to straighten. Simultaneously the right bi-metal strip bends to the right and so the contacts part rapidly and the flasher lamp goes out. The sequence continues as the left strip begins to bend to the right again and the right strip now having no current coil heating returns to the upright position (Fig. 10.13).

5   Trailers and caravans

1   The towbar assembly usually includes provision for extending the lighting and signalling facilities to the trailer. Requirements are that the number plate, rear lights and flashing indicators should work as for the

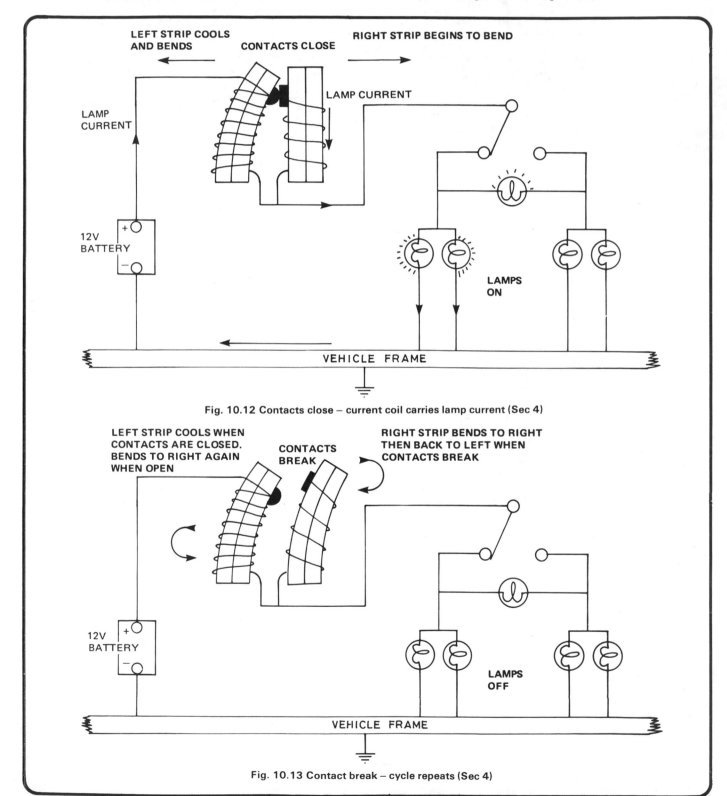

Fig. 10.12 Contacts close – current coil carries lamp current (Sec 4)

Fig. 10.13 Contact break – cycle repeats (Sec 4)

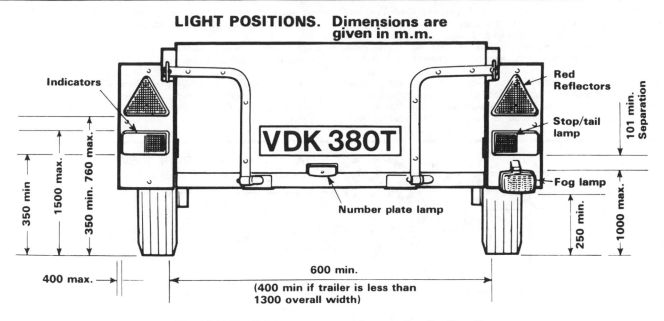

Fig. 10.14 The lighting arrangement for a small trailer (Sec 5)

parent vehicle. The recommended layout for a small goods trailer to conform to UK regulations is shown in Fig. 10.14.

2   Current to existing rear lights and indicators of a vehicle is conveyed via fuses and switches by wiring running along one or both sides of the boot (trunk). Each of the feed wires needs to be brought out to a standard socket into which the trailer electrics plug can be fitted. Some vehicle manufacturers anticipate the need for wiring extensions and use multi-connectors, but it is possible to tap off wires by the use of snap-on self-stripping connectors which obviate the need for soldering or crimping of terminations. The action of squeezing down the self-stripping connector cuts through some strands of cable, but trouble does not seem to arise. Connections to the parent vehicle socket are shown in Fig. 10.16.

Fig. 10.15 Snap-on self-stripping connector (Sec 5)

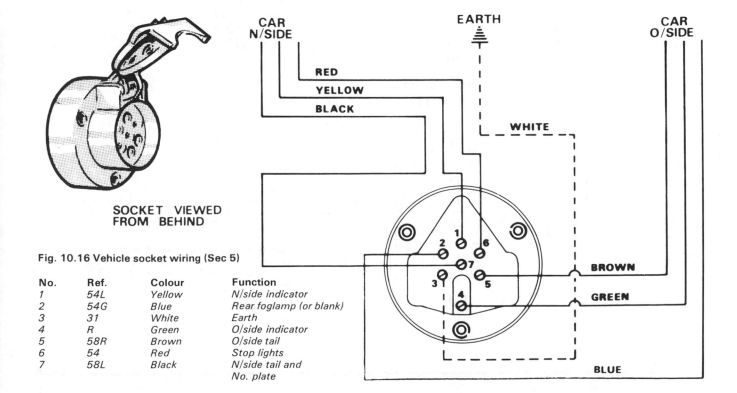

Fig. 10.16 Vehicle socket wiring (Sec 5)

No.	Ref.	Colour	Function
1	54L	Yellow	N/side indicator
2	54G	Blue	Rear foglamp (or blank)
3	31	White	Earth
4	R	Green	O/side indicator
5	58R	Brown	O/side tail
6	54	Red	Stop lights
7	58L	Black	N/side tail and No. plate

3   Trailer plug connections are shown in Fig. 10.17. Sufficient extra cable should be used to allow for the effect of sharp turns by the vehicle and trailer. Earthing via the ball and socket should not be relied upon, since the grease and continual movement would give lamp flickering. It is essential to use the earth connections to terminal 3.

4   The standard flasher unit will not function correctly with a trailer load, since the rate of flashing depends upon the current loadings per vehicle side. Lucas, Hella and Bosch supply heavy duty flasher units designed to work with the additional trailer electrical loading. Note

that an extra warning light, visible to the driver, must be fitted to indicate that the trailer flashers are working properly (Fig. 10.18).

5   An alternative is to employ a relay mounted near the rear of the towing vehicle, typical being the 'Transflash' unit, Fig. 10.19.

6   Readers wishing to pursue the subject of trailer lighting and other regulations are referred to the Trailer Manual available from Mechanical Services Ltd, Belmont Road, Lancashire, UK. Telephone Bolton 58434.

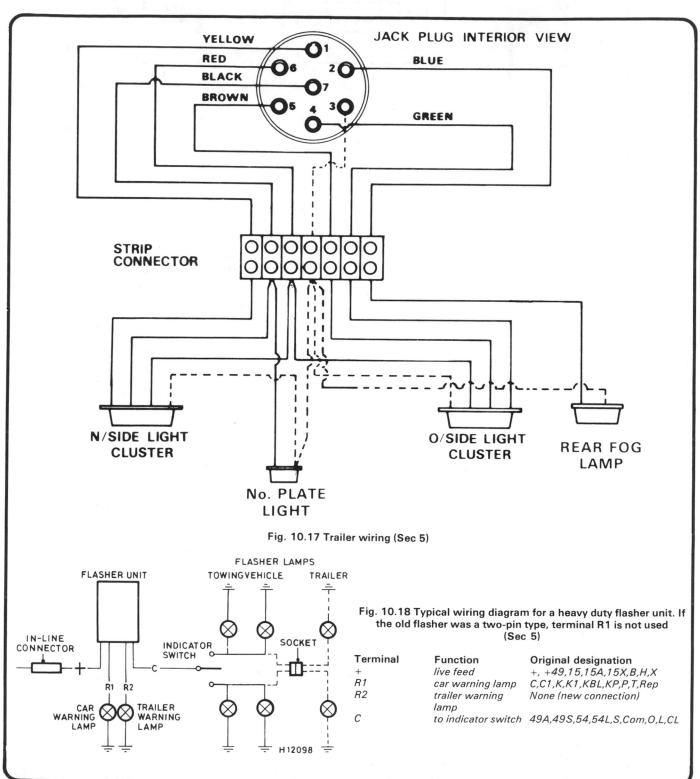

Fig. 10.17 Trailer wiring (Sec 5)

Fig. 10.18 Typical wiring diagram for a heavy duty flasher unit. If the old flasher was a two-pin type, terminal R1 is not used (Sec 5)

Terminal	Function	Original designation
+	live feed	+, +49,15,15A,15X,B,H,X
R1	car warning lamp	C,C1,K,K1,KBL,KP,P,T,Rep
R2	trailer warning lamp	None (new connection)
C	to indicator switch	49A,49S,54,54L,S,Com,O,L,CL

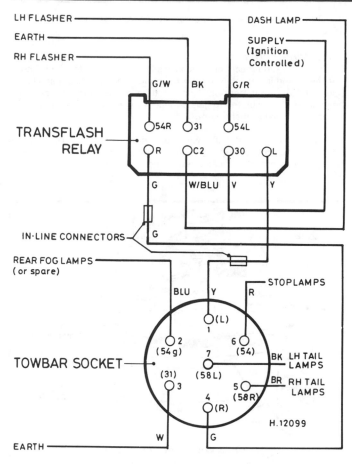

Fig. 10.19 Wiring diagram for connecting a standard seven-pin towbar socket (type 12N) to 'Transflash' relay and car wiring (Sec 5)

Socket is viewed from the wire entry side

BK	Black	R	Red
BLU	Blue	V	Violet
BR	Brown	W	White
G	Green	Y	Yellow

6 Horns

1 A horn is a legal requirement on motor vehicles in most countries. In general three types of horn may be met:

  (a) high frequency horns
  (b) wind-tone horns
  (c) air horns

2 With the exception of the air horn, vibratory motion of a diaphragm to create sound waves is produced by a form of electric bell mechanism, in which an iron armature is attracted to the iron core of a solenoid working off the vehicle 12 volt supply. The movement of the armature breaks open the contacts so current and magnetic attraction cease; the armature returns to its original position under spring tension and the cycle repeats (Fig. 10.20). This principle of operation applies to both high frequency (HF) and wind-tone horns.

The high frequency (HF) horn
3 The HF horn has been in existence since the 1920's with little change (Fig. 10.21). A vibratory circuit drives a thin diaphragm to give a low frequency note of about 300 vibrations per second (300 hertz). A second vibrator called a tone disc is also driven, but will give rise to a high frequency sound of about 2000 vibrations per second (2000 hertz). The low notes have the property of distance penetration while the high notes can be heard above traffic roar.

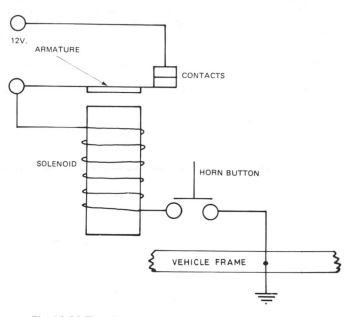

Fig. 10.20 The electromagnetic vibrator principle (Sec 6)

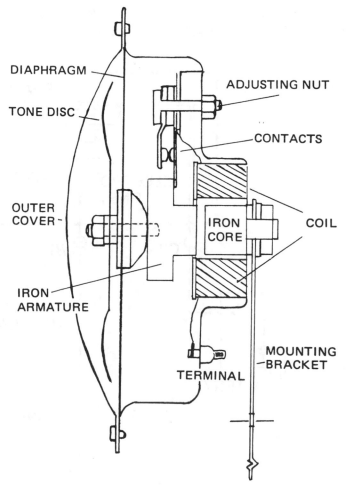

Fig. 10.21 High frequency horn (Sec 6)

4   When the horn button is pressed, the coil energises the electromagnet, the armature is attracted to it and hits it (see Fig. 10.21). The movement breaks the contacts, the armature releases and the contacts again close – a repeating process for so long as the horn button is pressed.

5   The mechanical shock of the armature/magnet impact makes the tone disc ring. The tone disc vibrates at an overtone frequency with the diaphragm, so that the two tones produce a resultant sound which has penetration without being too harsh.

6   It is possible to connect two or more horns in parallel to produce a greater sound level and to mix tones for a pleasing effect.

7   Adjustment is usually effected at the rear of the HF horn (Fig. 10.22).

Wind-tone horns

8   The operating mechanism is basically the same as for the HF horn, but the sound is passed into a horn wound in a spiral like a snail shell (Fig. 10.23). The dimensions and the flare of the horn trumpet have been carefully calculated to give a mellow tone in the same manner as an orchestral wind instrument.

9   To obtain a good note, wind-tone horns are often operated in pairs. The current load is high, and so a relay may be used to keep heavy cables out of the car interior and minimize voltage drop (Fig. 10.24).

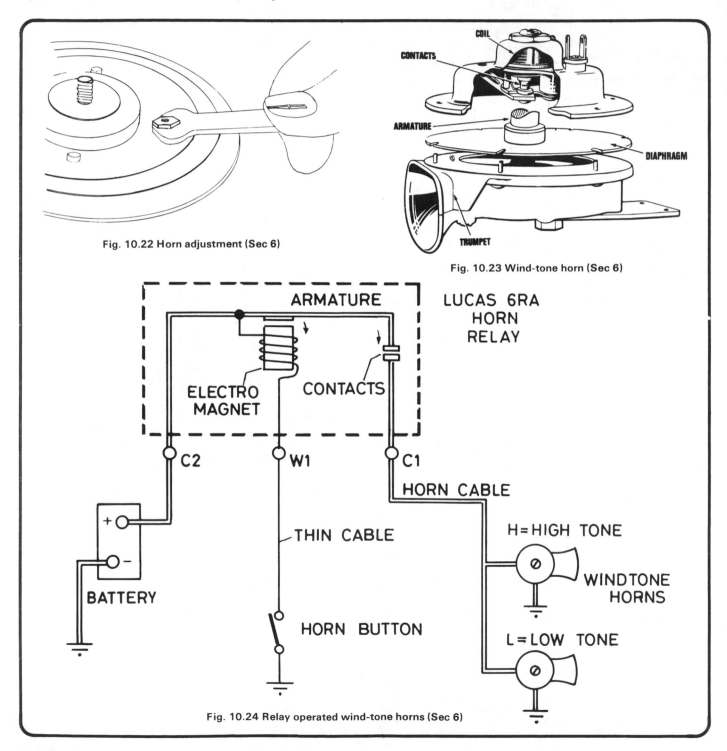

Fig. 10.22 Horn adjustment (Sec 6)

Fig. 10.23 Wind-tone horn (Sec 6)

Fig. 10.24 Relay operated wind-tone horns (Sec 6)

Air horns

10 Air horns are simple in principle. Air or gas is pumped under pressure to a chamber which is closed at one end by a diaphragm; the diaphragm pressure against the annular end of the horn prevents the escape of the air or gas.

11 When the pressure is high enough the diaphragm is pushed to the left, Fig. 10.25, and air/gas is released into the horn. The pressure drops and the diaphragm closes — the cycle repeats. If the pressure is supplied by a pump then the horn button controls the pump motor either directly or by a relay.

12 Pumps can be simple in just supplying pressure to the horn, but can also be led out to various timed horns in sequence by a rotary valve in order to play a tune. Such equipment is on sale, but it should be pointed out that the use of a horn combination producing more than one note is illegal in the UK.

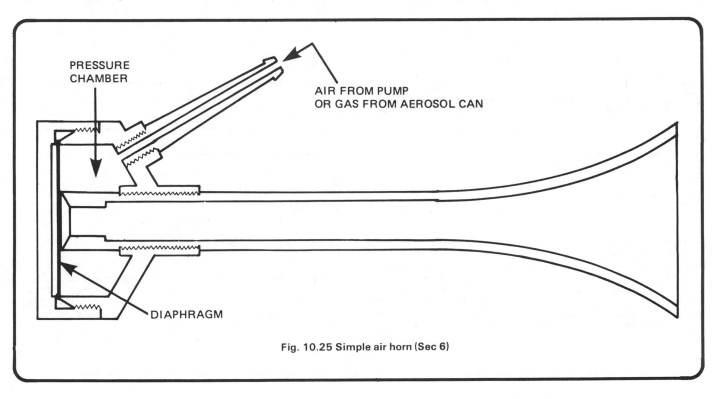

PRESSURE CHAMBER

AIR FROM PUMP OR GAS FROM AEROSOL CAN

DIAPHRAGM

Fig. 10.25 Simple air horn (Sec 6)

Chapter 11 Screen wipers

Contents

1 Wiper motors

1   Wiper moters are mainly of the permanent magnet field type (Fig. 11.1) with earlier vehicles using a shunt wound field form (Fig. 11.2). Permanent magnets are now well developed and are of the high-energy ceramic type set in a cylindrical yoke of laminated steel. The advantages of permanent magnet motors are that the cost of a wound field is eliminated with the gain of lower input current requirement and greater reliability.

2   Permanent magnet motors may be single-speed or two-speed. Single-speed motors have a pair of commutator brushes 180° apart, but the two-speed motor has three brushes, the additional brush being set at a small angle from one of the others and identifiable by being narrower at the top than the other two. The supply voltage is switched to this third brush to obtain higher speed wiping (Fig. 11.3).

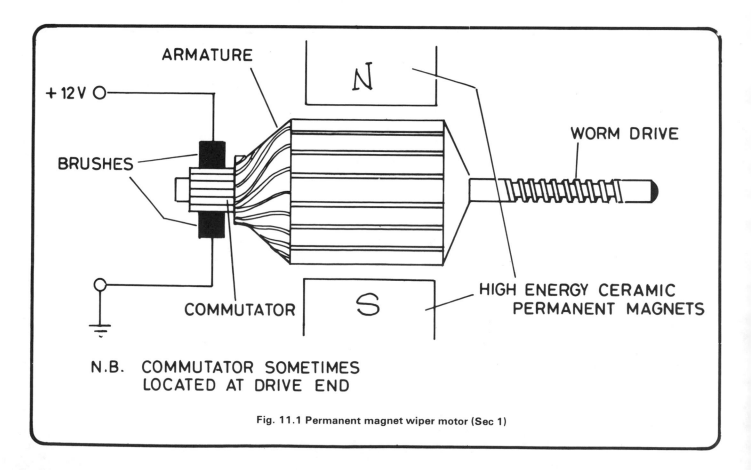

Fig. 11.1 Permanent magnet wiper motor (Sec 1)

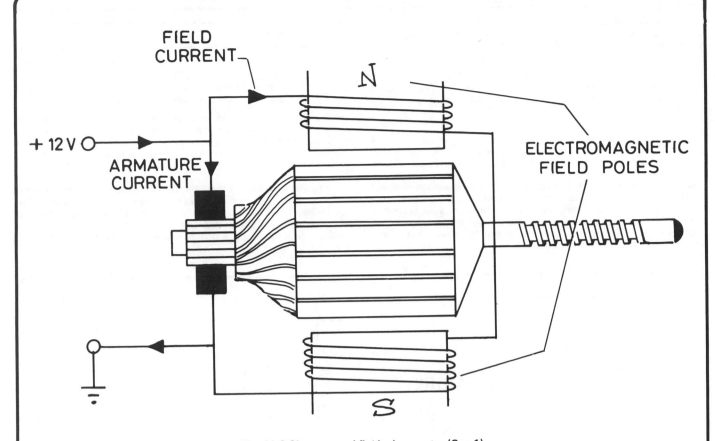

Fig. 11.2 Shunt wound field wiper motor (Sec 1)

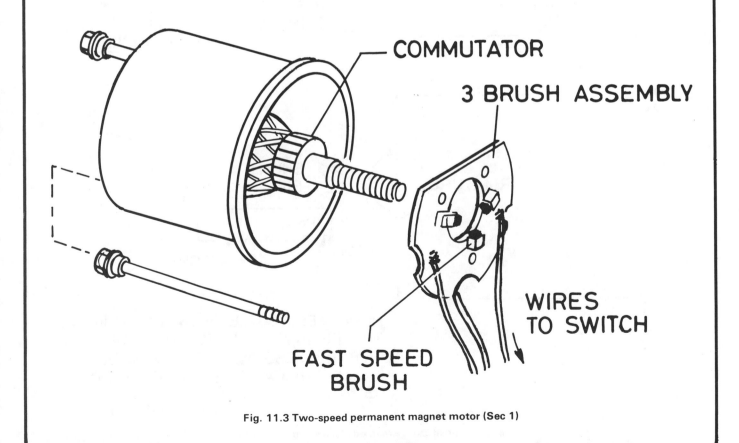

Fig. 11.3 Two-speed permanent magnet motor (Sec 1)

3   Two-speed operation of a shunt wound motor is possible by the inclusion of a switchable series resistor in the shunt, or by including a resistor in the main supply lead, Fig. 11.4.

4   Normally the wiper motor is connected directly to an auxiliary output fuse so that it becomes live when the ignition is on. Special arrangements are made to bring the wiper blades to a park position on switching off.

5   Protection of the wiper motor is desirable under conditions of overload which might occur, for example if the wiper blades are frozen to the windscreen. Since the motor would be prevented from rotating there would be no back emf, and consequently a heavy current would overheat the armature. A thermal switch working on the bi-metal principle is sometimes found connected in series with the supply to the wiper motor. Under sustained overload the bi-metal strip heats and bends, thus opening a pair of contacts, switching off the motor. As the switch cools, the supply is reconnected; the motor is switched on and off cyclically until the fault cause is cleared.

2   Wiper drives

1   Three types of drive from the motor to the wiper blades are in use:

   (a)   The link system (Fig. 11.5)
   (b)   The rack drive (Fig. 11.6)
   (c)   The crank and linkage method (Fig. 11.7)

In all cases the motor drive operates through a worm gear to develop the necessary torque at a suitable speed for the windscreen, ie about 50 wipes per minute for single-speed motors and 50 and 70 wipes per minute for two-speed motors. Here a 'wipe' is defined as one go-and-return movement, or one complete cycle.

2   The link systems are more efficient than the rack drive, but suffer the disadvantage of being difficult to house under the dashboard. The less efficient rack drive is probably used more frequently because of this problem. On some installations the rack is fairly flexible, but others have the rack running in a rigid tube preformed to the shape required for a particular vehicle.

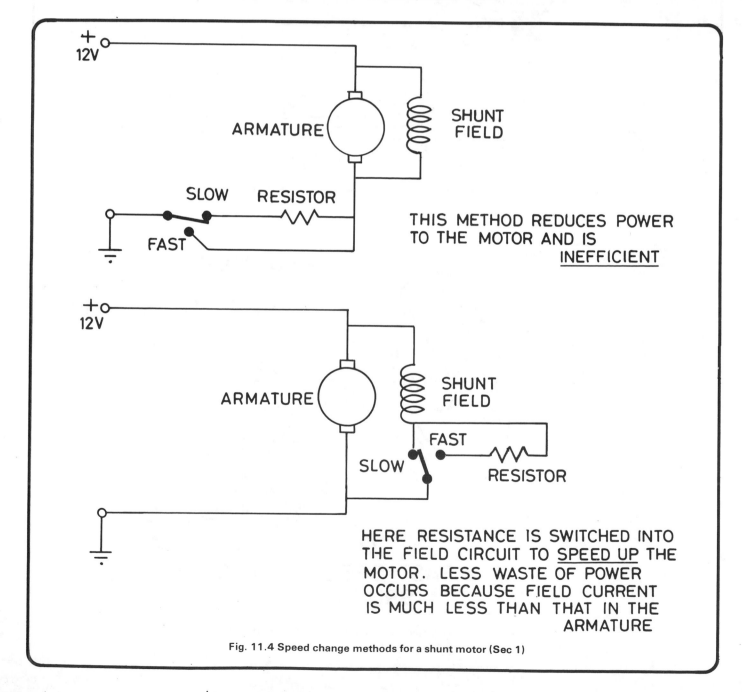

Fig. 11.4 Speed change methods for a shunt motor (Sec 1)

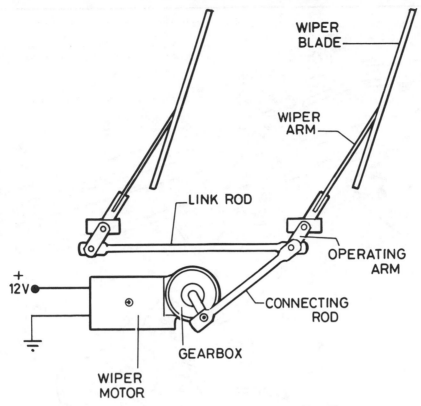

WIPER
BLADE

WIPER
ARM

LINK ROD

OPERATING
ARM

+
12V

CONNECTING
ROD

GEARBOX

WIPER
MOTOR

Fig. 11.5 Link system for wiper drive (Sec 2)

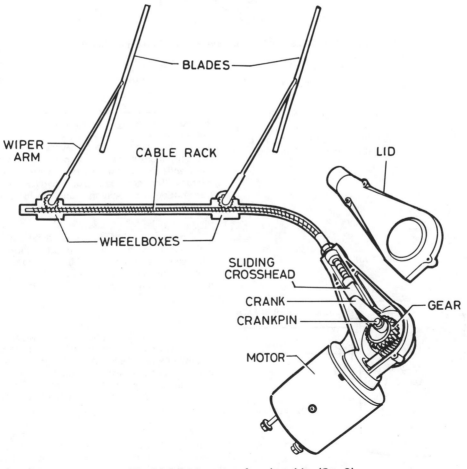

BLADES

WIPER
ARM

CABLE RACK

LID

WHEELBOXES

SLIDING
CROSSHEAD

CRANK

CRANKPIN

GEAR

MOTOR

Fig. 11.6 Rack system for wiper drive (Sec 2)

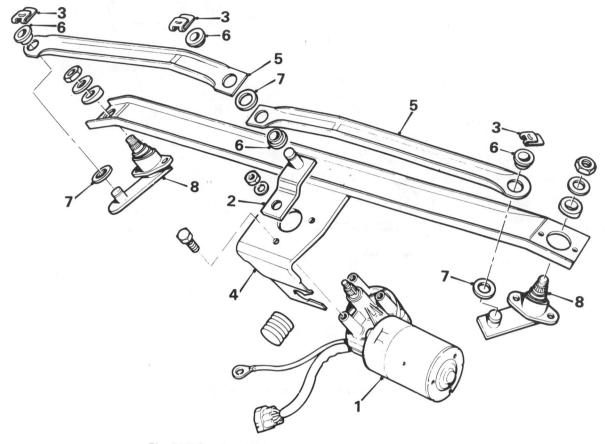

Fig. 11.7 Crank and linkage system for wiper drive (Sec 2)

1 *Wiper motor*	3 *Clip*	5 *Link*	7 *Washer*
2 *Crank lever*	4 *Mounting bracket*	6 *Bush*	8 *Pivot housing*

3   Reference to Fig. 11.6 will show the rack passing through small gearboxes (or wheelboxes) after the take-off for the wiper arms. The rack is pushed and pulled alternately by the action of the pin, connecting rod and main gearwheel. (Detail is given in Fig. 11.8).

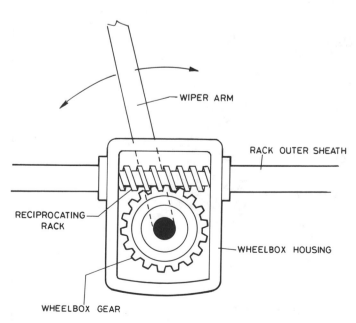

Fig. 11.8 Wiper wheelbox (Sec 2)

3   Park switching – permanent magnet motors

1   A wiper motor used on several vehicles is the Lucas 14W which is a permanent magnet two-speed motor with flexible rack drive. The shaft ends in a worm gear driving a moulded gearwheel in a diecast gearbox. The gear carries a pin over which a connecting rod fits, transmitting reciprocating motion to the wiper rack.

2   On the underside of the gearwheel is a cam operating a two-stage limit switch. Reference to Fig. 11.9 shows this special limit switch with contacts A and B, which are so arranged that the cam first switches the blade away from contact A, followed by a small gap when the blade is not in contact with A or B and finally makes contact with B.

3   When the driver switches off the wiper, contacts 2 and 5 are made and current will flow to the armature because the switch blade is still in contact with terminal A. As the gearwheel proceeds the cam breaks the switch contact with A resulting in the motor slowing down. At this stage there is no supply to the motor. The motor will have sufficient momentum to run on until the blade touches contact B.

4   This short circuits the armature to earth; the motor armature, rotating under its magnetic poles, is acting as a generator and when the armature is shorted out a current will flow requiring power to flow out of the armature. This can only come from the rotational energy of the armature, which thus abruptly decelerates to standstill. This is the principle of regenerative braking.

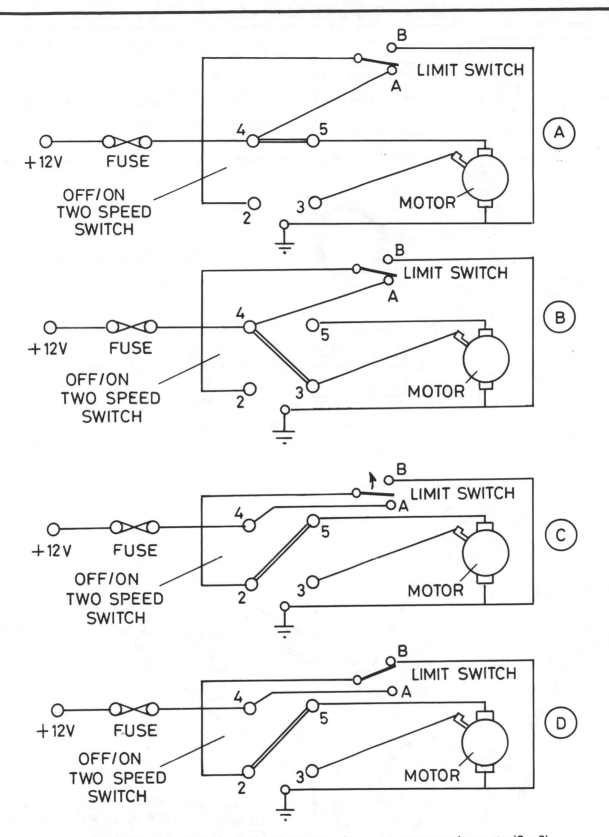

Fig. 11.9 Park and on/off switching of a two-speed permanent magnet wiper motor (Sec 3)

A   Normal speed wipe
B   High-speed wipe
C   Off — switch blade
    has left terminal A,
    but not reached
    terminal B

D   Off — switch blade
    contacts terminal B.
    The motor brakes
    regeneratively

4 Park switching – wound field motors

1   Self-parking of wiper blades is due to a park switch housed in the wiper gearbox. The cover has an insulated disc on its underside, and set in this disc is a brass circular track with a small cut-out so that it does not form a complete circle.

2   A spring finger is attached to the rotating crankpin and the finger runs in contact with the brass track (Fig. 11.10). When the driver switches the wiper switch off the motor continues to drive until:

(a) the rotating finger comes to the gap in the brass track and switches the motor off
(b) the wiper blades have reached the park position

The insulated disc is adjustable (Fig. 11.11) to make condition (a) coincide with (b).

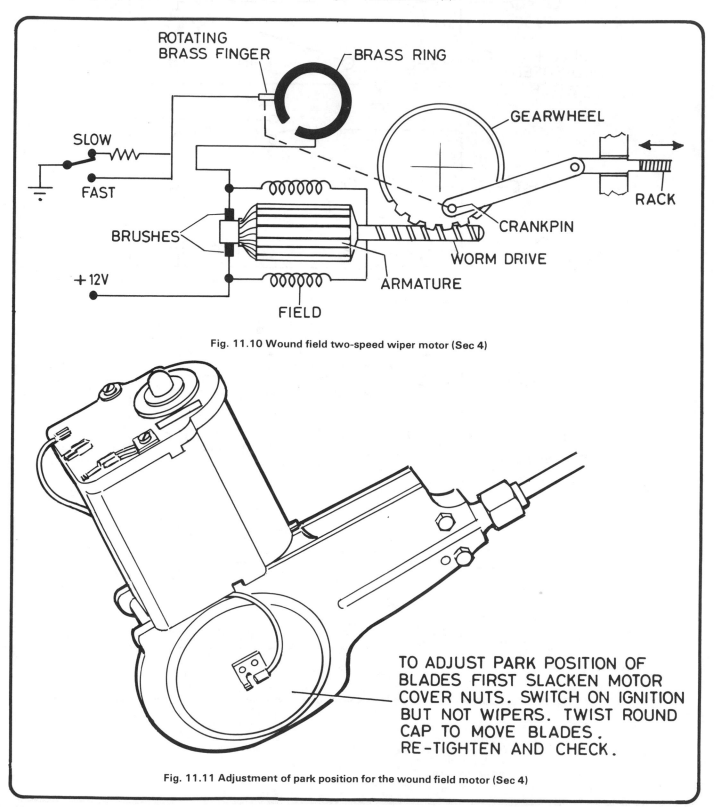

Fig. 11.10 Wound field two-speed wiper motor (Sec 4)

TO ADJUST PARK POSITION OF BLADES FIRST SLACKEN MOTOR COVER NUTS. SWITCH ON IGNITION BUT NOT WIPERS. TWIST ROUND CAP TO MOVE BLADES. RE-TIGHTEN AND CHECK.

Fig. 11.11 Adjustment of park position for the wound field motor (Sec 4)

5 Intermittent wiping

1   The requirement for intermittent wipe is most felt on those days when the rain has ceased but roads are still wet. Nearby traffic throws up dirty specks which do not call for continuous wiper action. Under these circumstances an occasional wipe of the screen is required.

2   A wound field wiper motor is capable of being single-wipe operated by a spring-loaded toggle switch. The driver presses and releases the switch, the motor starts and is switched off by the automatic park switch at the end of the cycle.

3   Permanent magnet motors will not work with this type of switch because the park switch will have a short circuit across the armature in the rest position. Manual pulse switching is possible, but at the expense of more complex connections.

4   Electronic intermittent wipe devices are available as accessories, and as original equipment. Most aftermarket devices have a combined control knob which switches the device on/off and also determines the time interval between wipes; on original equipment the 'intermittent wipe' is one position on the control switch, this being usually a stalk type on the steering column. Typically delay periods can be 2 to 30 seconds, this being selected by the driver to suit conditions.

6 Wiper service

1   A number of wiper motors are sealed and are not intended for repair in the event of trouble. It may be possible to take such motors apart, but unfortunately dealers will not stock any spares, although it may be possible to replace brushes by filing down a set intended for other equipment. Most Lucas models are capable of being serviced, however.

2   A most common fault with wipers is that of worn brushes, which should typically be about 5 mm long. The high speed brush should not be worn so that the narrow section has disappeared (Fig. 11.12).

3   Permanent magnet motor brush sets are available mounted on a plastic board (Fig. 11.3), and for the wound field motor brushes are set in two holders linked by a pressure spring (Fig. 11.13).

4   **Armatures** are not easily repaired, and if inspection shows signs of blackening, or the commutator has worn through (it is too thin to lathe-skim) then a replacement armature will be required. Stripping down requires care and the procedure varies according to make, but in general look out for the parking switch wires which can be jammed inside the motor during disassembly. Mark the correct position of the parking switch in order that it can be reassembled correctly, and check that there is armature endfloat of about 0.25 mm (0.01 inch). Endfloat can be adjusted on some models by shim washers, or by an adjuster screw which should be locked by a nut and/or a thread-locking compound.

5   **Gearboxes** can be checked for obvious stripped gears. Check that the packing grease is actually around the gear; after a period of operating the gear cuts a hole in the grease which then surrounds but does not touch the gear.

6   If a main gearwheel has to be renewed ensure that the correct one is purchased, since the angle of wipe depends on the location of the crankpin hole. A number on the wheel gives the angle of wipe, eg 130°.

7   It is important to replace the washers associated with the gearwheel exactly as they were, especially the crinkled washer underneath the gear. Ideally the special grease recommended by the manufacturers should be used.

8   **Motors failing to switch off** is not an uncommon fault, and is often due to a faulty parking switch or possibly the parking switch/motor wire shorting to earth. Sometimes a motor will switch off under heavy load conditions, eg with a dry screen, low battery voltage or the vehicle on tickover speed (when the dynamo does not charge), but refuses to switch off perhaps when running fast on a slippery screen. It is worth trying an adjustment of the parking switch before condemning it, however.

9   **Slow or standstill operation** of the blades can be due to a jammed rack or, in the case of a linkage mechanism, a linkage member dropping off. In the latter case a free rod flailing about has been known to go right through the bodywork.

10 To check the rack, remove the gearbox cover and disconnect the rack from the gear-drive. Then push and pull the rack to see if the wipers move; if the rack operates the wipers only a moderate force (about 6 lbf) should be needed. If the system is stiff the rack should be pulled out (remove the blades first) and greased with high melting

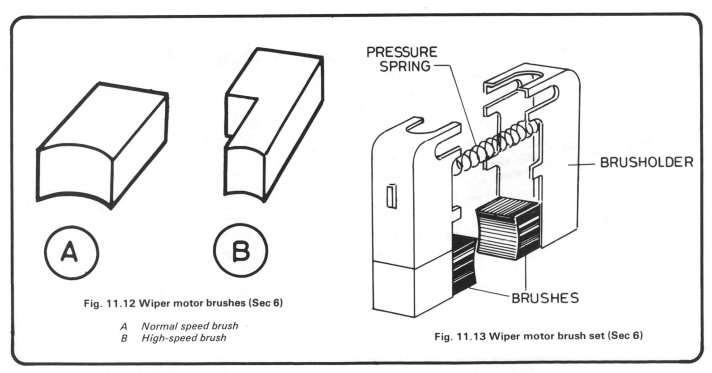

Fig. 11.12 Wiper motor brushes (Sec 6)

A   *Normal speed brush*
B   *High-speed brush*

Fig. 11.13 Wiper motor brush set (Sec 6)

point (HMP) grease. An occasional spot of glycerine (not oil) on the shaft where it emerges from the body is beneficial.

11 **A worn rack and pinion** can result in slack movement of the wiper arms causing the blades to hit the screen trim at the bottom end of travel or even to fail to work completely, although the motor will be heard operating fast. The rack and the pinion in a wiper wheelbox (ie behind the blade) operate over a fixed and limited range, and it is possible to defer the day for complete renewal by turning the pinion through a half turn and by turning over the rack. This way both will engage on unworn sections.

12 To do this, first remove the wiper arms and blades. In the wiper gearbox remove the circlip holding the connecting rod to the crankpin located in the main gear. Lift off the connecting rod and, after pulling the rack back far enough to clear both wheelboxes, that is when no longer engaging the pinions, turn the rack over 180° and refit after turning the wiper spindles by 180° each also. Since pulling back the rack will rotate the wiper spindles by several turns, make alignment marks for the starting point of the gear engagement with the rack.

13 If the gears in the wheel boxes are too far worn, then replacements are available, the boxes being fixed by the nut behind the wiper arm.

7 Wiper blades

1 The deterioration of blades is gradual and it is only when replacements are fitted that the fall-off in performance can be appreciated. Clues to the need for replacement are streaking marks, showing that the thin wipe edge has been cut and is ragged, and also areas of the screen which are missed altogether.

2 It is recommended that blades are changed annually, and the choice is between complete blade units or refills. Before opting for the cheaper refill it is worth checking to see if the remainder of the blade is worth using again. Pins and fixings in the blades can become badly worn, giving rise to sloppy action on the screen, which can ultimately result in the metal parts coming into contact with the glass and

causing scratches. When replacement rubbers are bought, it is as well to buy them with the metal backing strips, since these have a significant effect in keeping the rubber in contact with the glass. Check that the blades are of the same type, fitting and length as those being replaced (Figs. 11.14 and 11.15).

3 Springs built into the wiper arms will weaken in time and replacement is advisable if there is any suspicion of tension loss. The designers place regard on these often forgotten items for, if the tension is too great, the rubber drag is too much for the motor, but if too weak the blades will lift off the screen, especially in windy conditions.

4 Wiper judder is very annoying and can be tracked down to several causes, but most probably is due to the lack of parallelism of the wiper arm with the screen, resulting in the blade being pulled one way but pushed the other way. To check, remove the blades and look at the arm end; this should be parallel with the glass surface at mid-wipe position. It is worth trying a judicial bending of the arm to achieve this condition.

8 Windscreen washers

1 Many vehicles now have electrically driven pumps for the production of screen wash jets. The motors are 12 volt permanent magnet types driving a centrifugal water pump, and may be mounted on top of the water container or located separately.

2 The pump is self-priming and has an inlet tube filter. It is designed to work over a wide temperature range of the order of 80°C down to −20°C, assuming that the water is protected by a suitable antifreeze.

3 Little can be done to service these units and replacement is necessary in the event of failure. The performance is typically such that the current loading is 2.8 amperes at 13.5 volts, when the pump will deliver 1.3 pints per minute at a pressure of 10 lbf per square inch.

4 Screen wash motors are sometimes connected to intermittent wipe switches so that a single jet of water coincides with the intermittent wipe.

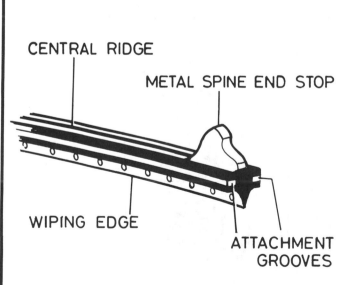

Fig. 11.14 Shape of wiper rubber (Sec 7)

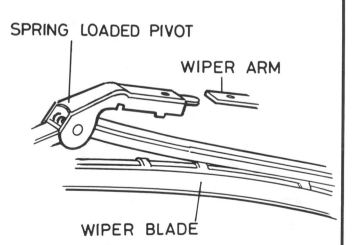

Fig. 11.15 Bayonet-type wiper arm fixing (Sec 7)

Chapter 12 Radio interference suppression

Contents

1 Interference

1   Interference to radio, television and communication equipment may result from apparatus in which changes or interruption to current flow occur. Motor vehicle equipment includes a number of interference-generating items, in particular the ignition system, starter and dynamo commutators, rectifiers, switches, wiper motors, voltage regulators and electric petrol pumps.

2   In early days of radio, transmitters worked by high voltage sparks, so it is hardly surprising that the ignition system of an automobile gives rise to radiation – in this case unwanted, and likely to cause interference to nearby television sets, and the vehicle's own receiving equipment, if any. Fig. 12.1 shows the equivalent of an ignition system in which two spark gaps (at the distributor rotor and the plugs) are associated with the coil and HT lead inductances and the stray capacitance of coil, leads and the plugs.

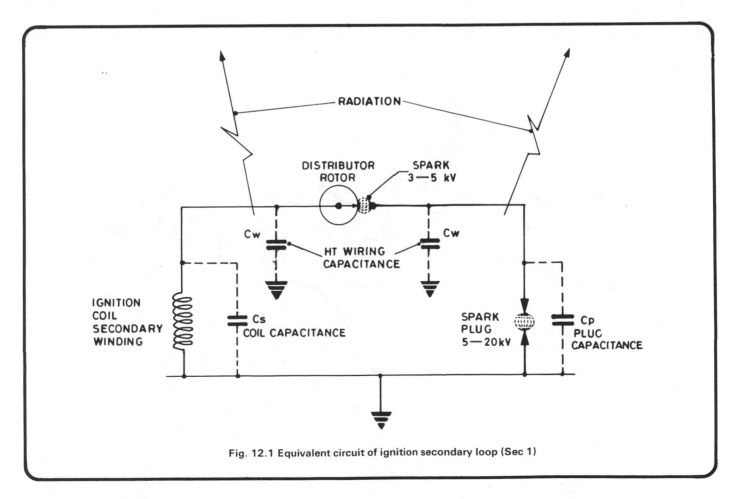

Fig. 12.1 Equivalent circuit of ignition secondary loop (Sec 1)

3   All these components contribute to a form of radio transmitter, generating waves with frequencies ranging from as low as 150 kilohertz (long wave band) through to 600 megahertz, but with maximum effect in the range 40 to 100 megahertz.

4   The circuit capacitances shown are responsible for most of the interference. When the plug fires, the voltage just before sparking can be several kilovolts: this drops abruptly to a sparking voltage of only a few hundred volts, and the stored energy in the stray capacitances C_s, C_w and C_p is discharged in a time period in the order of 1 microsecond.

5   Radiation from inside an engine compartment is to some extent shielded by the bonnet (hood) and surrounding metalwork, but only if all parts are properly connected (or bonded). If not, metal parts in the radiation path which are wholly or partly insulated can act like aerials which re-radiate interference. This can apply to all sorts of items in a vehicle, such as metal parcel shelves; test bonding with an earthed braid is often the only way of locating the culprit.

6   Interference can reach in-car radio and other equipment by conduction through cables, and a simple test with radio receivers is to pull out the aerial plug. If the interference disappears or reduces substantially the path is by radiation, but if the noise remains it is reaching the receiver by conduction (Fig. 12.2).

2 Legal suppression requirements

1   All vehicles manufactured in the UK must comply with regulations relating to the levels of interference. EEC regulations are now implemented by all members, together with other European countries.

2   It is illegal to replace suppression equipment on a vehicle in such a way as to reduce the interference protection to below legal requirements.

3   Resistive HT cables do not reduce engine performance and should not be replaced with wire HT cabling.

3 Radio installation

1   In the installation of a radio receiver in a vehicle, it is important to check that good earth connections are made, and that wiring is as short as possible. Metal-to-metal contact is vital, and bolting down a receiver or an aerial onto a painted surface will not do. An older vehicle should be checked for corrosion at earth terminations if interference becomes a new problem.

2   Radio receivers should be given the best possible signal, with the aerial mounted in a good position – having least chance of engine interference pick-up and adequate screening from bodywork. In this respect aerials should be of good quality and windscreen stick-on types avoided. Roof aerials, although requiring extra trouble to fit, are away from the radiation field around the bonnet and are also above the vehicle so as to be able to pick up radio signals from any direction without the car body obstructing the path.

3   Never use the aerial down-lead braiding as the only earth for the equipment – the power supply should have a good separate earth point.

4   Receivers are provided with a variable trimmer to match the set to the aerial. Considerable reduction in the signal-to-noise ratio will result if this adjustment is not carried out to the manufacturers instructions.

5   Detailed installation information will be given by the radio supplier, and much will depend upon the type of vehicle and desired aerial position. However, the principles of good earthing, shortest earth leads and good aerial position will apply in all cases.

6   Further notes on installation are to be found in Section 8 of this Chapter, which relates to VHF/FM receivers.

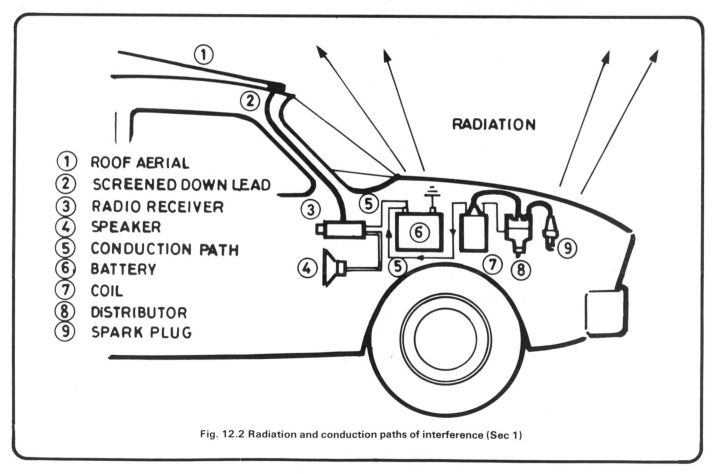

RADIATION

① ROOF AERIAL
② SCREENED DOWN LEAD
③ RADIO RECEIVER
④ SPEAKER
⑤ CONDUCTION PATH
⑥ BATTERY
⑦ COIL
⑧ DISTRIBUTOR
⑨ SPARK PLUG

Fig. 12.2 Radiation and conduction paths of interference (Sec 1)

4 Suppression methods – ignition

1 Ignition interference is normally heard as a crackle which varies with engine speed.

2 Suppressed HT cables are supplied as original equipment by manufacturers and will meet regulations as far as external interference is concerned. Resistive HT cable has a core of graphite-impregnated woven rayon or silk, with a PVC or synthetic rubber insulation.

3 Such cable comes in two grades, one having a higher resistance per unit length, but plug leads will be arranged to have a resistance of about 10 000 ohms for standard cases (Fig. 12.3). It may be necessary to use higher values in cases of bad interference, such as occurs with glass-fibre bodies where no metal screening occurs.

4 Occasionally vehicles will be found using fixed resistors to each plug, in conjunction with low resistance wire cable. Their performance at VHF is insufficient and they should be replaced by resistive HT cable.

5 A capacitor of 1 μ F (microfarad) connected from the LT supply side of the ignition coil to earth will complete basic ignition interference treatment. The capacitor should be specifically for this job and a good earth made under one of the coil fixing bolts by scraping away any paint. **Never** connect a capacitor on the contact breaker side of the coil, as the points will fail after a short time. The length of wire between the capacitor and its connector should never be altered, since it is critical at higher radio frequencies.

5 Suppression methods – line-borne interference (conduction)

1 Interference from wipers, washers, heater blower, flashers and stop-lamps is frequently taken to the receiver by the vehicle wiring. This should be confirmed by removing the aerial lead, replacing it with a dummy aerial consisting of a polystyrene capacitor of 62 to 82 pF connected to earth at the receiver input.

2 With the engine running check for separate noises over the wavebands, switching on the accessories separately. A choke fitted into the receiver supply lead will probably effect a cure (Fig. 12.4). If not, separate suppression of the offending item will be necessary.

3 Low-priced radio equipment might benefit from the fitting of a 1000 microfarad 16 volt electrolytic capacitor connected from the radio side of the choke down to the radio chassis. **Note**: *polarity is important when using electrolytic capacitors.*

6 Suppression methods – re-radiation

1 If ignition interference persists after the basic treatment of Section 4, it is possible that a part of the vehicle is picking up radiation and, acting as an aerial, is then re-radiating.

2 This can be located by systematically going over the vehicle using an earth strap and connecting suspected items to a good earth on the vehicle. Possible re-radiators include:

Exhaust pipes
Parcel trays
Doors or panels
Engine-to-body
Front suspension
Gear lever – especially French and Italian cars
Steering column – especially French and Italian cars

Once tracked down, permanent bonding down with an earth strap is required.

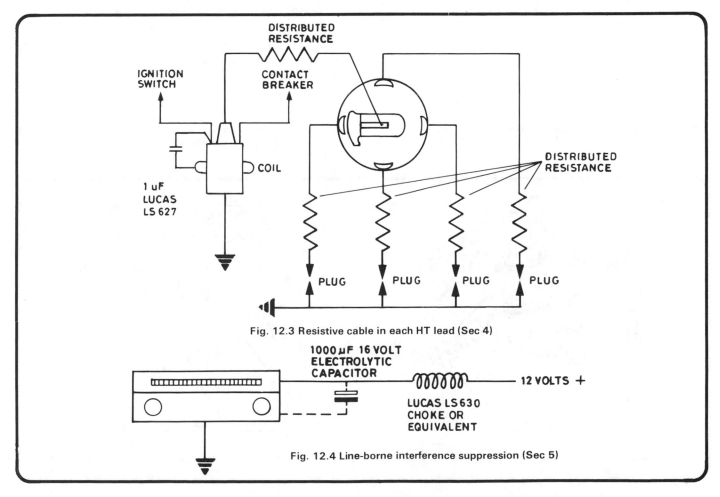

Fig. 12.3 Resistive cable in each HT lead (Sec 4)

Fig. 12.4 Line-borne interference suppression (Sec 5)

7 Suppression methods – other equipment

Symptom	Remedy
Alternators and dynamos Whine varying with engine speed	Connect a 1 μ F capacitor from terminal D to earth for a dynamo, or connect a 3 μ F capacitor from the main output (thick cable) terminal to earth for an alternator (Fig. 12.5)
Instrument stabiliser	Connect a 3A in-line choke in the stabiliser feed (B terminal). If necessary connect a 1 μ F capacitor to earth, as shown in Fig. 12.6. Finally try a second 3A choke in the instrument line
Voltage regulator Whine or crackle that cuts in as speed rises, and drops out at low speeds or when the lights are switched on (generally not apparent at idling speeds)	Lucas ACR, Delco, Bosch and Femsa alternators; fit a 1 μ F capacitor between the warning lamp terminal (IND) and earth. For dynamo systems fit a 1 μ F capacitor between the control box D terminal (the main output lead from the dynamo to the box) and earth (Fig. 12.7) Never connect capacitors from field terminal to earth
Wiper motor Crackling when the motor is switched on (when testing, wet the screen to preserve the blades)	Connect the wiper motor body to earth using a bonding strap. For permanent magnet and wound field motors use a 7A choke assembly (Fig. 12.8)
Electronic tachometer Ignition noise persists after normal suppression	If the noise disappears when the tachometer lead is disconnected, suppress the lead by inserting a 3A in-line choke (Fig. 12.9) at the coil/distributor end
Horn	A capacitor and choke combination is effective if the horn is connected directly to the 12V supply. The use of a relay is an alternative remedy, as this will reduce the length of interference-carrying leads (Fig. 12.10)
Electrostatic noise Crackles in the receiver output – caused by the build-up of static electricity in non-driven wheels	It is possible to fit spring-loaded contacts between the wheels and the vehicle frame – a dealer will advise on the availability of this method
Crackles in the receiver output, and also electric shocks to people touching the car	Changing a tyre sometimes helps – because of tyres' varying electrical resistance. In difficult cases a trailing flex which touches the ground will cure the problem. If this is not acceptable it is worth trying conductive tyre paint on the tyre walls
Miscellaneous Including clocks, screenwashers, heater motors, electric fuel pumps, flashers, stop lamps	Try a 1 μ F capacitor from feed to earth (or from both wires to earth for heater motors). If necessary, chokes of the appropriate current rating can be added

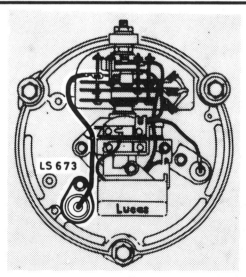

Fig. 12.5 Suppression of alternator interference (Sec 7)

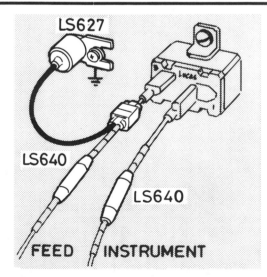

Fig. 12.6 Suppression of instrument stabiliser interference (Sec 7)

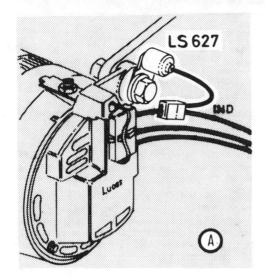

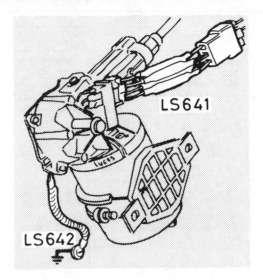

Fig. 12.8 Suppression of wiper motor interference (Sec 7)

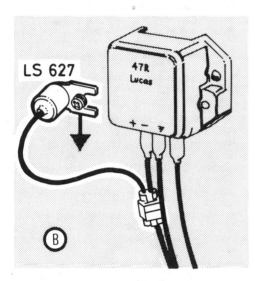

Fig. 12.7 Suppression of voltage regulator interference (Sec 7)

A   Alternator systems   B   Dynamo systems

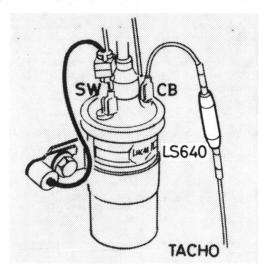

Fig. 12.9 Suppression of electronic tachometer interference
(Sec 7)

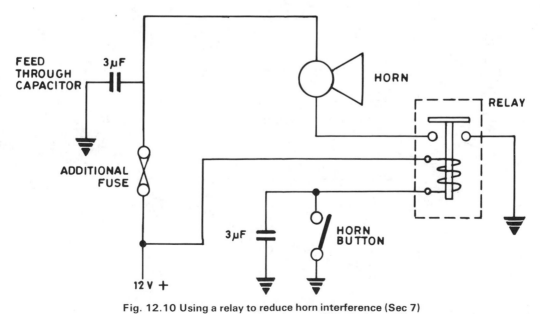

Fig. 12.10 Using a relay to reduce horn interference (Sec 7)

8 VHF/FM broadcasts

1 Reception of VHF/FM in an automobile is more prone to problems than the medium and long wavebands. Medium/long wave transmitters are capable of covering considerable distances, but VHF transmitters are restricted to line of sight, meaning ranges of 10 to 50 miles, depending upon the terrain, the effects of buildings and the transmitter power.

2 Because of the limited range it is necessary to retune on a long journey, and it may be better for those habitually travelling long distances or living in areas of poor provision of transmitters to use an AM radio working on medium/long wavebands.

3 Most forms of interference occur in the form of amplitude changes, in that a received radio signal would have superimposed on it an interference impulse tending to make the combined received signal momentarily larger.

4 VHF transmissions in the UK send information not by variation of the amplitude level – amplitude modulation (AM), but by varying the frequency of transmission by a small fraction in accord with the microphone signal, hence the name frequency modulation (FM).

5 FM receivers have a limiting device which holds the amplitude of the signal voltage in the set at a constant level so when an unwanted pulse is received it is chopped off by the limiter. It is this single factor which accounts for the success of receivers working on very high frequency (VHF) for they are, in fact, working over a band where ignition interference reaches a peak. However, the protection against interference by the FM receiver limiter depends upon the received signal being above a certain minimum level.

6 When conditions are poor, interference can arise, and some of the suppression devices described in Section 4 of this Chapter fall off in performance at very high frequencies unless specifically designed for the VHF band. Available suppression devices include reactive HT cable, resistive distributor caps, screened plug caps, screened leads and resistive sparking plugs such as the Champion RN9Y. Fortunately original equipment manufacturers incorporate suppression components in alternators and regulators.

7 Recent developments in VHF/FM receiver design include:

(a) **Muting,** in which incoming signal strength is measured by a circuit which silences the receiver when signal is weakened by hills or buildings. This eliminates the FM noise which is characteristic of signal loss; the system also cuts out FM noise between stations when tuning.

(b) **Interference absorption circuits** which identify unwanted pulses of interference and reject them.

(c) **Stereo switching** – stereo signals need to be about ten times greater in strength than for mono reception. When the received signal in stereo is too weak the set is switched over to mono reception mode automatically, thus eliminating unnecessary noise.

(d) **Automatic search tuning.** Designed for accurate tuning of a programme, the receiver uses a phase-locked loop (PLL) circuit which holds the tuner on a chosen signal. Tuning accurately by manual operation can require attention which is a distraction from driving and this system eliminates the hazard.

(e) **Stereo reception control (SRC).** A more refined version of (c), which progressively mixes the stereo channels into mono. It also trims the frequency response to minimise interference and noise, until the signal returns to a level which is sufficient to operate on full stereo again (Fig. 12.11).

8 For VHF/FM receiver installation the following points should be observed:

(a) Earthing of the receiver chassis and the aerial mounting is important. Use a separate earthing wire at the radio, and scrape paint away at the aerial mounting.

(b) If possible, use a good quality roof aerial to obtain maximum height and distance from interference generating devices on the vehicle.

(c) Use of a high quality aerial down-lead is important, since losses in cheap cable can be significant.

(d) The polarisation of FM transmissions may be horizontal, vertical, circular or slanted. Because of this the optimum mounting angle is at 45° to the vehicle roof.

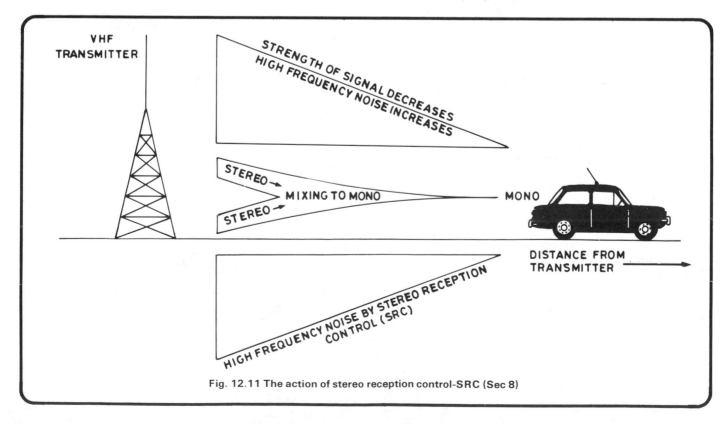

Fig. 12.11 The action of stereo reception control-SRC (Sec 8)

9   VHF/FM signals are reflected by hard objects, such as hills and buildings, giving rise to the possibility that a vehicle aerial may receive the signal both directly and from the reflector (Fig. 12.12). The length of the reflected path will be longer than the direct path, and the resultant signal voltage at the aerial may rise, fall and even disappear altogether with the vehicle motion. This phenomenon is due to the difference of phase between the two alternating voltage signals, and is characterised by a popping sound. Such reflection effects occur also with TV receivers (ghosting), but their aerials are directional and can be adjusted to minimise the effect. The motor vehicle has the disadvantage of using a simple aerial, and because the vehicle is mobile there is always the likelihood of this effect.

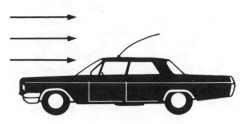

Fig. 12.13 A thin aerial bends, resulting in a distorted radiation pattern (Sec 9)

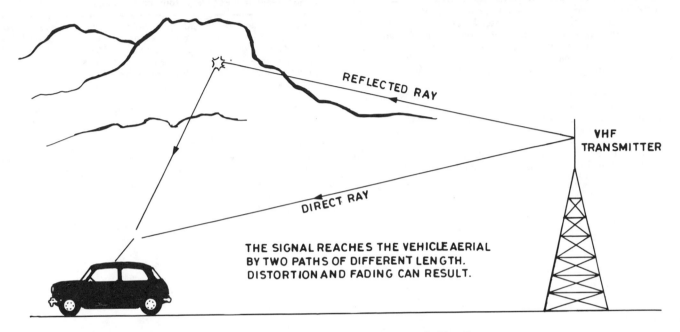

REFLECTED RAY

DIRECT RAY

VHF TRANSMITTER

THE SIGNAL REACHES THE VEHICLE AERIAL BY TWO PATHS OF DIFFERENT LENGTH. DISTORTION AND FADING CAN RESULT.

Fig. 12.12 The effect of reflected signals (Sec 8)

9   Citizens' Band radio (CB)

1   In the UK, CB transmitter/receivers work within the 27 MHz and 934 MHz bands, using the FM mode. At present interest is concentrated on 27 MHz where the design and manufacture of equipment is less difficult. Maximum transmitted power is 4 watts, and 40 channels spaced 10 kHz apart within the range 27.60125 to 27.99125 MHz are available.

2   Aerials are the key to effective transmission and reception. Regulations limit the aerial length to 1.5 metres, so tuning the aerial is necessary to obtain optimum results. The choice of a CB aerial is dependent on whether it is to be permanently installed or removable, and the performance will hinge on correct tuning and the location point on the vehicle. Common practice is to clip the aerial to the roof gutter or to employ wing mounting where the aerial can be rapidly unscrewed. An alternative is to use the boot (trunk) rim to render the aerial theftproof, but a popular solution is to use the 'magmount' – a type of mounting having a strong magnetic base clamping to the vehicle at any point, usually the roof.

3   Aerial location determines the signal distribution for both transmission and reception, but it is wise to choose a point away from the engine compartment to minimise interference from vehicle electrical equipment.

4   The 1.5 metre aerial is subject to considerable wind and acceleration forces. Cheaper units will whip backwards and forwards (Fig. 12.13) and in so doing will alter the relationship with the metal surface of the vehicle with which it forms a ground plane aerial system. The radiation pattern will change correspondingly, giving rise to break up of both incoming and outgoing signals.

5   Interference problems on the vehicle carrying CB equipment fall into two categories:

(a)   Interference to nearby TV and radio receivers when transmitting
(b)   Interference to CB set reception due to electrical equipment on the vehicle

6   Problems of break-through to TV and radio are not frequent, but can be difficult to solve. Mostly trouble is not detected or reported because the vehicle is moving and the symptoms rapidly disappear at the TV/radio receiver, but when the CB set is used as a base station any trouble with nearby receivers will soon result in a complaint.

7   It must not be assumed by the CB operator that his equipment is faultless, for much depends upon the design. Harmonics (that is, multiples) of 27 MHz may be transmitted unknowingly and these can fall into other user's bands. Where trouble of this nature occurs, low pass filters in the aerial or supply leads can help, and should be fitted in base station aerials as a matter of course. In stubborn cases it may be necessary to call for assistance from the Licensing Authority, or, if possible, to have the equipment checked by the manufacturers.

8   Interference received on the CB set from the vehicle equipment is, fortunately, not usually a severe problem. The precautions outlined elsewhere in this Chapter apply, but there are some extra points worth noting. It is common practice to use a slide-mount on CB equipment enabling the set to be easily removed for use as a base station, for example. Care must be taken that the slide mount fittings are properly earthed and that first class connection occurs between the set and slide-mount.

9   Vehicle manufacturers in the UK are required to provide suppression of electrical equipment to cover 40 to 250 MHz to protect TV and VHF radio bands. Such suppression appears to be adequately effective at 27 MHz, but suppression of individual items such as alternators/dynamos, clocks, stabilisers, flashers, wiper motors, etc, may still be necessary. The suppression capacitors and chokes available from auto-electrical suppliers for entertainment receivers will usually give the required results with CB equipment. Details are to be found in earlier Sections of this Chapter.

10 Glass-fibre bodied vehicles

1   Such vehicles do not have the advantage of a metal box surrounding the engine as is the case, in effect, of conventional vehicles. It is usually necessary to line the bonnet, bulkhead and wing valances with metal foil, which could well be the aluminium foil available from builders merchants. Bonding of sheets one to another and the whole down to the chassis is essential.

2   Wiring harness may have to be wrapped in metal foil which again should be earthed to the vehicle chassis. The aerial base and radio chassis must be taken to the vehicle chassis by heavy metal braid. VHF radio suppression in glass-fibre cars may not be a feasible operation.

3   In addition to all the above, normal suppression components should be employed, but special attention paid to earth bonding.

11 Suppression methods – electronic ignition

1   Manufacturers of electronic ignition sets build in a certain level of suppression, but this does not relieve the need for suppressing HT leads.

2   In some cases it is permitted to connect a capacitor on the LT supply side of the ignition coil, but not in every case. Makers instructions should be carefully followed, otherwise damage to the ignition semiconductors may result.

12 Suppression methods – fluorescent tubes

1   Caravans and public transport vehicles use fluorescent tubes which may give rise to radio and television reception troubles. Both lamp fittings and cables can give rise to interference due to the pulsating nature of the lamp discharge and the presence of harmonics. In addition, the inverter which converts the vehicle voltage to suit the tubes is non-linear and, accordingly, an interference generator.

2   Location of caravan aerials is important to reduce interference pick-up and obtain maximum signal strength.

3   Interference may be attenuated by the use of 7 ampere line chokes in the supply lines close to the invertor. Open mesh screening of the tube itself may be necessary in persistent cases.

Chapter 13 Air conditioning

Contents

1 Introduction

1   It might be thought that air conditioning of an automobile interior is only desirable in hot countries, but there are several advantages to its installation in vehicles operating in temperate climates.

2   A well-known property of air conditioning is that of cooling the air in the vehicle passenger space, but there are other factors which make the installation a practical and worthwhile proposition even for small cars. Advantages are:

(a)   interior cooling in summer
(b)   dehumidifying of air
(c)   demisting of all windows in winter
(d)   filtering of smoke and other airborne pollution
(e)   minimizing of fatigue for driver and passengers

3   Because air is treated by the air conditioning unit it is fit for recirculation in the passenger compartment. To allow for air changes, about 15% of the air reaching the passengers comes in as fresh, the remainder being circulated by the air conditioning system.

4   Inside the vehicle the installation is compact and unobtrusive, as evidenced in Fig. 13.1 This shows a Salmon Diavia Artico unit fitted to a BMW 5-Series.

Fig. 13.1 Air conditioning control panel on Salmon Diavia Artico unit fitted to BMW 5-Series (Sec 1)

2 Principles of air conditioning

The Fahrenheit system is used in this Section, since it accords with most of the available literature.

Heat is movable

1   All will be familiar with the household refrigerator in which the food compartment is cooled, and at the back of the refrigerator is a radiator which gets hot. The refrigerator is extracting heat from the interior and passing it, via a pumping system, out to the condenser. One way of thinking of this process is to visualise heat being pumped from one area to another.

2   Air conditioning the interior of a motor vehicle works in the same way. Heat is extracted from the passenger compartment air, ie, it is cooled, and the heat is pumped round to a condenser which passes the transmitted heat to passing external air, just like a car engine radiator.

3   Heat will pass from one object to another providing there is a temperature difference. The hotter object loses heat to the colder object. Transfer of heat by objects in contact is common. An example could include the hardening of steel, in which heated steel is plunged into water; the steel loses heat to the water – net result being that the steel temperature falls and the water temperature rises.

4   Similarly the human body runs at an internal temperature of 98.4°F, but the comfort range is 70°F to 80°F. If an object at lower temperature than this is touched it is said to be cold because heat is transferring from the human body to the object. Transference of heat in this way is said to be by CONDUCTION.

5   Heat will also transfer by RADIATION, which means that heat is given off in the form of waves just like light or radio waves. No physical material is necessary for such heat movement – the heat from the sun reaches Earth after travelling through 93 000 000 miles of empty space.

6   If a hot object is immersed in a gas or a liquid at a lower temperature, then heat will be removed from the surface of the hot object and shifted about by movement of the liquid or gas itself. This form of heat transference is by CONVECTION.

7   The car radiator is really mis-named, for most of the heat is removed by the air passing over the honeycomb elements and being conducted and convected away, although there will be some radiation loss. A better name might be 'heat exchanger'.

Change of state

8   Many substances can be changed from solid to liquid to vapour

(gas) by the application of sufficient heat. Each stage is a change of state. It is noteworthy that to reverse the process heat is given off from the substance.

9   The most commonly observable change of state is that of water, which may easily be transformed from ice to water to steam and vice versa. In air conditioning the process of change of state from liquid to vapour is of particular interest, but water is not the substance used.

Latent Heat of Vaporisation

10   If sufficient heat is applied to, say, water the temperature rises to boiling point (212°F or 100°C), this figure being applicable at mean sea level pressure. If the heat continues to be applied the temperature does not rise any further – so where does the heat go?

11   The answer is that it is used in converting water at 212°F (100°C) to water vapour (steam) at 212°F (100°C). It is found that every pound of water converted to steam requires 970 BTU (British Thermal Units) of heat (one BTU is defined as the amount of heat required to raise the temperature of 1 lb of water through 1°F). This is called the Latent Heat of Vaporisation.

12   The process is reversible; if 1 lb of steam condenses to become water the steam gives off 970 BTU of heat. This is the Latent Heat of Condensation and is the same BTU value as the Latent Heat of Vaporisation. Water is unsuitable as a refrigerant, but illustrates the idea of change of state conveniently.

Refrigerant R12 (Freon)

13   The working fluid in automobile air conditioning systems is R12 (or Freon). Like water, R12 will change from liquid to vapour and vice versa, but will do so at the more convenient temperature of −21.6°F (−29.8°C), this being its boiling point.

14   At a temperature above this, R12 changes from liquid to vapour, and in so doing absorbs a quantity of heat from the car interior. The boiling point depends upon the system pressure, and Fig. 13.2 shows the relationship.

15   Finally it should be mentioned that compression of a gas or vapour generates heat (the action of a bicycle pump illustrates this – Fig. 13.3), but this is also a reversible process, and when the gas or vapour is allowed to expand the temperature will fall.

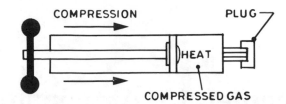

COMPRESSION PRODUCES TEMPERATURE RISE

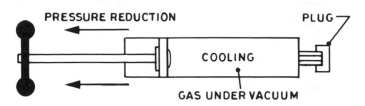

PRESSURE REDUCTION CAUSES COOLING

Fig. 13.3 The link between compression and temperature (Sec 2)

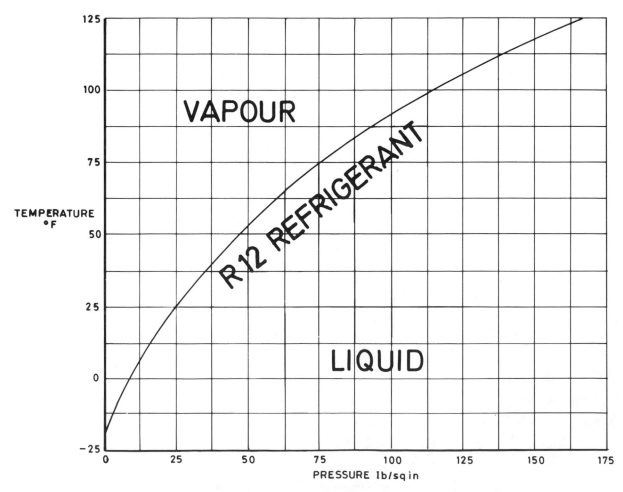

Fig. 13.2 The pressure-temperature relationship for the refrigerant R12 (Sec 2)

3   The practical air conditioning system

1   About 2 lb weight of R12 refrigerant is circulated around a closed circuit by a belt-driven compressor pump, delivering a pressure of the order of 150 to 250 psi.

2   Referring to Fig. 13.4, the refrigerant flows from the compressor in vapour form to the condenser, which is often located in front of the car radiator and has its own cooling fan.

3   The condenser receives the refrigerant vapour which, in passing through the finned pipes exposed to ram air, cools and changes state into liquid form. The latent heat given up is carried away by the air passing over the condenser. Usually the ram air (ie airflow due to vehicle motion) is augmented by the condenser cooling fan.

4   The liquified refrigerant emerges from the condenser and flows to the receiver drier which removes any moisture from the system. The receiver drier also stores any excess liquid.

5   After drying, the refrigerant passes through an expansion valve which regulates the flow of vapour through the evaporator coil. The expansion valve also causes the refrigerant pressure to fall rapidly, and with it the refrigerant temperature.

6   The expansion valve nozzle atomises the liquid refrigerant which can easily absorb latent heat and change from an atomised liquid into a vapour. This heat comes from the car interior and is picked up from the air in the passenger compartment as the air is forced over the evaporator. The R12 absorbs a large amount of heat in this change of state, and thus keeps the car interior cool.

7   The fins on the evaporator are so cold that the moisture in the car air condenses on them and runs down a drain hole in the floor. With this action a high proportion of dust and smoke particles are also removed from the air.

8   At the evaporator outlet the R12 vapour is drawn into the condenser at low pressure, and the cycle repeats.

9   The required temperature is set by a dashboard thermostat control which in turn controls the compressor engagement. It is estimated that a single pass of air removes 80% of all airborne impurities and also achieves a substantial reduction in humidity.

4   Components

Compressor pump

1   An example of a high quality compressor for automobile air conditioning systems is that made by Sankyo International and shown in Fig. 13.5. This five cylinder compressor is made to fine tolerances and is the wobble-plate type in which the inclined, rotating wobble-plate pushes the pistons in sequence. Each cylinder has inlet and outlet reed valves operating in a common cylinder head onto which the high and low pressure side fittings are mounted.

2   Compressor pumps require lubrication which is provided by oil in the refrigerant system. Failure can occur if the hoses or coils have a leak and the oil is lost via the leak. The lubrication is by a positive pressure system, which uses the pressure difference between suction intake and crankcase to give film lubrication to all working parts. No oil pump is required.

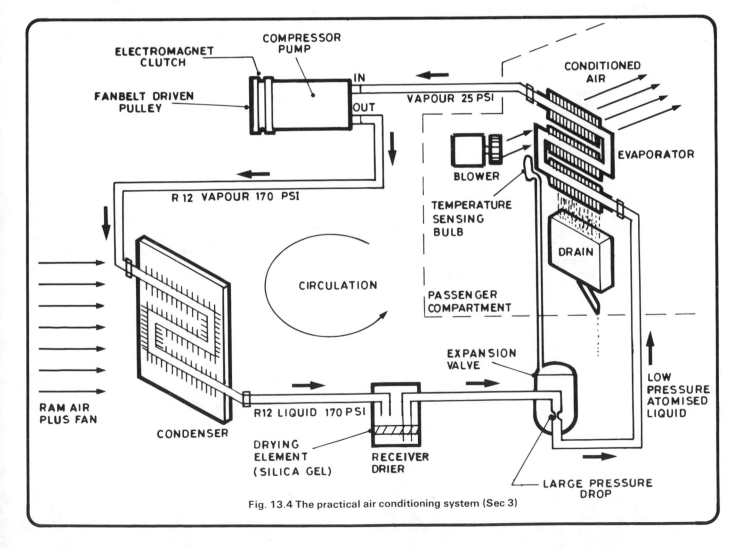

Fig. 13.4 The practical air conditioning system (Sec 3)

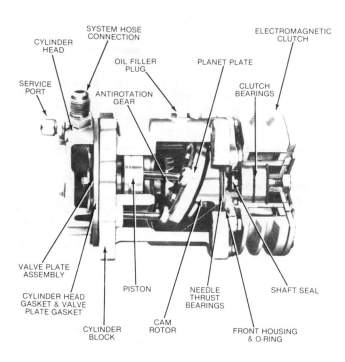

Fig. 13.5 A compressor pump (Sec 4)

3   The working outlet pressures can be of the order of 240 psi but typically about 170 psi is used. It is essential that the pump should deal only with R12 as a vapour and not as a liquid, and means of achieving this are discussed under the sub-section on the evaporator.

4   The engine loading is not insignificant and may require up to 5 hp (3.73 kW) for a 180 psi output at 3000 rpm. The vehicle engine speed may drop slightly at idle when the pump load occurs by the switching on of the electromagnetic clutch.

Receiver drier

5   This device is usually mounted near to the condenser from which it receives high pressure liquid flow. The receiver drier acts as a storage tank, holding the refrigerant (R12) until required by the evaporator.

6   A second function is to remove moisture from the refrigerant by the use of a dessicant, usually in the form of silica gel. Removal of moisture is very important because it is harmful to air conditioning components, especially since it combines with R12 to form hydrochloric and hydrofluoric acid. There is also the possibility that moisture may reach the expansion valve and freeze solid, blocking the flow of R12.

Condenser

7   This consists of a coil carrying the refrigerant at high pressure and giving maximum contact with passing air by having thin cooling fins. The condenser is mounted directly in front of the radiator and has the full ram airflow, this being due to the forward motion of the car and the fan.

8   As the R12 flows down the coil, about two-thirds of the length contains heat-laden vapour and the remainder the R12 in liquid form. At the point of change of state there is the maximum heat given off.

Evaporator

9   Like the condenser, this consists of a refrigerant-carrying finned coil to form a heat exchanger. It differs mainly in its compactness, for it has to find a space in the passenger compartment below or behind the dashboard.

10   The evaporator receives refrigerant from the expansion valve in the form of a low-pressure, cold, atomised liquid. Because of the natural movement of heat from a hotter to a colder body, heat from the passenger compartment will be absorbed by this refrigerant in being passed over the fins by the blower. In addition, and of much greater effect, when the liquid vaporises the latent heat will be extracted from the passing air, which will then be cooled. The refrigerant then becomes a low-pressure saturated vapour before reaching the pump inlet.

11   A sensing tube is in contact with the evaporator matrix and feeds back to the expansion valve, which is thus controlled to pass the right amount of R12 so that the evaporator output is always vapour, not a liquid.

Expansion valve

12   There are several types of expansion valve but all have the same sort of action. The valve performs three functions:

(a)   Metering action – the metered orifice in the valve reduces the pressure of the incoming liquid R12. This is achieved by passing the liquid through the nozzle orifice, for it then sprays out to give an atomised spray which quickly becomes a saturated vapour on passing into the evaporator.

(b)   Modulating action – the valve is required to supply the right amount of R12 so that correct evaporation takes place at a later point in the circuit.

(c)   Control – the valve must respond quickly to the temperature conditions in the vehicle and cope with the changes of refrigerant required by altering the control to the expansion valve orifice.

Chapter 14 Vehicle wiring and the electrical tool kit

Contents

1 Routing of wiring

1 For convenience of manufacture, wires are taped together into a loom and emerge at the most convenient point near to the electrical device to which attachment is to be made. The loom is routed through the vehicle so as to use minimum lengths of wire or cable, partly from the point of view of cost and partly to minimise the inevitable volt-drop in the wiring.

2 Manufacturers identify cables by colouring the insulation, sometimes with two colours, but unfortunately there is no universal code; however, there is standardisation in the major manufacturing countries so that all vehicles made in that country will use the same coding system.

3 Taping the separate cables into the form of a loom gives mechanical strength. This is important in the motor vehicle because vibration can cause wire fracture if the vibration amplitude is large enough. Cables emerging from the loom will be cut to the correct lengths to reach the required point and then may be terminated. The form of termination depends upon the application, but bullet plugs and sockets, Lucar blades, snap-in line connectors, eyelets, post connectors and self-stripping types are most frequently met (Figs. 14.1 and 14.2).

	DESCRIPTION	OVERALL DIA.
	SOLDER TYPE	4·75 mm (0·187")
	CRIMP TYPE, SUITABLE FOR CABLE 14/0·25 mm (14/0·010") PT AND SPT	4·75 mm (0·187")
	CRIMP TYPE, SUITABLE FOR CABLE 14/0·30 mm (14/·012") PT	4·75 mm (0·187")
	CRIMP TYPE, SUITABLE FOR CABLE 28/0·30 mm (14/·012") PT	4·75 mm (0·187")
	CRIMP TYPE, SUITABLE FOR CABLE 44/0·30 mm (44/·012") PT	4·75 mm (0·187")
	SLEEVE TERMINAL $\frac{3}{16}$" DIA.	

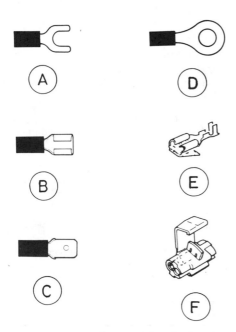

Fig. 14.1 Typical connectors for auto-electrical equipment (Sec 1)

A	Fork	D	Eyelet
B	Lucar female	E	Lucar piggy back
C	Lucar male	F	Self-stripping connector

	DESCRIPTION
	2-WAY SNAP-IN CABLE CONNECTOR (MAY BE USED WITH $\frac{9}{32}$" SINGLE CABLE CLIP)
	4-WAY CABLE CONNECTOR (COMMON CONTACT)
	6-WAY CABLE CONNECTOR (INSULATED)
	6-WAY CABLE CONNECTOR (COMMON CONTACT)
	10-WAY CABLE CONNECTOR (INSULATED)

Fig. 14.2 Snap-in bullet connectors (Sec 1)

A	Male	B	Female

4   Instrument panel wiring is now frequently in the form of a printed circuit board (PCB). The PCB is a sheet of insulating board which has a thin copper foil sheet bonded to both sides. The 'wire routes' are drawn out by photographic means and the unwanted copper stripped away by etching or other means leaving only the required conducting paths. It is possible to joint points on the back and front of the board by through pins, •which are then soldered. Connectors specially designed to grip and make contact on the board result is a much cheaper method of making the instrument panel connections (Fig. 14.3). Care must be taken to ensure that no current overload occurs on a PCB, because the copper foil quickly blows like a fuse.

Fig. 14.3 A typical instrument panel printed circuit board attached to the rear of an instrument cluster (Sec 1)

5   Connections can be troublesome, and it is worth checking the PCB plug and socket if intermittent faults occur. Sometimes capless bulbs are used in the board as indicator lamps and special attention should be given to ensuring good connections.

6   Should a copper foil strip be damaged and broken, it is possible to bridge a gap with thin tinned fuse using the minimum amount of soldering iron heat.

2   Cable sizes

1   It is important that the cross-sectional area of the copper wire is large enough to carry the current without overheating. Additionally the volt-drop in the wire must be low enough to ensure correct operation of the equipment to which it is connected. For all this, on the grounds of cost the manufacturer will use the minimum size of cable which is consistent with the above requirements.

2   Rarely is the cable made of one single copper wire, because it would be difficult to bend round corners and, in any case, might fracture with vibration. Cables are made up of strands of copper wire (often tinned) twisted in a slow spiral and then covered with an insulator which is extruded like toothpaste.

3   Both metric and inch measurements are in use in automobiles, depending upon the country of origin, but the principles of choosing the correct size are the same. The manufacturer will use a cable which is the minimum size to do the job (a thought to bear in mind when adding accessories) the criteria being:

(a)   the volt-drop on full load must not be too great
(b)   the cable heating must be within specified limits

4   In order to carry current to meet condition (a) the copper cross-sectional area must be sufficient; cable heating (b) will also depend upon the cross-sectional area, but additionally the factor of the cable's ability to get rid of the heat is important. A single cable exposed to air can be used to carry a much higher current than if it were bunched up with other cables as a part of a loom. Cables that carry current for only a short time can be worked at a higher current density, but here the permitted volt-drop is the important consideration.

5   Wires are graded by denoting the number of strands and the diameter of a single strand; for example, 14/0.01 (inch) has 14 strands, each of which has a diameter of 0.01 inch. In the case of metric cables the same idea is used so 16/0.2 (metric) indicates 16 strands, each of diameter 0.2 mm.

3   Volt-drop and current ratings

1   In the accompanying tables, Fig. 14.4, it is assumed that the current density is 5500 amperes per square inch of copper for up to 44/0.012 inch size, and 4500 amperes per square inch for larger sizes.

Size	Inch cables current rating (A)	Volt drop (V/ft/A)
23/0.0076	5.75	0.00836
9/0.012	5.75	0.00840
14/0.010	6.00	0.00778
36/0.0076	8.75	0.00534
14/0.012	8.75	0.00540
28/0.012	17.5	0.00770
35/0.012	21.75	0.00216
44/0.012	27.5	0.00172
65/0.012	35	0.00116
97/0.012	50	0.0008
120/0.012	60	0.00064
60/0.018	70	0.00057

Size	Metric cables current rating (A)	Volt drop (V/m/A)
16/0.20	4.25	0.0371
9/0.30	5.5	0.02935
14/0.25	6.0	0.02715
14/0.30	8.5	0.01884
21/0.30	12.75	0.01257
28/0.30	17.0	0.00942
35/0.30	21.0	0.00754
44/0.30	25.5	0.006
65/0.30	31.0	0.00406
84/0.30	41.5	0.00374
97/0.30	48.0	0.00272
120/0.30	55.5	0.0022
80/0.40	70.0	0.00182

Fig. 14.4 Cable volt-drop and current rating (Sec 3)

2   The current ratings shown may be reduced to 60% for cables run in a loom (or bunched together), and also in the case of continuously-loaded cables of 28/0.012 inch and above.

3   A working guide to the choice of cable size can be based on five cable sizes:

Inch Units	Metric Units (mm)	Current Rating (Amps)	Use
14/0.012	14/0.3	8.75	General applications such as park and tail lamps, stop lamps, flasher indicator circuits and radio/cassettes
28/0.012	28/0.3	17.5	Heavier loads, eg headlamps, horns, heated rear windows, cigar lighters
44/0.012	44/0.3	27.5	Dynamo charging cable
65/0.012	65/0.3	35	Alternator charging circuit
84/0.012	84/0.3	41.5	Alternator charging circuit

4   Cable coding

1   Colour coding of cables is useful, identifying wires or leads which are routed through the motor vehicle. Although there is generally standardisation of colours in a particular country, unfortunately each country uses a different set of colours. The chart shows standards used in many of the vehicles imported to the UK (Fig. 14.5).

CHARGING – IGNITION – STARTING SYSTEMS

BASIC CABLE COLOURS (SUPPLEMENTARY/ TRACER COLOURS INDICATED IN CIRCLE ON MATRIX BELOW)

COUNTRY OF ORIGIN	VEHICLE MANUFACTURERS											
GERMANY	AUDI, PORSCHE, VW.	COIL TO DIST		W LAMP FEED		COIL FEED	STARTER SOL FEED	COIL FEED STARTER MAIN FEED				
	BMW	BALLAST TO COIL COIL FEED	ALT EARTH ALT D NEG TO REG	ALT D - TO REG REG TO W LAMP			STARTER FEED ALT OF TO REG COIL TO DIST	STARTER FEED ALT OF TO REG COIL TO DIST				
	MERCEDES	ELCT UNIT TO DIST COIL TO DIST	ALT D NEG TO REG	REG TO W LAMP	COIL FEED STARTER SOL FEED		BALLAST FEED BALLAST IGN TO SOL					
	OPEL	COIL TO DIST COIL TO TACHO	ALT D NEG TO REG ALT EARTH	W LAMP FEED			STARTER SOL FEED ALT OF TO REG COIL FEED STARTER FEED	ALT OUTPUT ALT D NEG TO REG				
FRANCE	CITROEN	ALT EXC TO REG ALT EARTH REG EARTH		REG TO EXC COIL TO DIST	REG - COIL FEED		W LAMP IND FEED STARTER SOL FEED COIL FEED	REG - TO COIL	ALT EARTH			
	CHRYSLER/SIMCA		ALT IND REG ALT D NEG				COIL FEED ALT EXC TO REG W LAMP TO REG ALT OUTPUT		SOL FEED			
	PEUGEOT	TACHO FEED	STARTER SOL FEED ALT OUTPUT				ALT OUTPUT	ALT + STARTER SOL FEED			COIL FEED	
	RENAULT	GEN EXC TO REG		ALT EXC TO REG REG - TO BATT	MAIN OUTPUT		REG FEED COIL FEED	ALT - TO BATT DYN OUTPUT STARTER SOL FEED ALT EARTH DYN NEG	ALT EARTH ALT D TO REG REG TO BATT		COIL FEED	
ITALY	ALFA ROMEO	ALT TO REG D REG TO W LAMP	ALT TO REG D		ALT TO W L IND		ALT OUTPUT	STARTER SOL FEED COIL TO DIST ALT F	TACHO FEED			COIL FEED
	FIAT	TACHO FEED ALT OF TO REG	ALT GEN OUTPUT STARTER MAIN FEED				STARTER SOL FEED	REG TO W LAMP STARTER MAIN FEED COIL TO DIST	W LAMP FEED		COIL FEED COIL FEED	
	LANCIA					COIL FEED	ALT IND ALT OUTPUT STARTER SOL FEED	ALT D NEG TO REG REG EARTH	DYN FEED			
SWEDEN	DAF	ALT OF TO REG STARTER SOL FEED	D - TO REG	COIL FEED	COIL TO DIST D NEG TO REG REG TO W LAMP		D - TO REG VARIOUS EARTHS COIL TO DIST	REG TO W LAMP				
	SAAB	BALLAST FEED COIL TO DIST	COIL TO DIST			ALT D - TO REG STARTER SOL FEED	ALT D - TO REG ALT D - TO W LAMP STARTER MAIN FEED	D NEG REG BALLAST TO COIL	MAIN OUTPUT COIL FEED			
	VOLVO	ALT OF TO REG	BALLAST TO SOL	SOL FEED COIL FEED			ALT OUTPUT D - W LAMP STARTER FEED	ALT EARTH COIL TO DIST				
JAPAN	DATSUN	BALLAST FEED	REG TO ALT NEG				ALT OUTPUT D - TO REG W LAMP STARTER FEED	COIL FEED STARTER SOL FEED	ALT OUTPUT REG TO ALT F MAIN OUTPUT			
	HONDA			COIL TO DIST				STARTER SOL FEED COIL FEED	ALT FIELD W LAMP FEED ALT OUTPUT			
	MAZDA	TACHO FEED			TACHO FEED			AMMETER FEED STARTER SOL FEED COIL FEED	ALT OUTPUT			
	TOYOTA	REG TO W LAMP		REG TO W LAMP			BALLAST TO STARTER	COIL FEED COIL TO DIST	STARTER SOL FEED REG TO IGN ALT OUTPUT			

KEY TO ABBREVIATIONS

ALT – ALTERNATOR
DYN – DYNAMO
GEN – GENERATOR
SOL – SOLENOID
DIST – DISTRIBUTOR
REG – REGULATOR
W-L – WARNING LAMP
ELCT – ELECTRONIC - ELECTRONIC IGNITION UNIT
NEG – NEGATIVE
IGN – IGNITION
EXC – EXCITOR
TACHO – TACHOMETER
BATT – BATTERY

EXAMPLES:
SUPPLEMENTARY COLOUR
MAIN COLOUR
CIRCUIT

AUDI → COIL TO DISTRIBUTOR
BMW ● → BALLAST TO COIL
SAAB ○ → BALLAST FEED

© Lucas Electrical Limited 1978
Lucas Electrical Limited
Parts and Service Division
Great Hampton Street
Birmingham B18 6AU

Fig. 14.5 Wiring colour codes for imported vehicles (Sec 4)

2 In the United Kingdom the British Standard BS-AU7 determines colour coding of automobile wiring (Fig. 14.6). Lucas use a 7 colour set in which plain colours – purple, green, blue, red, white, brown and green are supplemented by a further group using a base colour with a thin line trace of a different colour, thus:

Black   –   earth (ground) connections

Green   –   feeds to auxiliary devices controlled by the ignition switch, eg wipers, flashers, etc

White   –   base colour for ignition circuits

Red   –   sidelights (parking lights) and rear lights

Blue   –   with white trace – main beam headlamp
with red trace – dip (meeting) beam headlamp

Purple   –   auxiliary devices not fed via the ignition switch, eg horn, interior light

Brown   –   main battery feed

Other colours are used, according to equipment specifications, eg light green, pink, slate.

Colour		Destination
Main	Tracer	
Brown		Main battery feed
Brown	Blue	Control box (compensated voltage control only) to ignition and lighting switch (feed)
Brown	Red	Compression ignition starting aid to switch. Main battery feed to double pole ignition switch (a.c. alt. system)
Brown	Purple	Alternator regulator feed
Brown	Green	Dynamo 'F' to control box 'F'. Alternator field 'F' to control box 'F'
Brown	Light Green	Screenwiper motor to switch
Brown	White	Ammeter to control box. Ammeter to main alternator terminal
Brown	Yellow	Dynamo 'D' to control box 'D' and ignition warning light. Alternator neutral point
Brown	Black	Alternator warning light, negative side
Brown	Pink	
Brown	Slate	
Brown	Orange	
Blue		Lighting switch (head) to dipper switch
Blue	Brown	
Blue	Red	Dipper switch to headlamp dip beam. Headlamp dip beam fuse to right-hand headlamp (when independently fused)
Blue	Purple	
Blue	Green	
Blue	Light Green	Screenwiper motor to switch
Blue	White	Dipper switch to headlamp main beam (subsidiary circuit — headlamp flasher relay to headlamp). Headlamp main beam fuse to right-hand headlamp (when independently fused). Headlamp main beam fuse to outboard headlamps (when outboard headlamps independently fused). Dipper switch to main beam warning light
Blue	Yellow	Long range driving switch to lamp.
Blue	Black	
Blue	Pink	Headlamp dip beam fuse to left-hand headlamp (when independently fused)
Blue	Slate	Headlamp main beam fuse to left-hand headlamp or inboard headlamps (when independently fused)

Colour		Destination
Main	Tracer	
Blue	Orange	
Red		Side and tail lamp feed
Red	Brown	Variable intensity panel lights (when used in addition to normal panel lights)
Red	Blue	
Red	Purple	Map light switch to map light
Red	Green	Lighting switch to side and tail lamp fuse (when fused)
Red	Light Green	Screenwiper motor to switch
Red	White	Panel light switch to panel lights
Red	Yellow	Fog lamp switch to fog lamp
Red	Black	Parking switch to left-hand side lamp
Red	Pink	
Red	Slate	
Red	Orange	Parking light switch to right-hand sidelamp
Purple		Accessories fused direct from battery
Purple	Brown	Horn fuse to horn relay (when horn is fused separately)
Purple	Blue	
Purple	Red	Boot light switch to boot light
Purple	Green	
Purple	Light Green	
Purple	White	Interior light to switch (subsidiary circuit — door safety lights to switch)
Purple	Yellow	Horn to horn relay
Purple	Black	Horn or horn relay to horn push
Purple	Pink	
Purple	Slate	Aerial lift motor to switch UP
Purple	Orange	Aerial lift motor switch DOWN
Green		Accessories fused via ignition switch (subsidiary circuit fuse A4 to hazard switch (terminal 6))
Green	Brown	Reverse lamp to switch
Green	Blue	Water temperature gauge to temperature unit
Green	Red	Left-hand flasher lamps
Green	Purple	Stop lamps to stop lamp switch
Green	Light Green	Hazard flasher unit to hazard pilot lamp
Green	White	Right-hand flasher lamps
Green	Yellow	Heater motor to switch, single speed (or to 'slow' on two-speed motor)
Green	Black	Fuel gauge to fuel tank unit or changeover switch

Fig. 14.6 British standard wiring code for automobiles (Sec 4)

3   Handbooks are usually printed in black and white only, so the cable colours are identified by a lettering code, such as:

B	=	Black
U	=	Blue
N	=	Brown
R	=	Red
P	=	Purple
G	=	Green
S	=	Slate
W	=	White

When a cable has a base colour and a second colour spiral trace the

code is, for example:

WG = White with green trace

European vehicles using the DIN code will code cables as follows:

BL	=	Blue (Blau)
BR	=	Brown (Braun)
GE	=	Amber (Gelb)
GR	=	Grey (Grau)
GN	=	Green (Grün)
RT	=	Red (Rot)
SW	=	Black (Schwarz)
WS	=	White (Weiss)

Colour		Destination
Main	Tracer	
Green	Pink	Choke solenoid to choke switch (when fused)
Green	Slate	Heater motor to switch (or to fast) (on 2-speed motor)
Green	Orange	Low fuel level warning light
Light Green		Instrument voltage stabilizer to instruments
Light Green	Brown	Flasher switch to flasher unit 'L'
Light Green	Blue	Flasher switch to left-hand flasher warning light
Light Green	Red	Fuel tank changeover switch to right-hand tank unit
Light Green	Purple	Flasher unit 'F' to flasher warning light
Light Green	Green	
Light Green	White	
Light Green	Yellow	Flasher switch to right-hand flasher warning light
Light Green	Black	Screen jet switch to screen jet motor
Light Green	Pink	Flasher unit 'L' to emergency switch (simultaneous flashing)
Light Green	Slate	Fuel tank changeover switch to left-hand tank unit
Light Green	Orange	
White		Ignition control circuit (unfused) (Ignition switch to ballast resistor)
White	Brown	Oil pressure switch to warning light or gauge
White	Blue	Choke switch to choke solenoid (unfused). Rear heater fuse unit to switch. Electronic ignition TAC ignition unit to resistance.
White	Red	Solenoid starter switch to starter push or inhibitor switch
White	Purple	Fuel pump No. 1 or right-hand to change-over switch
White	Green	Fuel pump No. 2 or left-hand to change-over switch
White	Light Green	Screenwiper motor to switch
White	Yellow	Starter inhibitor switch to starter push. Ballast resistor to coil. Starter solenoid to coil
White	Black	Ignition coil CB to distributor contact breaker. Rear heated window to switch or fuse TAC ignition
White	Pink	Radio from ignition switch
White	Slate	Tachometer to ignition coil
White	Orange	Hazard warning feed (to switch)
Yellow		Overdrive

Colour		Destination
Main	Tracer	
Yellow	Brown	Overdrive
Yellow	Blue	Overdrive
Yellow	Red	Overdrive
Yellow	Purple	Overdrive
Yellow	Green	Overdrive
Yellow	Light Green	Screenwiper motor to switch
Yellow	White	
Yellow	Black	
Yellow	Pink	
Yellow	Slate	
Yellow	Orange	
Black		All earth connections
Black	Brown	Tachometer generator to tachometer
Black	Blue	Tachometer generator to tachometer
Black	Red	Electric speedometer
Black	Purple	
Black	Green	Screenwiper switch to screenwiper (single speed) relay to radiator fan motor
Black	Light Green	Vacuum brake switch to warning light and/or buzzer
Black	White	Brake fluid level warning light to switch and handbrake switch
Black	Yellow	Electric speedometer
Black	Pink	
Black	Slate	
Black	Orange	Radiator fan motor to thermal switch
Slate		Window lift
Slate	Brown	Window lift
Slate	Blue	Window lift
Slate	Red	Window lift
Slate	Purple	Window lift
Slate	Green	Window lift
Slate	Light Green	Window lift
Slate	White	Window lift
Slate	Yellow	Window lift
Slate	Black	Window lift
Slate	Pink	Window lift
Slate	Orange	Window lift

BS-AU7 Colour Code for vehicle wiring is reproduced by permission of the British Standards Institution, 2 Park Street, London W1A 2BS, from whom copies of the standard may be obtained.

Fig. 14.6 British standard wiring code for automobiles – continued (Sec 4)

5 Wiring diagrams

1   Automobile wiring diagrams vary considerably in format. Some are concerned only with the electrical connections (Fig. 14.7 – Austin Metro) while the diagram for the Volvo 343 (Fig. 14.8) shows the relative position of components on the vehicle. This method illustrates groups of cables which would be taped together to form a loom, but does allow tracing out a particular cable. Not so the wiring diagram of the Vauxhall Chevette (Fig. 14.9) which illustrates the cables going into a loom without the possibility of direct tracing; in this example the cable is identified at entry and exit points by a number.

Key to wiring diagram Fig. 14.7 for the Austin Metro (Sec 5)

1	Rear fog guard lamps	**47**	Hazard switch and warning light
2	Front fog lamps (if fitted)	**49**	Ballast resistor cable
3	Panel illumination lamp	**50**	Direction indicator flasher unit
4	Cigar lighter illumination lamp	**51**	Heated rear screen switch
5	L.H. tail lamp	**53**	Brake fluid level sensor
6	Number-plate lamp	**54**	Direction indicator switch
7	R.H. tail lamp	**55**	Brake failure warning light
8	L.H. side lamp	**56**	Reverse lamp switch
9	R.H. side lamp	**57**	Stop lamp switch
10	Headlamp dipped beams	**58**	Voltage stabilizer
11	Main beam warning light	**59**	Brake pad wear warning light
12	Headlamp main beams	**60**	Ignition warning light
13	Front fog lamp relay (if fitted)	**61**	Tachometer (if fitted)
14	Horn	**62**	Ignition coil
15	Starter motor	**63**	Brake pad wear sensors
16	Starter motor solenoid	**64**	Choke warning light
17	Rear fog guard lamp switch and warning light	**65**	Oil pressure warning light
19	Headlamp dip switch	**66**	Handbrake warning light
20	Headlamp flasher switch	**67**	Seat belt warning light
21	Horn-push	**68**	Fuel gauge
22	Front fog lamp switch and warning light (if fitted)	**69**	Water temperature gauge
23	Fuses	**70**	Direction indicator repeater lamps
24	Line fuses	**71**	R.H. front indicator
25	Main lighting switch	**72**	R.H. rear indicator
26	Battery	**73**	Indicator warning light
27	Auxiliary circuits relay	**74**	L.H. rear indicator
28	Rear screen wash/wipe switch (if fitted)	**75**	L.H. front indicator
29	Windscreen wash/wipe switch	**76**	Heated rear screen
30	Ignition/starter switch	**77**	Reversing lamps
31	Headlamp washer relay (if fitted)	**78**	Gearbox selector panel illumination (Automatics only)
32	Heater motor	**79**	Stop lamps
33	Rear screen wiper motor (if fitted)	**80**	Choke warning light switch
34	Windscreen wiper motor	**81**	Oil pressure switch
35	Cigar lighter	**82**	Handbrake warning light switch
36	Clock (digital on HLS models)	**83**	Passenger seat switch
37	Headlamp washer motor (if fitted)	**84**	Passenger seat belt switch
38	Rear screen washer motor (if fitted)	**85**	Driver seat belt switch
39	Windscreen washer motor	**86**	Fuel gauge tank unit
40	Radio (if fitted)	**87**	Water temperature transducer
41	Interior lamp and switch	**88**	Radiator cooling fan
42	Heater motor switch	**89**	Radiator cooling fan thermostat
43	Door switches	**90**	Distributor
44	Brake failure warning lamp relay	**91**	Heater control illumination
45	Alternator	**92**	Panel switch illumination
46	Hazard warning flasher unit		

Cable colour code

B	Black	**N**	Brown	**S**	Slate
G	Green	**O**	Orange	**U**	Blue
K	Pink	**P**	Purple	**W**	White
LG	Light green	**R**	Red	**Y**	Yellow

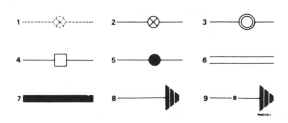

Key to symbols used in wiring diagrams

1   When fitted
2   Connector
3   Instrument printed circuit connector
4   Fuse board printed circuit connector
5   Sealed joint
6   Instrument printed circuit
7   Fuse board printed circuit
8   Component earthed through fixings
9   Component earthed with cable

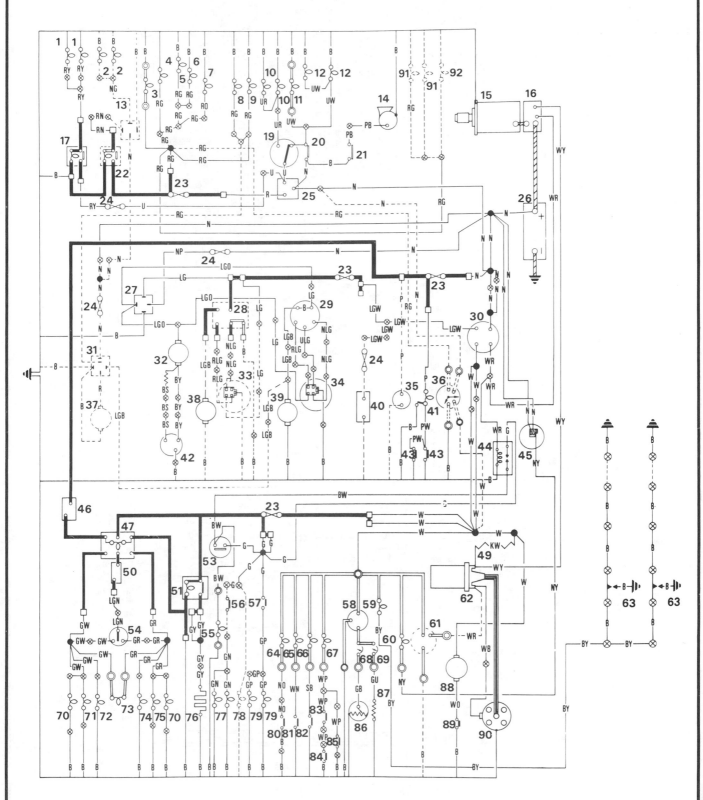

Fig. 14.7 Wiring diagram for the Austin Metro (Sec 5)

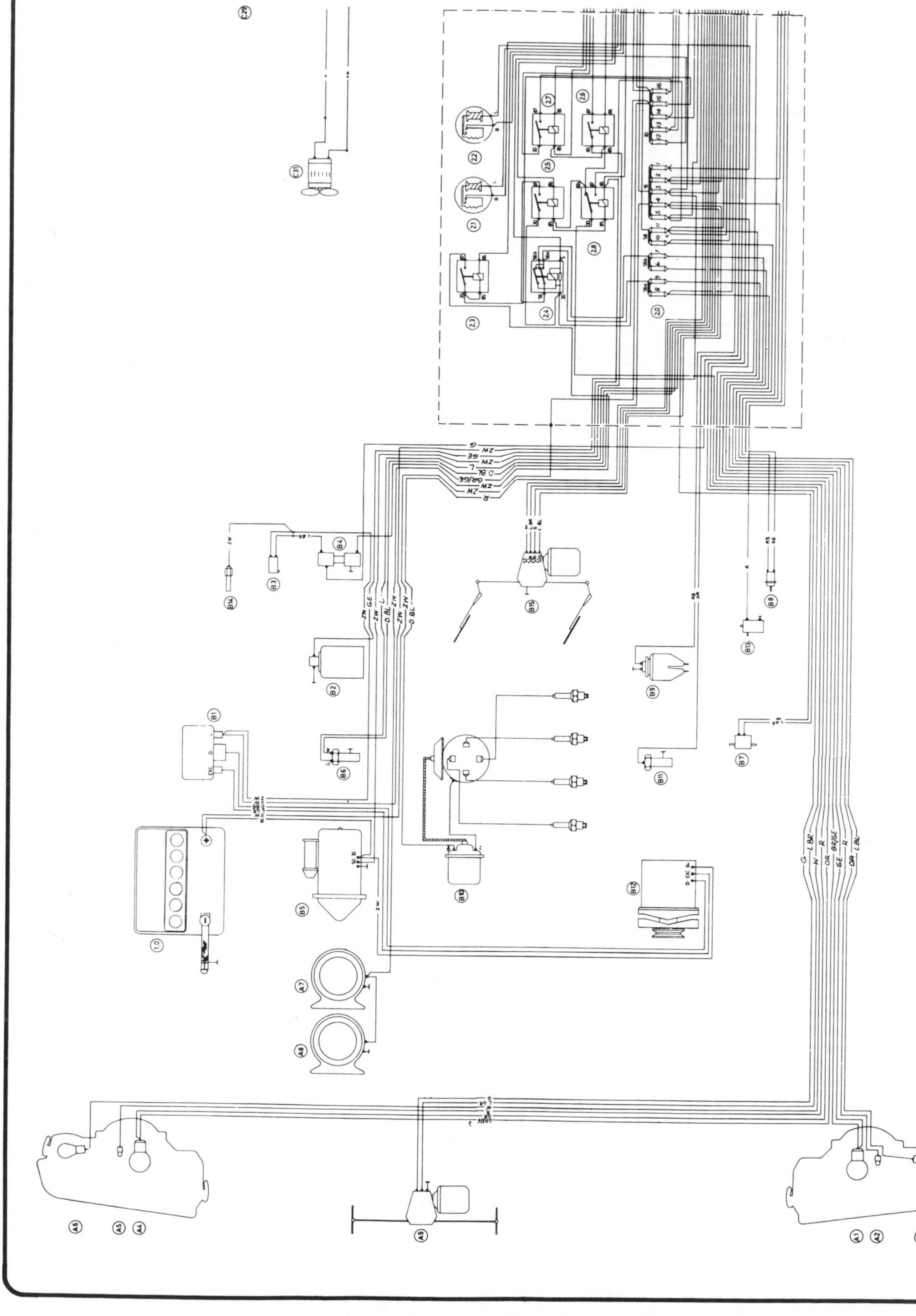

Fig. 14.8 Wiring diagram for the Volvo 343 (Sec 5)

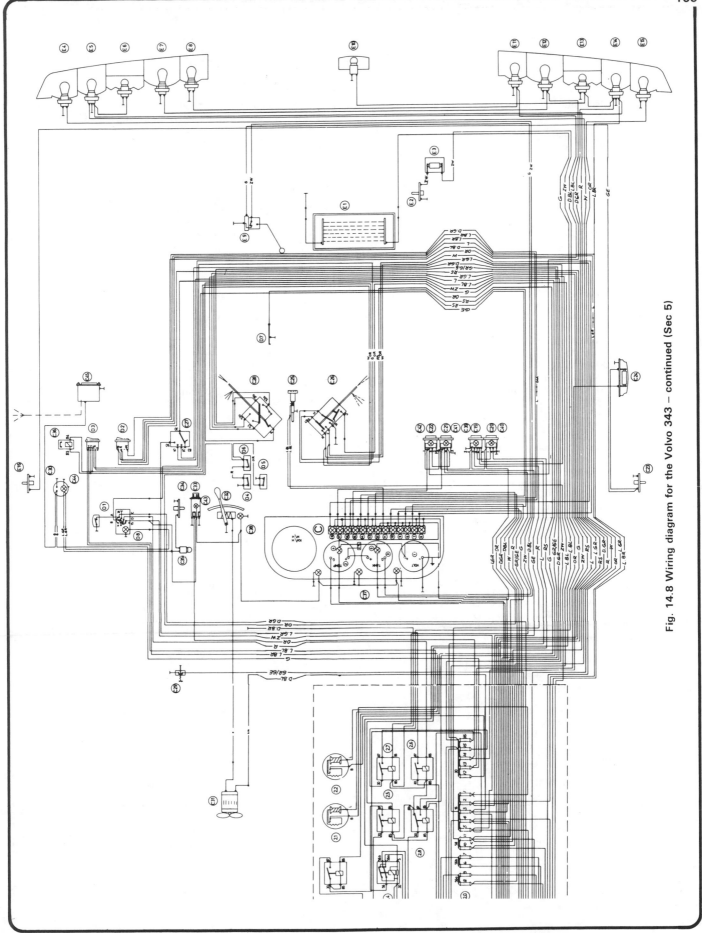

Fig. 14.8 Wiring diagram for the Volvo 343 – continued (Sec 5)

166

Key to wiring diagram Fig. 14.8 for the Volvo 343 (Sec 5)

A1   Headlamp main beam/dipped beam
A2   Parking light
A3   Direction indicator
A4   Headlamp main beam/dipped beam
A5   Parking lights
A6   Direction indicator
A7   Horn high-tone
A8   Horn low-tone
A9   Headlamp wiper motor (Nordic)

B1   Voltage regulator
B2   Water pump
B3   Microswitch
B4   4-way valve
B5   Starter motor
B6   Coolant temperature sender/switch
B7   Declutching valve
B8   Brake light switch
B9   Brake fluid level float
B10 Ignition coil
B11 Oil pressure sender
B12 Alternator
B13 3-way valve (Sweden)
B14 Pilot jet (Sweden)
B15 Windscreen wiper motor

C1   Voltmeter
C2   Temperature gauge
C3   Fuel gauge
C4   Coolant temperature warning lamp
C5   Fuel reserve indicating lamp
C6   Direction indicating lamp, left
C7   Parking light indicating lamp
C8   Handbrake warning lamp
C9   Oil pressure warning lamp
C10 Brake fluid level warning lamp
C11 Choke indicating lamp
C12 Seat belt indicating lamp
C13 Hazard warning installation indicating lamp
C14 Main beam indicating lamp
C15 Rear-warning foglamp, indicating lamp
C16 Low ratio hold indicating lamp
C17 Heated rear window indicating lamp
C18 Direction indicating lamp, right
C19 Switch for main beam/dipped beam
C20 Switch for parking lights
C21 Switch for heated rear window
C22 Switch for rear-warning foglamp
C23 Courtesy light door switch, left
C24 Courtesy light, car interior
C25 Choke
C26 Direction indicator switch
C27 Ignition switch
C28 Windscreen wiper switch
C29 Kickdown switch
C30 Clock
C31 Blower
C32 Blower rheostat
C33 Cigar lighter
C34 Switch for glove compartment light
C35 Lamp for glove compartment
C36 Direction indicator
C37 Lamp for instrument lighting

C38 Lamp for illumination of heater controls
C39 Lamp for illumination of main/dipped beam switch
C40 Lamp for illumination of parking lights switch
C41 Lamp for illumination of heated rear window switch
C42 Lamp for illumination of rear warning foglamp switch
C43 Lamp for illumination of cigar lighter
C44 Lamp for clock illumination (DL)
C45 Radio (optional)

D1   Selector lever switch
D2   Low ratio hold switch
D3   Switch for hazard warning installation
D4   Seat belt contact, left front
D5   Seat belt contact, right front
D6   Seat cushion contact, rear seat
D7   Handbrake switch
D8   Selector scale switch

E1   Heated rear window
E2   Boot light switch
E3   Boot light
E4   Direction indicator
E5   Tail light/brake light
E6   Tail light
E7   Rear-warning foglamp
E8   Reversing light
E9   Float
E10 Number plate light
E11 Reversing light
E12 Rear-warning foglamp
E13 Tail light
E14 Tail light/brake light
E15 Direction indicator
E16 Courtesy light door switch, right

1.0 Battery
2.0 Fusebox
2.1 Direction indicator
2.2 Hazard warning installation
2.3 Horn relay
2.4 Main beam/dipped beam relay
2.5 Vehicle lighting relay
2.6 Interlock (start inhibitor) relay
2.7 Heated rear window relay (DL)
2.8 Headlamp wash/wipe installation relay (Nordic)

Colour code

W   White
R   Red
OR   Orange
RS   Pink
D BR   Dark brown
L BR   Light brown
D BL   Dark blue
L BL   Light blue
D GR   Dark green
L GR   Light green
GR/GE Green/yellow
GE   Yellow
L   Lilac
G   Grey
ZW   Black

Key to wiring diagram Fig. 14.9 for the Vauxhall Chevette (Sec 5)

No.	Colour	Size	No.	Colour	Size
1	Brown	65/0.30	37	Green/purple	9/0.30
2	Brown	44/0.30	38	Green/light green	9/0.30
3	Brown	35/0.30	39	Green/white	14/0.30
4	Brown	14/0.30	40	Green/white	9/0.30
5	Brown/blue	35/0.30	41	Green/yellow	14/0.30
6	Brown/yellow	9/0.30	42	Green/black	9/0.30
7	Blue	35/0.30	43	Green/slate	14/0.30
8	Blue	28/0.30	44	Light green/brown	14/0.30
9	Blue/red	28/0.30	45	Light green/brown	9/0.30
10	Blue/red	14/0.30	46	Light green/black	14/0.25
11	Blue/light green	14/0.30	47	Light green/black	9/0.30
12	Blue/white	35/0.30	48	White	35/0.30
13	Blue/white	28/0.30	49	White	28/0.30
14	Blue/white	14/0.30	50	White	14/0.30
15	Blue/white	9/0.30	51	White/brown	9/0.30
16	Red	14/0.25	52	White/blue	28/0.30
17	Red/blue	9/0.30	53	White/red	28/0.30
18	Red/green	28/0.30	54	White/green	14/0.30
19	Red/light green	14/0.30	55	White/black	7/16/0.10
20	Red/black	9/0.30	56	White/black	28/0.30
21	Red/orange	9/0.30	57	White/black	9/0.30
22	Purple	35/0.30	58	Yellow/light green	14/0.30
23	Purple	28/0.30	59	Black	28/0.30
24	Purple	9/0.30	60	Black	14/0.30
25	Purple/brown	14/0.30	61	Black	14/0.25
26	Purple/white	9/0.30	62	Black	9/0.30
27	Purple/black	14/0.30	63	Black/white	9/0.30
28	Purple/black	9/0.30	64	Brown/white	0.75mm^2
29	Green	28/0.30	65	Yellow	0.75mm^2
30	Green	14/0.30	66	Grey	0.75mm^2
31	Green	14/0.25	67	Black	0.75mm^2
32	Green	9/0.30	68	Fusible link	14/0.30
33	Green/brown	9/0.30	69	Battery cable	37/0.75
34	Green/blue	9/0.30	70	Ground cable	16/16/0.30
35	Green/red	14/0.30	71	Resistance wire	●
36	Green/red	9/0.30			

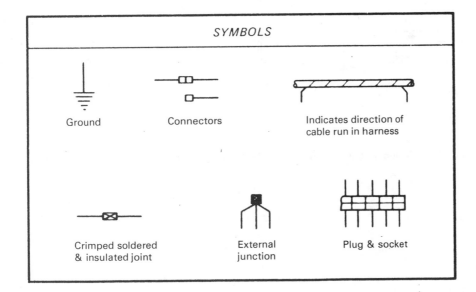

SYMBOLS

Ground

Connectors

Indicates direction of cable run in harness

Crimped soldered & insulated joint

External junction

Plug & socket

● Denotes single strand resistance wire giving a total of $2\,\Omega \pm 20\,\Omega$ routed between points A1 – A2 – A3
Resistance wire 1/0.71 or 22 S.W.G
Resistance per 25mm .0312 $\Omega \pm 5\%$

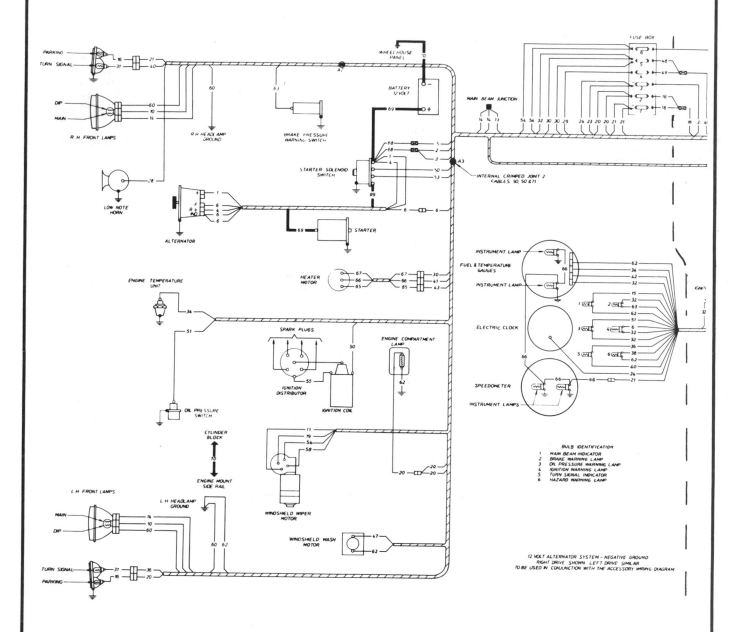

Fig. 14.9 Wiring diagram for the Vauxhall Chevette (Sec 5)

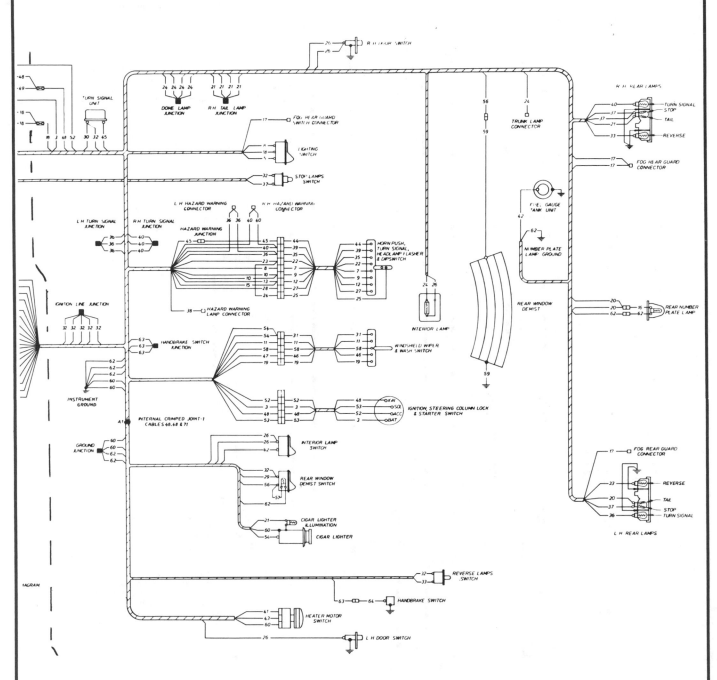

Fig. 14.9 Wiring diagram for the Vauxhall Chevette – continued (Sec 5)

INSTRUCTIONS FOR USING CURRENT FLOW DIAGRAMS

Note:
All **switches** and **contacts** are illustrated in the **mechanical off position.** The various contacts in a switch are shown in the current track to which they belong by function.

The grey area represents the relay plate with fuse holder

Numbers in yellow squares indicate that a wire is discontinued in the diagram and refer to the current track where it is continued.

Wire cross section in mm²

Terminals with the numbers which are on the actual parts.

Wiring colours (are shown in the actual colours to be found on the vehicle)

Numbers/number combinations These indicate the individual contacts in a multi-point connector, e.g. T 10/4
T 10 = ten-point connector
/4 = contact 4

Symbols (in this case: bulb)

Parts designation Using the legend you will be able to find which part in the current flow diagram is referred to by this symbol, e.g. W = interior light

Internal connections (thin lines) These connections are **not** to be found in the form of wires. Internal connections are however current-carrying connections. They make it possible to check the flow of current within a component or unit.

Numbers in circles indicate the locations of earthing points (see legend)

Current track numbers to help you find the parts in the current flow diagram (see legend)

Pictorial illustration of parts whose symbols are given in the current track above.

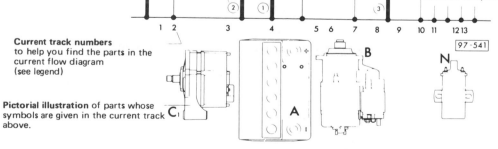

Fig. 14.10 Instructions for using Volkswagen current flow diagrams (Sec 5)

2 The VAG/Volkswagen system is unlike any conventional diagram; their current flow charts show individual circuits of the electrical system of a vehicle, divided up into current tracks. All components with their functional connections are shown; components are illustrated by symbols with thin lines indicating internal connections (Figs. 14.10 and 14.11).

3 The current flow chart shown is annotated for instructional purposes and given a few minutes study the advantages of the method become apparent. Probably the most advantageous point is the ease of following a wire feed to a component. Also the pictorial illustration at the foot of the current flow diagram assists location of the component on the vehicle.

Specimen legend

The same part designations are used in all current flow diagrams.

E.g.: A is always used for the battery or N for the ignition coil

Designation		in current track
A	— Battery	4
B	— Starter	5, 6, 7, 8
C	— Alternator	3
C 1	— Voltage regulator	3
F 2	— Door contact switch	2
N	— Ignition coil	10, 11
N 6	— Series resistance (for coil)	8
O	— Distributor	10, 11, 12, 13
P	— Spark plug connector	11, 12, 13
Q	— Spark plugs	11, 12, 13
S 7	— Fuse in fusebox	
T 10	— Connector, ten-point, on instrument panel insert	
W	— Interior light	

① — Earthing strap, battery/body

② — Earthing strap, alternator/engine

③ — Earthing strap, gearbox/chassis

Explanation of where a connection is to be found on the vehicle.

Number of current track to help you locate the part in the current flow diagram. Current track numbers are not given for fuses, wiring connections and earthing points.

Fig. 14.10 Instructions for using Volkswagen current flow diagrams – continued (Sec 5)

SYMBOLS USED IN CURRENT FLOW DIAGRAMS

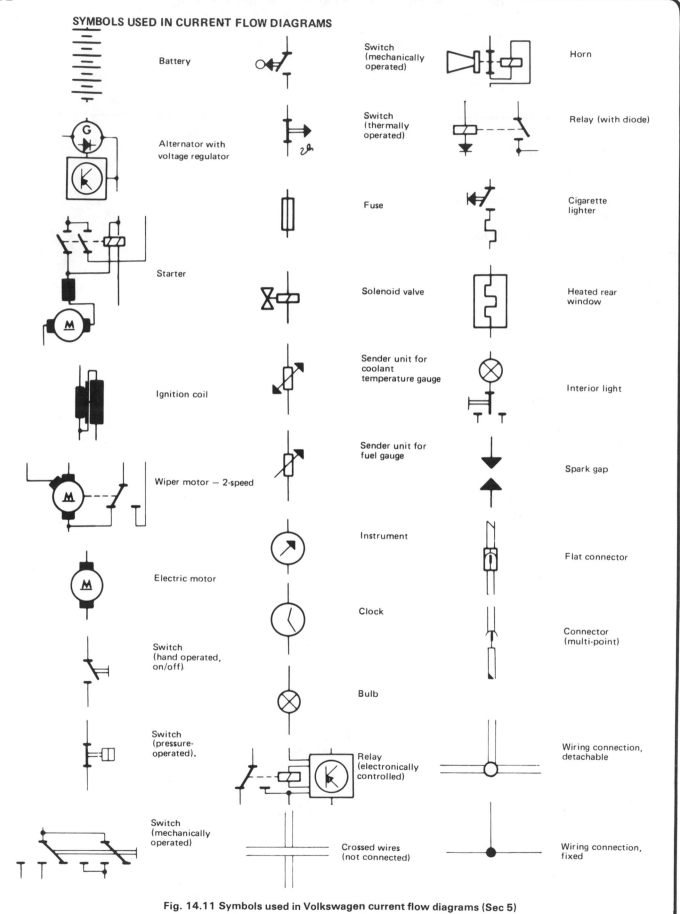

Fig. 14.11 Symbols used in Volkswagen current flow diagrams (Sec 5)

4   Symbols for electrical components found in automobiles vary according to the country of origin, but each diagram gives a key or a name near the symbol so usually there is no doubt. Cars of European Continent origin generally employ the German DIN system for symbols, a selection being given in Fig. 14.12.

5   Terminal marking on equipment and on corresponding circuit diagrams is useful for identification. The DIN system allots numbers and some letters to terminals of equipment and it pays to remember the more common of them when working on European vehicles. Certain code numbers are most important, so that any terminal marked 30 is live with no switch in the line, and so would be suitable for connection of certain accessories. 31 represents an earth terminal, and 31 b is used when an electrical load is operated by a switch in the return path to earth.

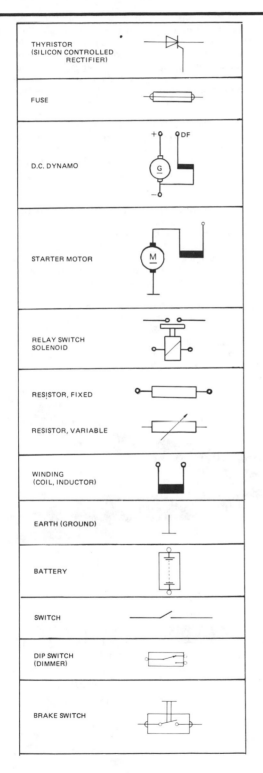

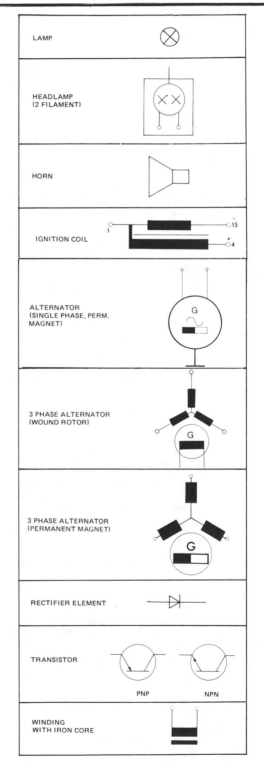

Fig. 14.12 DIN circuit symbols (Sec 5)

6 Fig. 14.13 gives a selection of code numbers used in vehicles employing DIN standards. For a comprehensive coverage of this subject the reader is referred to the Bosch Technical Instruction booklet 'Graphical Symbols and Circuit Diagrams for Automotive Electrics'.

Terminal Number	Wire leading from	To
1	Ignition coil	Contact breaker
4	Ignition coil ht	Sparking plug (or distributor)
15	Ignition switch	Ignition coil
or 15	Switch in line from battery +	Switched load
15a	CDI pulse coil	CDI trigger terminal
15/54	Main switch or ignition switch	Coil, warning light, fuse for daylight current consumers, i.e. brake lights, horn, flasher switch etc.
30	Battery +	Starter, ignition switch
30/51	Battery or generator	Relay switch
31	Battery –	Earth (ground)
31b	Switch	Earth (ground)
49	Ignition switch	Flasher unit
49a	Flasher unit	Turn indicator switch
50	Starter switch	Starter solenoid
51	Generator regulator	Battery, starter or main switch
54	See 15/54	
L54	Turn indicator switch	Left-hand turn indicator lamp
R54	Turn indicator switch	Right-hand turn indicator lamp
56	Lightswitch	Dipswitch
56a	Dipswitch	Main beam bulb and indicator bulb
56b	Dipswitch	Dipped beam bulb
57	Lightswitch	Parking light (city light US)
58	Lightswitch	Tail light, number plate light, side light
61	Generator regulator	Charge warning lamp
85	Relay switch winding	Earth (ground)
86	Relay switch winding	Battery (via switch or direct)
87	Relay switch with normally open contact	Accessory
87a	Ditto – closed contact	Accessory
B+	Battery positive	–
B–	Battery negative	–
D+	Generator +	Regulator
DF	Generator exciter winding	Regulator
L	Turn indicator switch	Left-hand turn indicator lamp
R	Turn indicator switch	Right-hand turn indicator lamp
UVW	Individual phase terminals	3-phase rectifier pack

Fig. 14.13 A selection of DIN terminal markings (Sec 5)

6 Connections

1 Good, clean connections are vital for trouble-free operation, particularly since certain electrical components will be exposed to weather. The braided earthing strap from the battery to the body carries all the current used in the motor vehicle. The bolted connection down to the body should be checked for corrosion and even the possibility of paint underneath the earthing terminal tag.

2 Battery connections can be a source of volt-drop and, when loaded by the starter motor current can go, momentarily, open-circuit giving a sharp 'click' sound from the starter solenoid but no drive – every auto-electrician meets this phenomenon at some time. Lugs and terminal posts should be kept clean, and any white 'fungus' removed. A trace of Vaseline on the lugs and posts will be helpful, and even better will be the special anti-corrosion grease now available in auto shops.

3 The heavy cable connection to the lug is sometimes by sweated joint and this can be the source of the break occurring on heavy current demand. This is best checked by putting a voltmeter or bulb onto the solenoid terminal and then moving the cable about at the lug end. Erratic movements of the voltmeter pointer, or the bulb going on or off, indicate a faulty joint.

4 Connectors of various types are used for joining parts of a circuit; the safest, but most trouble to make, is a soldered connection. Soldered joints require only that the wire and tags are scraped clean, and only resin flux (not acid flux such as Bakers fluid) is used, because of the danger of subsequent corrosion. The small soldering iron used in electronics is not generally suitable for auto-electrical work, and an iron of 65 to 150 watts rating is recommended.

5 Crimping of joints requires a tool which is a special form of pliers which crushes the wings of a connecting tag onto the bared wire surface (Fig. 14.14 and 14.15). The electrical connection can be very good, but trouble can arise if the wire and tag are not really clean. Volt-drop due to imperfect crimped joints is always a possibility, and should be checked where circuit malfunction occurs.

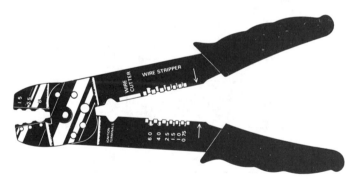

Fig. 14.14 Crimping tool (Sec 6)

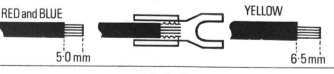

RECOMMENDED STRIP LENGTH

REMEMBER TO STRIP THE WIRE THE CORRECT DISTANCE FOR THE APPROPRIATE WIRE SIZE

RED and BLUE   YELLOW

5·0 mm   6·5 mm

MAKE SURE THE INSULATION BUTTS FIRMLY AGAINST TERMINAL BARREL

Completed crimps

THIS CRIMP GIVES AN IDEAL ELECTRICAL CONNECTION. MAKE SURE YOU CRIMP BOTH *CONDUCTOR* AND *INSULATION* CRIMPS

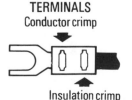

TERMINALS
Conductor crimp

Insulation crimp

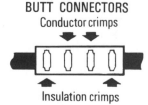

BUTT CONNECTORS
Conductor crimps

Insulation crimps

Fig. 14.15 Crimping hints (Sec 6)

7 Fuses

1   Many electrical circuits have protective devices so that in the event of a short circuit, the battery is isolated. The battery is capable of driving a high current into an accidental short-circuit and this may be sufficient to burn the insulation off cables, possibly buckle the battery plates, or cause a fire. The motor vehicle uses the fuse for such protection.

2   A fuse consists of a cartridge with contacts on either end and a strip of soft metal or length of tinned wire connected between them. When an overload occurs the fuse wire or strip will melt, breaking the circuit.

3   The fuse may be replaced, but the auto-electrician will need to find and rectify the cause, otherwise the new fuse will also melt.

4   Four types of fuse are presently in use on vehicles:

   (a)   Glass tubular fuses
   (b)   Ceramic base fuses
   (c)   Flat-bladed fuses
   (d)   Fusible links

It is to be noted that glass fuses are normally rated at their fusing value, but ceramic fuses are rated at the maximum continuous current that they can carry, being half of the fusing value.

5   Fig. 14.16 illustrates the fuses (a), (b) and (c) and gives codings and current ratings. Fuses shown are usually mounted on fuseboards and located in matching clips, but in-line fuses may be employed, usually for protection of an accessory installed as non-original equipment.

6   Fusible links are fitted by many vehicle manufacturers to prevent an outbreak of fire in the case of an accident, where wires might be cut or trapped by twisted metal. The link is a highly rated fuse connected in the main supply cable close to the battery and will fail in the event of a massive short-circuit in the wiring system. Some fusible links are easily replaced, but others have to be soldered in.

7   Little will normally go wrong with fuses, but occasionally they suffer from corrosion of the metal ends which gives rise to poor contact with the fusebox clips. A remedy is to clean them with emery paper or a small wire brush and give them a spray with an electrical cleaning and protective fluid.

8   Of interest is the thermal breaker which protects lighting circuits and consists of a bi-metal strip and a pair of contacts. Any large abnormal load in the lighting circuit will cause the bi-metal strip to heat and bend, eventually breaking the contacts open. The lighting load is therefore periodically switched on and off; the wiring system is protected, but the driver should have sufficient intermittent lighting to come to a halt safely. A typical unit used in one Vauxhall vehicle will pass 25 amperes, but with a current of 33 amperes should open within 30 to 180 seconds.

8   Adding extras

1   A wide range of electrical accessories is now on sale and care should be taken in ensuring that connections into the vehicle wiring system are appropriate and safe.

2   The item of equipment will usually come with its own cable, but this cable is often the thinnest that will do the job. It is worth checking on the current taken and to compare the supplied cable with the guide found earlier in this Chapter — if necessary, use a thicker grade.

FUSES (Flat Bladed)

Identification	Rating
Purple	3
Pink	4
Orange	5
Brown	7.5
Red	10
Blue	15
Yellow	20
White	25
Green	30

FUSES (ceramic type)

Identification	BSS Ratings
Length 25mm	AMP
Yellow	5
White	8
Red	16
Blue	25

FUSES (glass cartridge)

cone end   flat end

Identification	Lucas Ratings
Length 25.4mm (1")	
Cone end	AMP
Blue	3
Yellow	4.5
Nut Brown	8.0
Red on Green	10.0
White	35.0
Length 29.4mm (1^{5}/32")	
Flat end	
Red on Blue	2.0
Red	5.0
Blue on Green	8.0
Black on Blue	10.0
Light Brown	15.0
Blue on Yellow	20.0
Pink	25.0
White	35.0
Yellow	50.0

Fig. 14.16 Automobile fuses and ratings (Sec 7)

3   Wiring-in is dependent upon the type of vehicle, and it must be decided firstly whether the accessory will be connected to the battery supply or be wired through the ignition switch. Wiring to the supply has the danger that the accessory might accidentally be left on when the driver leaves the car, but equally it must be remembered that extra loads on the ignition switch or a lighting switch can cause contact trouble, leading to switch failure. It is a matter of judgement; as examples, heavy current items such as spotlamps, heated rear windows, foglamps and horns should use a relay.

4   The relay is an electrically-operated switch (see Chapter 1). The relay coil which closes the contacts magnetically takes a small current for operation, and several manufacturers market such a unit suitable for installation of car electrical extras. Fig. 14.17 shows the basic circuit of the relay together with terminal markings covering a range of manufacturers, and Fig. 14.18 shows the symbols found on a wiring diagram to represent the relay. Examples of relay applications are given below:

5   Driving (or spot) lamps are frequently fitted to enhance illumination, and in the UK the law states that these must be wired so as to extinguish when the headlights are dipped. A relay control is required and, in order to meet the condition above, the feed to the main beam should supply the relay coil (Fig. 14.19). A practical point on fitting is to note that Hella now market a replacement front grille and lamp set. This saves the tedious task of fitting with brackets or cutting holes in the bodywork.

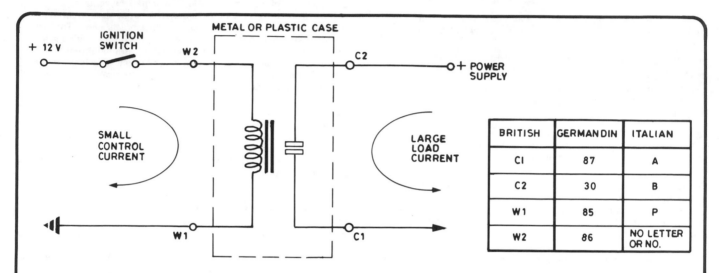

BRITISH	GERMAN DIN	ITALIAN
C1	87	A
C2	30	B
W1	85	P
W2	86	NO LETTER OR NO.

NB   THIS DIAGRAM SERVES TO ILLUSTRATE PRINCIPLE OF OPERATION IT IS NOT SYMBOLISED ON WIRING DIAGRAMS THIS WAY.

Fig. 14.17 Connections and marking of relays (Sec 8)

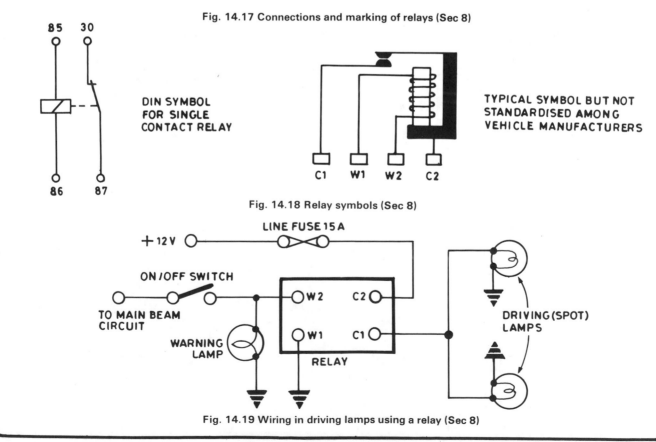

Fig. 14.18 Relay symbols (Sec 8)

Fig. 14.19 Wiring in driving lamps using a relay (Sec 8)

6   A heated rear window will take a minimum of 6 amperes and is a case for using a relay. It is preferable to supply the relay from an ignition switch controlled feed to obviate the risk of leaving the heater on (Fig. 14.20).

7   Wiring in a pair of horns calls for a relay since the current demand will be high. In the diagram (Fig. 14.21) the horn button is connected in the earth (ground) wire. If the existing horn is fed through a relay, it is possible to substitute the new horns or feed a second relay from the first.

8   Double connections can be of the plug-in bullet or the self-stripping types. In the case of the convenient self-stripping connectors make sure that the right size is chosen. For the Scotchlok type, colour blue is right for most automotive applications, but red is used for thinner cables, and brown or yellow for thicker cables.

9   Care must be taken not to overload the existing fusebox. Where several accessories are to be added and all must be fused, it is better to use an auxiliary fusebox. This can be fed from a relay which is itself fed from an ignition controlled supply (Fig. 14.22) and also provides more fused circuits supplied direct from the battery.

10   Fitting extras always involves finding a good earth. This may mean scraping paint back to the bare metal at the point chosen and it is always worthwhile to use a proper terminal. Corrosion can set in at such an earth point, so it is advisable to use a thin smear of anti-corrosion grease of the type recommended for battery terminals.

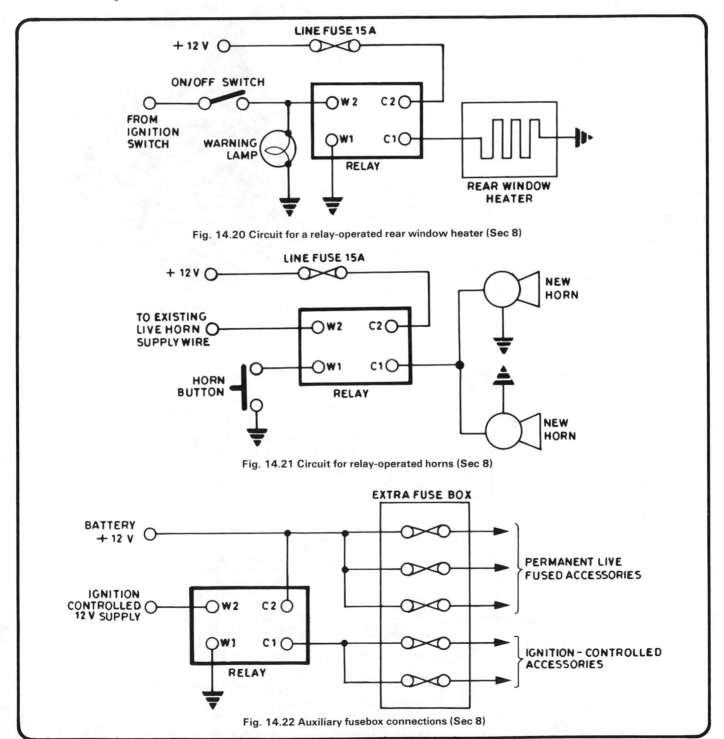

Fig. 14.20 Circuit for a relay-operated rear window heater (Sec 8)

Fig. 14.21 Circuit for relay-operated horns (Sec 8)

Fig. 14.22 Auxiliary fusebox connections (Sec 8)

9 Electrical tool kit

1   It is advantageous to keep a set of special tools just for electrical work, since there must be no possibility of oily tools being used anywhere on vehicle circuitry.

2   Here is a list to meet most needs:

Pocket knife (for scraping connections clean)
Plug spanner with rubber grip for plug tops
Electrician's screwdriver set
Cross-head screwdriver (chubby and 4 inch)
Engineer's combination pliers
HT cable pliers (optional)
Side-cutting pliers
Snipe-nosed pliers
Circlip pliers
Impact driver
Adjustable wire stripper
Crimping tool, with box of assorted connectors
Sets of Allen keys (Imperial and metric)
Ignition spanners
Flat file for dressing contact points
Spark plug feeler gauges and setting tool
Jump leads with heavy crocodile clips
Small bulb in holder with prod leads, to act as a test lamp
Rubber grommet kit
Hydrometer
Soldering iron (65 watt minimum, but 150 watt may be needed)

10 Test instruments and applications

Testmeters

1   Universal testmeters are available with ranges specially suited to automobile systems. Ranges for volts, amperes and ohms are normal, but it is rare for meters to be able to measure starter currents directly. In addition, many modern meters incorporate other functions such as dwell, points condition and engine speed (tachometer).

2   Readers are reminded of the danger in switching ranges on a multi-range meter without first disconnecting the leads from the circuit (see Chapter 1).

3   A useful yet inexpensive meter is shown in Fig. 14.23. This is a voltmeter with an ingenious circuit arrangement so that volts, ohms, dwell, points condition, engine timing and battery condition can be measured. Two of these are worthy of note:

4   Dwell measurement using this compact instrument is based on the average voltage between the ignition feed line and the distributor as the points open and close. The instrument pointer is not able to follow rapid variations and takes up a position on a scale which is an average of the square pulse of voltage at the input terminals (Fig. 14.24). This scale is calibrated in degrees of dwell angle.

Fig. 14.23 Sparktune testmeter (Sec 10)

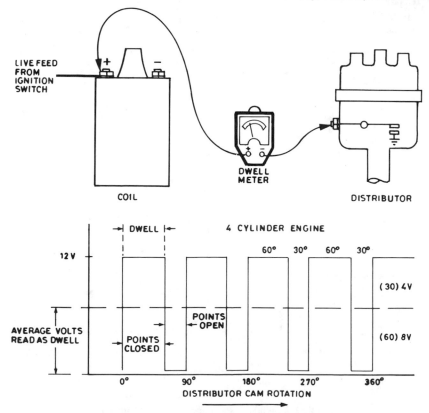

14.24 The use of average voltage to measure dwell (Sec 10)

5   The meter is first adjusted to read full scale whilst connected to the live feed terminal of the coil and earth with the engine turning over on the starter, but not running – the contact breaker lead being disconnected (Fig. 14.25). Next the meter is connected between the live feed terminal of the coil and the contact breaker terminal of the distributor. Note no connection exists between the coil contact breaker terminal and the distributor, so the engine will not fire (Fig. 14.25). The engine is again cranked, and the reading of the meter taken as degrees of dwell.

6   High resistance may be measured using the properties of a voltmeter, itself having a given resistance so that, for instance, if a resistive HT cable is connected in series with the meter across the vehicle battery, the current through the meter will be lower than without the added cable, and the pointer can be read on an ohms scale.

7   More sophisticated are the universal meters, some of which employ the latest silicon chip technology. The Gunson Testune is a good example of such a meter which will serve as a tachometer and measure dwell, amperes, volts, ohms and points condition. The method used for measurement of dwell is such that only a simple connection between contact breaker and earth is necessary. In this case the system is live and the engine running, so before voltage pulses can be measured it is necessary to remove transient spikes and to clip the height of the waves to a constant amplitude. This process is shown schematically in Fig. 14.26.

8   The Zener diode is used to maintain a stable voltage and give the waveform a constant amplitude. The Zener diode breaks down and begins to conduct as soon as a particular voltage is reached, ensuring that the designed level is not exceeded.

Stroboscopes

9   Stroboscopes for ignition timing are high-intensity flashing lamps in which the flashing rate is controlled by an ignition spark. With the engine running, the flashing light can be directed towards the engine timing marks on the fanbelt pulley or the flywheel, and has the effect of freezing the motion so that the marks appear to be stationary. The ignition distributor body can then be slowly moved until the correct alignment of the rotating timing mark and the fixed mark on the engine casting is achieved while the engine is running.

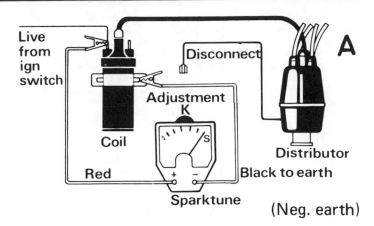

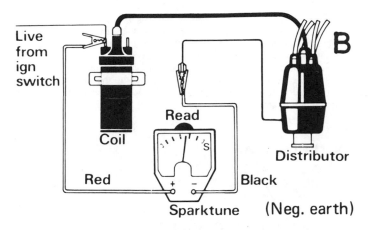

Fig. 14.25 Using the Sparktune (Sec 10)

A   Setting the meter
B   Reading the dwell angle

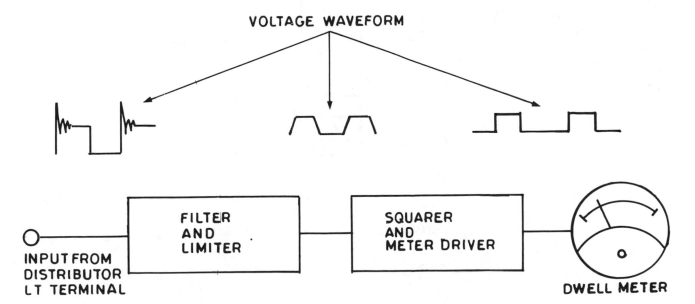

Fig. 14.26 The silicon chip dwell meter (Sec 10)

10 One type of strobscope is illustrated diagrammatically in Fig. 14.27. A fraction of the No 1 spark plug voltage is passed to the control grid of the xenon or neon tube by the probe lead and a capacitor. The main discharge electrodes of the tube are fed from a capacitor charged up from a high voltage dc supply. When the spark pulse reaches the control grid this is sufficient for the gas in the tube to break down, allowing current to flow through until the capacitor C is discharged. The current flow gives rise to an intense flash of light over a period of only microseconds. Xenon gives a whitish light, and is more intense than the red neon type of lamp, but the advantage is paid for in a higher cost.

11 Service data for many vehicles gives information for stroboscope timing only and can include the required advance at increasing speeds. It is therefore essential to be able to measure engine speed, and one manufacturer has combined the stroboscope with an ingenious measurement system to give a speed reading. The Gunson Tachostrobe is shown in Fig. 14.28, this having a variable-length vibrating wire, the oscillation rate being controlled by a thumb-wheel.

12 In the side of the stroboscope pistol is a prism which picks up some of the flashtube light and also the shadow of the vibrating wire. When the tube is flashing at the No 1 plug firing rate, the thumb-wheel is rotated until the vibrating wire comes into synchronisation, as shown by the shadow movement gradually slowing to near standstill. The thumb-wheel has a scale marked in revolutions per minute, and vibration is achieved by pulling the trigger every ten seconds or so; the trigger mechanism plucks the string as with a guitar.

13 **Great care must be taken when working on running engines using stroboscopes.** The visual impression that the fan is stationary has led to many accidents.

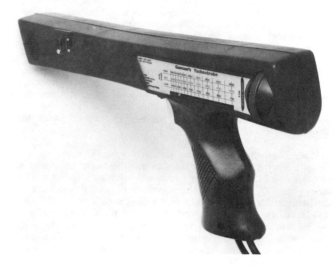

Fig. 14.28 The Tachostrobe (Sec 10)

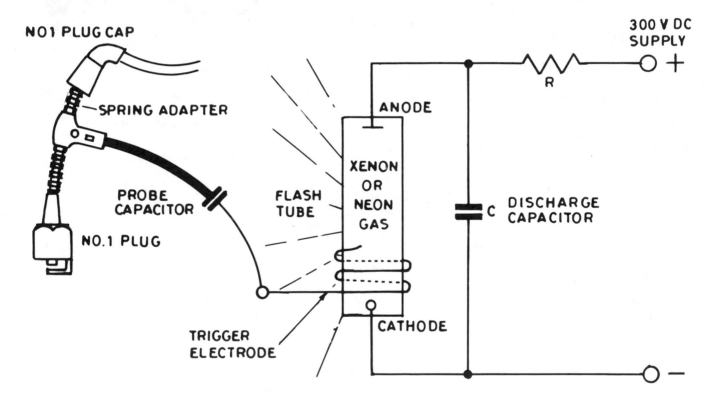

Fig. 14.27 Operation of a typical stroboscope (Sec 10)

Chapter 15 Diagnostic engine analysers

Contents

1 Introduction

1   Checking and locating engine faults may be greatly speeded up and made more precise by the use of engine analysers. Analysers are available in several types, ranging from portable units using indicator instruments to the sophisticated models with oscilloscope display facilities and digital/analogue instruments.

2   The facilities available depend upon the model and cost, but it is possible to:

    (a) measure voltage and current with precision
    (b) display screen patterns of waveforms showing the performance of generators and ignition systems. With some experience it is possible to recognise the fault and its location by examination of the pattern
    (c) measure the percentage of carbon monoxide in the exhaust gases, allowing precision adjustment of the carburettor
    (d) measure high and low resistance values with an ohmmeter reading in digital or analogue form
    (e) measure capacitance of the contact breaker capacitor and its possible leakage
    (f) measure and adjust ignition timing with the aid of a stroboscope
    (g) measure centrifugal and vacuum advance variation with engine speed
    (h) measure and display engine speed from the rate of sparking

3   The subject is too large to be treated fully here and so only a survey of the analyser can be given. Excellent courses are available, such as those provided by TI Crypton Ltd. at their Training School in Daventry, Northamptonshire, England. *Thanks are due to the Company for information in this Chapter.*

2 Voltmeter testing

1   The voltmeter built into the TI Crypton engine analyser (Fig. 15.1) is a high-grade moving-coil instrument with a large scale that may be read to at least 0.1 volt accuracy by the mechanic whilst making adjustments. Some equipment may additionally have a digital read-out facility.

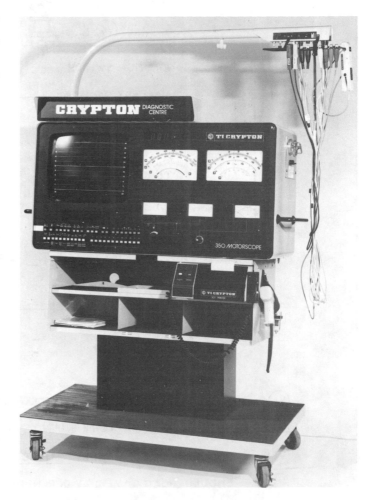

Fig. 15.1 The TI Crypton engine analyser (Sec 2)

2   Tests may be carried out by measuring the voltage relative to earth which, in this case, is a good metallic contact point on engine or bodywork. Voltages increase as the clip-on probe is attached to points up the circuit path to the battery supply point (Fig. 15.2).

3   Irregularities show the location of a high or low resistance component. For example, assuming the points are closed:

    (a)   if V_2 reads battery voltage, then there is a possibility of wrong connections between the ignition switch and the shorting terminal on the solenoid. The coil will be severely overloaded. It may be also that the coil primary winding is open circuit

    (b)   if V_1 exceeds the figures shown, the contacts may be in poor condition, exhibiting high resistance

    (c)   if V_3 is much below battery voltage, the ignition switch contacts may be high resistance

    (d)   corrosion on terminals or connecting tags, or poor connections under crimped joints, may account for volt-drops

The result of these malfunctions is that the ignition coil would not be receiving its designed voltage and ignition spark voltage will not be correct.

4   Note that this example is of a ballasted coil ignition circuit. The ballast resistor may be in one of several forms:

    (a)   as a resistive wire between the ignition switch and the coil feed terminal

    (b)   as a carbon resistor

    (c)   as a coiled wire resistor wound on a ceramic insulator

    (d)   as a temperature-dependent resistor, as used in certain French vehicles. This has low resistance when cold, giving full voltage to the coil at switch-on, but rises rapidly in resistance when the engine runs

5   Starter motor operation may drag down the coil voltage to an unacceptable level, leaving insufficient to produce a regular spark. Lowest possible readings of V_3 should be within 9 to 10 volts for an un-ballasted coil and 4.5 to 5.5 volts for a ballasted coil. If the measured voltage on cranking load is below these figures the trouble could be:

    (a)   faulty or discharged battery

    (b)   faulty starter motor

3   Oscilloscope displays

1   The most interesting feature of an analyser unit is the oscilloscope display, similar to a TV picture on one line. This is simply an electronic writing tool in which the spot traverses the screen at a constant speed and with a constant, controllable repetition rate.

2   Handwriting conveys information by horizontal movement plus a vertical motion, and so it is with the oscilloscope. The vertical motion is produced by a signal voltage applied to the cathode ray tube – this

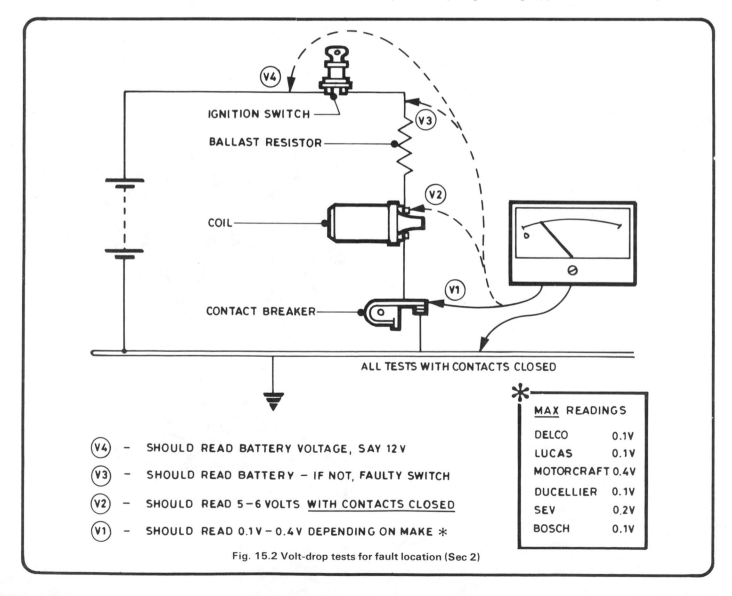

ALL TESTS WITH CONTACTS CLOSED

V4 — SHOULD READ BATTERY VOLTAGE, SAY 12 V

V3 — SHOULD READ BATTERY — IF NOT, FAULTY SWITCH

V2 — SHOULD READ 5–6 VOLTS WITH CONTACTS CLOSED

V1 — SHOULD READ 0.1V – 0.4V DEPENDING ON MAKE *

MAX READINGS	
DELCO	0.1V
LUCAS	0.1V
MOTORCRAFT	0.4V
DUCELLIER	0.1V
SEV	0.2V
BOSCH	0.1V

Fig. 15.2 Volt-drop tests for fault location (Sec 2)

could be the voltage at a spark plug or at the alternator terminal, for example.

3 Finally, handwriting can be seen because the ink on paper is a form of memory. In the case of the oscilloscope the brain perceives a picture of the whole line and not just the moving spot because (a) the eye has a retention facility, and (b) the spot on the phosphorous coating on the inside of the cathode ray tube face has an after-glow time which helps to create the visual impression of a continuous line.

4 Diagnosis by oscilloscope traces

1 Pictures may be displayed on the screen showing the coil primary voltage and the coil secondary voltage. The primary voltage is taken off at the coil CB terminal and the secondary voltage at a convenient HT point.

2 From the pictures an experienced operator can recognise many electrical malfunctions and also several of mechanical origin, such as inaccurate setting of the contact breaker gap, wear in the distributor, and contact breaker point bounce.

5 Oscilloscope fault diagnosis – primary circuit

1 Clipping the test probe onto the contact breaker side of the ignition coil primary will produce a picture similar to that of Fig. 15.3 for a system in good condition.

2 This shows the cycle of events taking place from 'points open' (left side of picture) to 'points close', and through to the next 'open' position. When the contact breaker points open, oscillations of electrical energy take place between the ignition coil primary and the capacitor (1).

3 At point (3) the oscillations jump to a different level and this shows that the spark has ceased at the plug. The oscillations remaining (2) die away as energy is dissipated in the form of heat.

4 At point (4) the contacts close and the height of the step represents the battery voltage. From (4) to (5) is the period of points closure and, if measured with a degree scale, is the dwell angle.

5 The whole oscilloscope pattern represents 1 cycle of sparking plug operation and, expressed in degrees, is 90° for a four-cylinder engine or 60° for a six-cylinder engine.

6 Other features detectable from the primary coil oscilloscope display include:

(a) capacitor condition
(b) HT suppression resistance values
(c) contact arcing
(d) shorted ignition coil or other faults

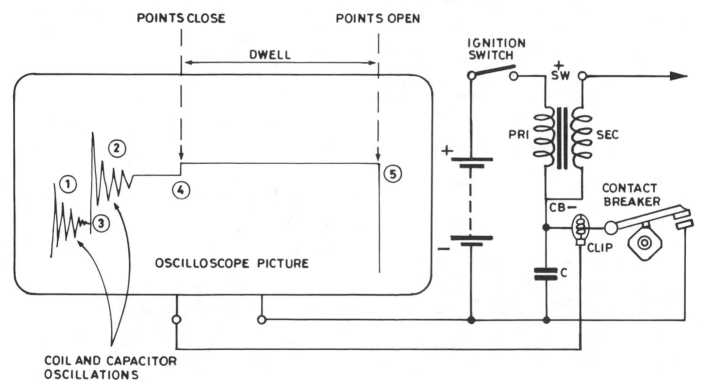

Fig. 15.3 Primary ignition circuit oscilloscope waveform (Sec 5)

For the significance of points 1 to 5 see text

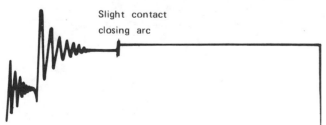

Fig. 15.4 Normal arcing for a new contact breaker (Sec 6)

6 Oscilloscope fault diagnosis – contact breaker

1 This subject is extensive, and only a few interpretations of the screen trace can be given here. The contact breaker can be subject to several faults, largely due to its being a mechanical device and prone to wear.

2 When new, the contact surfaces have high spots due to the manufacturing process. As the contacts wear in for the first few miles of operation there will be a small amount of 'hash' on the trace at the contact breaker close point (Fig. 15.4).

3   As the contacts wear further, pitting and piling will occur, with the earth contact usually losing metal and the live contact acquiring it. Arcing may occur, but other factors producing similar traces include:

(a)   over-lubrication in the distributor
(b)   misalignment of contacts
(c)   wrongly connected ballast resistor
(d)   use of incorrect coil

Fig. 15.5 shows a trace covering all of these faults.

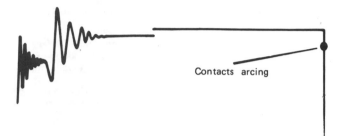

Fig. 15.5 Indication that the contact breaker needs renewing (Sec 6)

4   The pip of metal on the points is not, in itself, detrimental to the ignition function and need be removed only when setting the points gap by feeler gauge. However, if the dwell angle is used for setting, the points may remain undisturbed and the overall life will be increased considerably.

5   Contact bounce can cause misfiring, and is likely to be due to a weak tension spring or the wrong points set having been fitted. Bounce will also start at a lower speed if the gap is too big. Fig. 15.6 shows the oscilloscope picture due to contact bounce; this will be confirmed if the hash worsens with speed. Lack of cam lubrication can produce a similar effect.

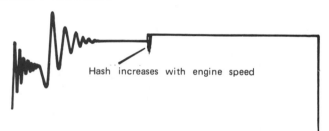

Fig. 15.6 Indication of contact bounce (Sec 6)

7   Oscilloscope fault diagnosis – dwell angle

1   This topic, referred to elsewhere in this book, is of prime importance to the proper running of the engine. Dwell angle is the angle of distributor rotation over which the contacts are closed for one ignition spark cycle (refer to Chapter 6, Section 9 for full details).

2   Adjustment of the contact breaker gap will alter the dwell; adjustment is made by stopping the engine and altering the gap until the correct dwell is obtained.

3   Measurement by oscilloscope is not the only method available, however; portable instruments and some analysers have pointer scales to give dwell readings directly. An example of the dwell angle display for a six-cylinder engine is shown in Fig. 15.7.

4   Distributor cam wear tends to reduce the points gap for a given dwell angle, and eventually the state may be reached where the gap is so small that the points scarcely open. This signifies the end of the distributor life.

5   Dwell overlap – the difference in dwell angle between one ignition

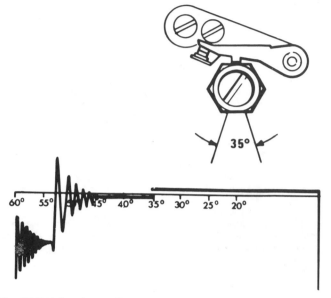

Fig. 15.7 Using the oscilloscope to measure dwell angle on a six-cylinder engine (Sec 7)

cycle and the others on the same cam – is possible, the main reasons being:

(a)   unequal cam lifts
(b)   bent distributor shaft
(c)   backlash between crankshaft and distributor drives
(d)   resonance (vibration) between crankshaft and distributor gears

6   Dwell angles of a faulty cam profile in which one cam face gives 65° and the next 57° dwell for a nominal 60° are shown in Fig. 15.8, together with the screen picture which, in this case, displays all four traces superimposed. The 8° overlap may be identified.

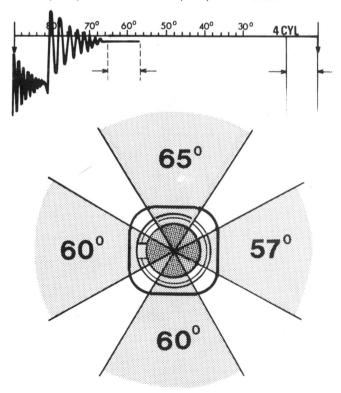

Fig. 15.8 Dwell overlap (Sec 7)

7   Dwell variation with different angles of advance may be measured by running the engine with and without the vacuum pipe attached. Such variation should not exceed 3° for a typical distributor and, if greater, could be due to the baseplate, which should be renewed. It is also possible that the distributor shaft may be worn and needs to be renewed (Fig. 15.9).

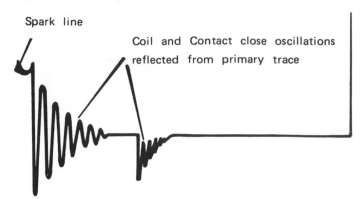

Fig. 15.11 Normal ignition secondary circuit waveform (Sec 8)

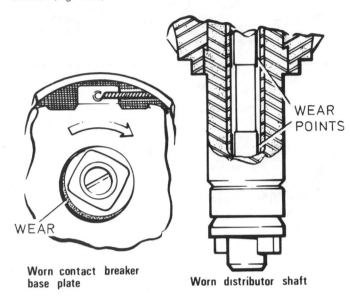

Fig. 15.9 Components responsible for dwell variation (Sec 7)

end (Fig. 15.10). A screen picture showing normal operation is shown in Fig. 15.11.

2   The coil is a special form of transformer, and this means that primary oscillations will appear in the secondary circuit. Only the spark line at the left-hand side of the trace is a direct reading of the secondary circuit, the remainder is a mirror image of the primary voltage.

3   From the secondary trace four useful tests can be performed:

   (a)   coil polarity
   (b)   coil secondary winding condition
   (c)   main HT lead condition
   (d)   plug lead and plug insulation condition

In the first three tests, one ignition cycle is displayed, but (d) must have all cycles superimposed, this being achieved by controls on the front panel of the analyser.

8   Oscilloscope fault diagnosis – secondary circuit

1   Connections to the coil HT lead are made by an adaptor which may be connected at the coil tower end of the HT line or the distributor

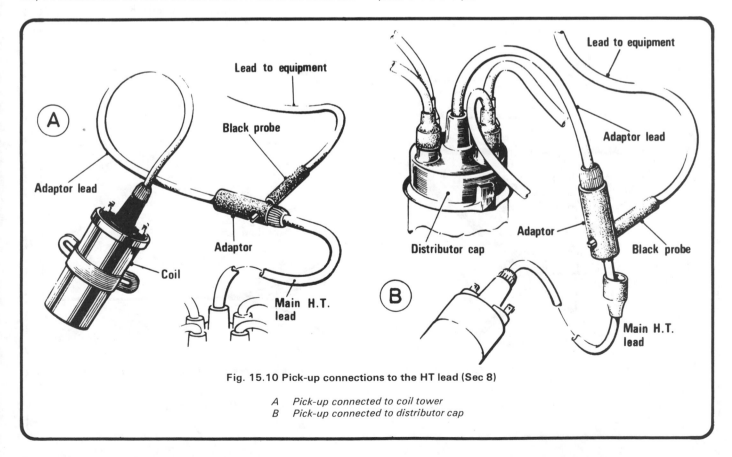

Fig. 15.10 Pick-up connections to the HT lead (Sec 8)

A   Pick-up connected to coil tower
B   Pick-up connected to distributor cap

4   **Coil polarity**: Reversed coil polarity results in a higher voltage requirement at the plugs – see Chapter 7. The oscillograms are shown in Fig. 15.12.

5   **Coil secondary winding condition**: The secondary wire is only 0.005 inch diameter, and a break is possible. Sparks will jump a small break, but the operational efficiency will rapidly deteriorate (Fig. 15.13).

6   **HT lead condition**: Breaks in an HT lead can occur, but will not be noticed, if small, except for misfiring under heavy load conditions. Fig. 15.14 shows traces for small and large HT lead breaks. Sometimes graphite resistance HT leads will become very high resistance, the fault again being insufficient to cause total ignition failure, but misfiring under load.

7   The position of the HT pick-up is important; at the distributor end of the main lead it will show breaks in the HT lead, but connected at the coil end will show lead resistance.

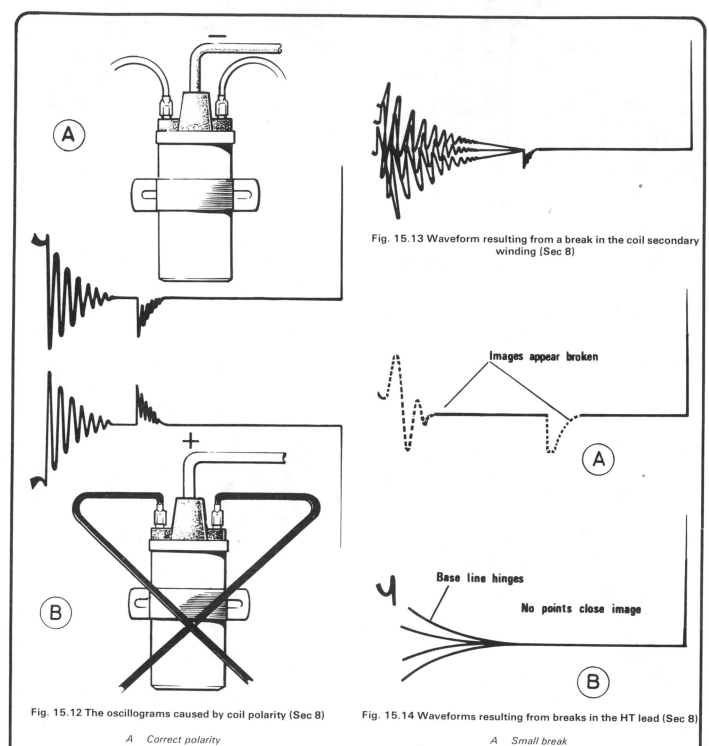

Fig. 15.13 Waveform resulting from a break in the coil secondary winding (Sec 8)

Images appear broken

Base line hinges

No points close image

Fig. 15.12 The oscillograms caused by coil polarity (Sec 8)

A   *Correct polarity*
B   *Reversed polarity*

Fig. 15.14 Waveforms resulting from breaks in the HT lead (Sec 8)

A   *Small break*
B   *Large break*

8 **Plug lead and plug insulation condition:** For this test HT traces from all sparks are superimposed on the screen. A trace showing a system in good condition is shown in Fig. 15.15. A break in one spark plug lead, but still allowing the plug to fire is shown in Fig. 15.16.

9 High circuit resistance is fairly common, and shows up as an increase in the slope downwards, from left to right, of the spark line (Fig. 15.17). Although this condition is often due to high resistance HT cables, it can show up due to carbon paths in the distributor cap, or on the spark plug insulator. Analysers with a display facility giving all secondary traces, one above the other, will show which is the offending lead (Fig. 15.18).

10 Several other fault conditions may be detected by the secondary display, including cracked plug insulation, open circuit plug leads and oiled-up sparking plugs.

9 Oscilloscope fault diagnosis – secondary spark voltage

1 Most analysers have the facility for measuring the breakdown voltage of each sparking plug. The most convenient method is to display in parade form the plug firing voltages, for any irregularity shows up immediately (Fig. 15.19). A display such as Fig. 15.20

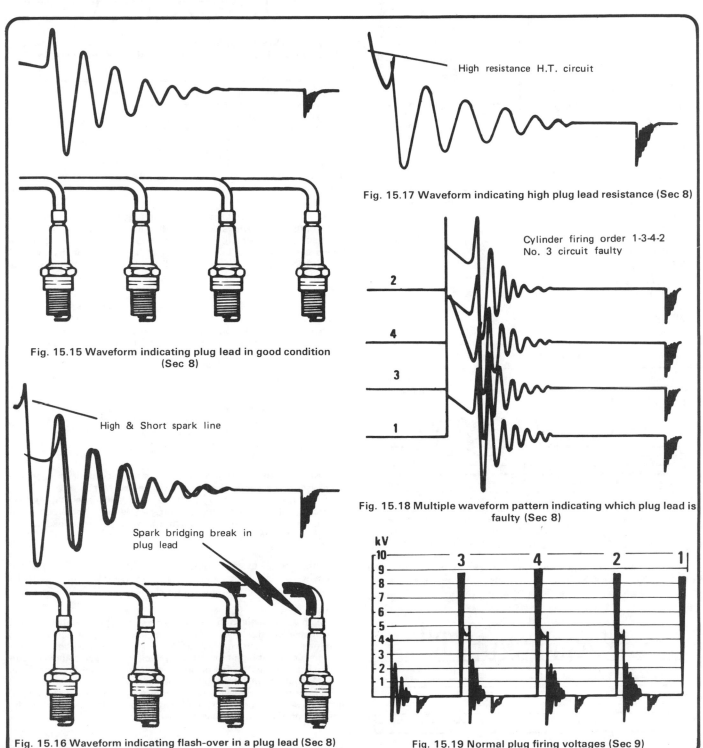

Fig. 15.15 Waveform indicating plug lead in good condition (Sec 8)

High & Short spark line

Spark bridging break in plug lead

Fig. 15.16 Waveform indicating flash-over in a plug lead (Sec 8)

High resistance H.T. circuit

Fig. 15.17 Waveform indicating high plug lead resistance (Sec 8)

Cylinder firing order 1-3-4-2
No. 3 circuit faulty

Fig. 15.18 Multiple waveform pattern indicating which plug lead is faulty (Sec 8)

Fig. 15.19 Normal plug firing voltages (Sec 9)

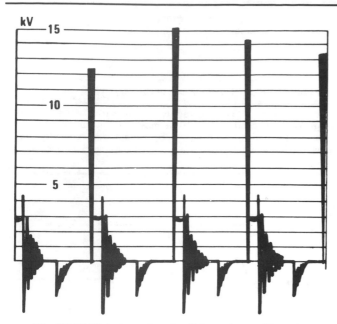

Fig. 15.20 High, irregular plug firing voltages (Sec 9)

would require plug examination, since the firing voltages are too high and non-uniform.

2   Plugs should normally fire in the range 8 to 14 kilovolts, with variation between plugs not to exceed 3 kV. The reasons for over voltage could be:

(a)   plug gaps too wide (reset)
(b)   wide rotor gap (replace rotor)
(c)   plug electrodes rounded (file square)
(d)   weak mixture (adjust carb)

10   Oscilloscope fault diagnosis – alternator

1   Connections to the main output lead of the alternator and earth will give a display of the output voltage showing the characteristic ripple in Fig. 15.21.

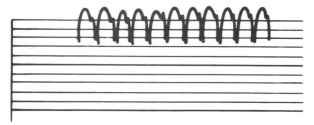

Fig. 15.21 Serviceable three-phase alternator waveform (Sec 10)

2   Connections to the regulator F terminal and earth will show the regulator square wave in Fig. 15.22. Modern alternators sometimes give pictures less rectangular than shown.

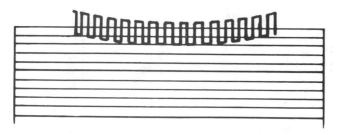

Fig. 15.22 Normal square wave produced by regulator (Sec 10)

3   Single-phase alternators are now in use in some French cars, and the oscillogram in Fig. 15.23 is characteristic of the full-wave rectification of a sine wave.

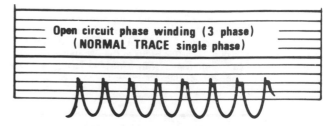

Fig. 15.23 Waveform for a serviceable single-phase (or a faulty three-phase alternator with open-circuit phase winding) (Sec 10)

11   Exhaust analysis

1   One of the most common pollutants in urban air is carbon monoxide (CO). This is a colourless, odourless gas of about the same density as air. When inhaled, this poisonous gas enters the bloodstream, where it replaces the oxygen needed to carry on the body's metabolism. If breathed in low concentrations it brings on headaches and a slowing down of physical and mental activity. At high concentration it kills quickly.

2   Some CO is produced wherever material containing carbon is burned, the most serious source of the gas being from motor vehicle exhaust systems. If petrol can be burnt completely, very little carbon monoxide is produced, but under normal running conditions a vehicle not fitted with any emission control device produces a considerable quantity of carbon monoxide.

3   To understand why carbon monoxide is present in vehicle exhaust gases it is necessary to consider the fuel burning process. Practically all normal fuels are compounds of hydrogen and carbon only, ie hydrocarbons. Burning is really an oxidisation process, and if the correct amount of oxygen for the particular fuel is supplied, all the carbon oxidises to carbon dioxide (CO_2) and all the hydrogen oxidises to water (H_2O).

4   This chemically correct ratio of about three parts of oxygen to one part of fuel, by weight, is called the stoichiometric ratio. However, since oxygen constitutes only about one-fifth of air, the correct air/fuel ratio, by weight, works out to be about 15:1.

5   When the mixture is too rich there is insufficient air for complete combustion and some of the fuel will not be burned at all, or only partly burned. Since hydrogen has a great affinity for oxygen, the hydrogen will take its full share of oxygen, leaving the carbon short. Consquently, a proportion of carbon monoxide will be formed as well as carbon dioxide.

6   Other products of incomplete combustion are acetylene and aldehydes which are responsible for the unpleasant smell from the exhaust of a vehicle warming up on choke.

7   With weak mixtures there is an excess of oxygen and the amounts of carbon monoxide and unburned fuel are greatly reduced. Excess weakness will impair combustion, but another disadvantage of weak mixtures is that at high temperature the excess oxygen combines with nitrogen and forms oxides of nitrogen, particularly nitrogen peroxide (NO_2), another pollutant which is obnoxious.

8   In general, the weaker the mixture the greater the proportion of nitrogen peroxide produced, up to a certain air/fuel ratio when the combustion temperature falls too low to form NO_2.

9   The variation of exhaust emission products with differing air/fuel ratios is illustrated in Fig. 15.24.

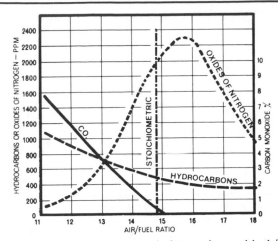

Fig. 15.24 Variation of exhaust emission products with air/fuel ratio (Sec 11)

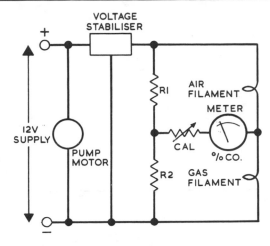

Fig. 15.25 Combustion-type CO analyser (Sec 12)

12 Carbon monoxide (CO) tester

1   Measurement of the percentage carbon monoxide (CO) in the exhaust gas is important since, in many countries, emission control standards are in force. Where no official standards exist, most vehicle manufacturers state the limits of % CO for tuning purposes. Two types of CO tester are in use.

2   **The infra-red tester** works on the principle that gases will absorb infra-red radiation at a wavelength which is characteristic of the gas. In this instrument infra-red radiation from a heated wire is directed through two tubes, one containing no carbon monoxide and the other filled with exhaust gas. Measuring devices at the far end of the tubes compare the strengths of received infra-red radiation, and the result is displayed on a meter scaled in % carbon monoxide.

3   **The combustion tester:** this type of emission tester operates by burning the combustible gases remaining in the exhaust and measuring the heat produced by the combustion. In one model, an electrically driven diaphragm pump draws exhaust gas and air through calibrated jets provided with replaceable filters. The mixture is pumped through a combustion chamber containing a heated platinum filament which burns the combustible gases.

4   The heat of combustion raises the temperature of the filament still further. Its electrical resistance is compared with that of a similar hot filament surrounded by only air. The increased resistance of the gas filament unbalances a bridge circuit, causing a meter deflection proportional to the percentage of CO present in the exhaust gases.

5   To smooth out pulsations in the gas flow, a buffer chamber or reservoir is inserted between the pump and the combustion chamber.

6   The voltage applied to the bridge circuit must be very well stabilised to avoid inaccuracy due to supply voltage variations.

7   Fig. 15.25 shows the instrument in diagrammatic form. The two filaments form a matched pair and have equal resistance when no CO is present. Resistors R1 and R2 are also equal, so that the bridge is balanced when CO is absent and no current flows through the meter. When the exhaust gases contain CO, the heat of combustion raises the temperature of the gas filament, thereby increasing its resistance. This unbalances the bridge causing current to flow through the meter, the scale of which is calibrated to read percentage of CO by volume.

8   Since the hot filament burns all combustible gases, it is important to remove as much hydro-carbon content from the exhaust gas as possible. This is achieved by surrounding the hot gas filament with a fine filter. Carbon monoxide can diffuse readily through the filter to reach the hot filament, but only a small proportion of the relatively more dense hydro-carbons are able to do so. The bulk of the hydro-carbon content of the exhaust gases thus bypasses the filament and is ejected into the atmosphere.

9   The infra-red instrument is precise and relatively expensive, but has the advantage of measuring % CO only, whereas the combustion meter measures the combustion heat from both CO and hydrogen in the exhaust, but is scaled in % CO on the assumption that the proportion of CO and hydrogen is constant – a reasonable assumption for most conditions.

10   **Use of the CO tester:** The method of making CO measurements varies slightly with the type of instrument being used. As an example the use of a combustion type CO meter will be described. The vehicle should first be checked to ensure that the engine is running correctly, with ignition timing, distributor dwell angle, spark plugs, etc, set to the manufacturer's recommended figures. Note that before attempting to make any CO measurements, the engine must be brought to its normal working temperature and must be running at its normal idling speed.

11   Stand the exhaust gas condenser unit on the ground in an upright position near the vehicle tail pipe. The purpose of the condenser is to cool the exhaust gases and to remove moisture. Attach one end of the hose to the gas inlet on the CO tester and the other end to the condenser. Push the probe into the exhaust pipe to a distance of one foot (Fig. 15.26).

12   Observe the meter reading and, if necessary, adjust the carburettor mixture screw until the required percentage CO is obtained. While adjusting the carburettor the engine must remain at the correct idling speed, and sufficient time must be allowed for the exhaust gas to reach the gas cell (up to half a minute in some cases).

Fig. 15.26 Condenser unit and probe (Sec 12)

Index

Printed by
Haynes Publishing Group
Sparkford Yeovil Somerset
England